THE AWE-INSPIRING RITES
OF INITIATION

The Awe-Inspiring Rites of Initiation

The Origins of the RCIA

Edward Yarnold, S.J.

SECOND EDITION

A Liturgical Press Book

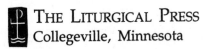
THE LITURGICAL PRESS
Collegeville, Minnesota

Published in Great Britain by T&T Clark Ltd,
59 George Street, Edinburgh EH2 2LQ, Scotland

This edition published under license from T&T Clark Ltd by
The Liturgical Press, Collegeville, Minnesota 56321

First published 1994

Library of Congress Cataloging-in-Publication Data

Yarnold, Edward.
    The awe-inspiring rites : the origins of the R.C.I.A. / by Edward
Yarnold. – 2nd ed.
        p.   cm.
    Prev. ed. published under title: The awe-inspiring rites of
initiation. 1971.
    Includes bibliographical references.
    ISBN 0-8146-2281-X
    1. Baptism–Sermons.   2. Confirmation–Sermons.   3. Lord's Supper–
Sermons.   4. Sermons, Greek–Translations into English.
5. Initiation rites–Religious aspects–Christianity–Sermons.
6. Initiation rites–Religious aspects–Christianity–History of
doctrines–Early church, ca. 30-600.   I. Title.   II. Title: Awe-inspiring rites of
initiation.
BV812.Y37   1993   93-17450
265'. 13'09015–dc20   CIP

Typeset by Trinity Typesetting, Edinburgh
Printed and bound in Great Britain by Cromwell Press, Wiltshire

To my colleagues
and generations of students
at Oxford and Notre Dame

Contents

Preface

The first edition of this book was published as long ago as 1972, just too early to take account of the new Rite of Christian Initiation of Adults, the Latin text of which was promulgated in the same year. This new edition has accordingly been recast so that it now corresponds throughout with the RCIA. At the same time the opportunity has been taken to introduce many other changes, the most important of which are a clearer and more accurate account of the three anointings, and a more correct explanation of the scrutinies.

'The awe-inspiring rites' – the words recur several times in these pages. Without being unfaithful to the Greek, I might have called this book 'The Spine-chilling Rites of Initiation'. It takes the form of a collection of sermons, all preached about the second half of the fourth century, explaining the sacraments of baptism, confirmation and Holy Communion by which a Christian became a full member of the Church. The ceremonies took place at night, some of them in the dark, after weeks of intense preparation; they were wrapped in secrecy, and the candidate knew little about them until just before, or even after, he had received them. Everything was calculated to inspire religious awe, to make these rites the occasion of a profound and life-long conversion.

Cyril, Ambrose, Chrysostom and Theodore, the Fathers who preached these sermons, thought of themselves as guiding the neophytes into knowledge of the Christian mysteries. This is the meaning of the description 'mystagogic' which is generally applied to them.[1] In the last section of the Introduction a comparison is drawn between the Greek mystery-religions and these rites of Christian initiation. The Christian mystagogic

---

[1] Cyril in fact describes his instructions as *mustagogiai* (MC 2.1).

preacher corresponds to the Greek hierophant who explained the mysteries to those undergoing initiation at Eleusis.

The aim of this book is first of all the convenience of students of the liturgy. Some of the sermons it contains are not easily available in English translation; it seemed therefore a useful undertaking to collect them together with introductions and notes. Secondly, since the modern RCIA was composed after the model of the fourth-century liturgy, those who are engaged in the catechumenate today may find that a book about ancient practice helps them better to understand the modern rite, and that they have something to learn from the study of the catechetical methods which were practised at the golden age of liturgical history. The ideas these sermons contain still have their validity, even though they are sometimes expressed in a style which has aged and which are based on a less critical understanding of scripture than is possible for us today. In particular we should ask ourselves whether the note of religious dread or awe is, as has sometimes been suggested, an un-Christian distortion of the simple primitive gospel, or whether it is an essential element in a balanced attitude to God. One of the authors of these homilies touches on this question, and explains that sacred fear is not incompatible with the love of God.[2] Thirdly, I hope that this book will transport the reader back to an enviable age when people were so sensitive to symbols that the liturgy could be left to speak for itself, even before the preacher had given any explanation.

Christian initiation is a complex process, and can be viewed in several lights. It is a process of developing conversion, or, more positively, of spiritual growth; it is a progressive deepening of the candidate's membership of the Christian community. In these sermons we see another aspect of initiation: it is an experience, above all an experience of awe, calculated to sink into the depths of the candidate's psyche and to produce a lasting transformation there.

I wish to express my thanks here to my colleagues Robert Murray, S.J., and Kevin Donovan, S.J., who both read the book

---

[2]Theodore of Mopsuestia, BH 5.28.

in typescript and made many helpful suggestions which enabled me to improve the presentation and to add many valuable references; also to my four patient co-translators, the late James Walsh, S.J., Dr P. G. Walsh, Michael Bossy, S.J. and (once again) Robert Murray.

Abbreviations

Where the context makes the sense clear, I have sometimes referred to the four Fathers whose work forms the body of this book as CJ, A, JC and T respectively. Other abbreviations used are:

ACW: *St John Chrysostom: Baptismal Instructions*, ed. P. W. Harkins (Ancient Christian Writers, 31). Westminster Maryland, and London, 1963.

BH: The *Baptismal Homilies* of Theodore of Mopsuestia, i.e. his last five catechetical instructions.

DACL: *Dictionnaire d'archéologie chrétienne et de liturgie*, Paris, 1907-1953.

DS: *Enchiridion Symbolorum*, ed. H. Denzinger and A. Schönmetzer, S.J. 33rd edn., Barcelona etc., 1965.

JTS: *Journal of Theological Studies.*

M: The *Mystagogic Catecheses* of St Cyril of Jerusalem.

PG: Patrologia Graeca, ed. J.-P. Migne.

PL: Patrologia Latina, ed. J.-P. Migne.

RAC: *Reallexikon für Antike und Christentum*, Stuttgart, 1950ff.

RCIA: Rite of Christian Initiation of Adults.

S: The *De Sacramentis* of St Ambrose

SL: *The Study of Liturgy*, 2nd edn., ed., C. Jones, G. Wainwright, E. Yarnold, and P. Bradshaw, London and New York, 1992.

Whitaker: E. C. Whitaker, *Documents of the Baptismal Liturgy*, 2nd edn., London, 1970.

1

The Ceremonies of Initiation
The RCIA and the Fourth Century

The four sets of sermons that form the main part of this book were preached during the fourth century in Milan, Jerusalem and Antioch.[1] Despite the different languages in which they are written and the local variations of rite, the initiation ceremonies described in them conform in essentials to a common pattern. With the help of these sermons, together with some other evidence, we are able to arrive at a detailed picture of the stages by which a person entered the Church at this time.

The ceremonies described in these sermons are all connected with the baptism of adults. But this is not to say that infant baptism was unknown at this time. J. Jeremias[2] has set out a wealth of evidence which indicates a widespread practice of infant baptism from early times. Hippolytus, for example, envisages that some of the candidates will be children too young to answer for themselves.[3] Jeremias argues that in the fourth century, however, there was a movement favouring the postponement of baptism;[4] and indeed in the four sets of sermons in the present book the impression is

---

[1]Concerning the place where Theodore's sermons were delivered, cf. p. 165.

[2]*Infant Baptism in the First Four Centuries* (London, 1960), especially pp. 11-18. Not all scholars, however, agree with all Jeremias' interpretations of his texts. See, for example, K. Aland, *Did the Early Church Baptize Infants?* (London, 1963).

[3]*Ap. Trad.* 21.4, I have adopted G. Dix's numbering through this book.

[4]*Op. cit.* Chap. 4.

1

inescapable that adult baptism was normal, almost invariable even, in Jerusalem, Milan and Antioch.[5]

The modern RCIA was composed as an adaptation of the rites of the early Church to twentieth-century needs. The rite in use today consists of four *periods:* (1) evangelization and precatechumenate, (2) catechesis, (3) purification and enlightenment, and (4) mystagogy. As gateways through which one passes from one period to the next, there are three '*steps*': (a) acceptance into the order of catechumens, (b) election or enrolment, (c) the sacraments of initiation. We shall consider these periods and steps in order, taking the headings of the modern rite as a framework into which to fit a description of the ceremonies on which the Fathers of the fourth century were commenting.[6]

FIRST PERIOD: PRECATECHUMENATE

In the modern rite the precatechumenate consists of inquiry on the part of the candidate and evangelization on the part of the Church. We have little indication how this period was conducted in the early church.

FIRST STEP: ACCEPTANCE INTO THE ORDER OF CATECHUMENS

The chief elements of the modern rite are the candidate's first acceptance of the Gospel (a Bible may be given as a symbol of

---

[5]Jeremias (*op. cit.*, pp. 94-95) shows that infant baptism was taken for granted by Ambrose (*De Abraham*, ii.81, 84; PL 14.495, 497) and Chrysostom (*In Gen.*, 40.4; PG 53.373. See also the quotation from a lost baptismal homily by Chrysostom preserved in Augustine, *Contra Julianum Pelagianum*, i. 6. 21-22; PL 44. 654-656).

[6]Unfortunately there is not a standard system for numbering the paragraphs of the RCIA. I have followed here the system adopted in the 1983 Latin edition of the Rite. Although the English edition (St Thomas More Centre, London, 1988), the Irish (Columba Press, Blackrock, 1986), and the American (Pueblo, New York, 1988) give different paragraph numbers, they all note the numbers of the Latin text in the margin.

this acceptance), the sponsors' affirmation of their willingness to assume their responsibilities, and the signing of the candidate with the cross. The ancient rite was like the modern one in several ways, as St Augustine's recollections show:

> I was signed with the sign of His Cross and seasoned with His salt straight from the womb of my mother, who had great hope in You.[7]

These words of St Augustine refer to the ceremony by which a candidate was admitted into the number of the catechumens. The saint himself was admitted unusually early. The reason, perhaps, was his mother's peculiar piety, or (to use his own words) her 'great hope'. His serious illness in childhood was apparently not the reason for this early enrolment, for this illness came later, when he was old enough to ask for baptism.[8] St Ambrose also alludes to a similar preliminary initiation which includes the signing of the candidate with the sign of the cross and the administration of salt.[9]

Besides prayers, there appear to be four elements in the ceremony as practised in the West:

(i) The sign of the cross was made, probably on the candidate's forehead;

(ii) Salt was given him;

(iii) Hands were laid upon him;

(iv) The candidate was exorcised.

---

[7] *Confessions*, i.11.17.

[8] 'When I was still a boy and one day developed a fever with dilatation of the stomach and was likely to die, you saw, O Lord, (for you were already my guardian) the eagerness and faith with which I begged for baptism …' (*loc. cit.*). St Augustine seems to refer to the same ceremonies in other places, e.g. *De Catechizandis Rudibus* (26.50; PL 40.344) and *De Peccatorum Meritis et Remissione* (ii.26.42; PL 44.176). In another place he seems to imply that exorcism forms part of this first step (*Contra Cresconium Donatistam*, ii.5.7; PL 43.471).

[9] The sign of the cross is mentioned in M20, the salt in *Expos. Ev. Luc.* 10.48 (PL 15.1815). There A addresses the water, which begins the first and completes the final rites. The sequel shows that salt counts as water: 'decaying meat is preserved for a long time by the sprinkling of salt'.

(i)   The sign of the cross. St Augustine, explaining the Creed to the candidates for baptism, urged them to believe boldly that Christ was crucified for men:

> Do not hesitate, do not be ashamed. When you first believed, you received the sign of Christ on your forehead, the home of shame. Remember your forehead and do not be afraid of another man's tongue.... Do not then be afraid of the shame of the Cross.[10]

The symbolism has another, probably more ancient, significance. Slaves and soldiers bore a mark on the hand or the forehead to show to whom they owed service.[11] The Christian was signed on the forehead to show that he belonged to Christ. St Augustine makes play with this meaning in a panegyric of the martyr St Stephen. 'But the Lord, who had put him in uniform and passed him as fit and placed his mark not on his hand but on his forehead, was watching his soldier from above.'[12]

This sign of the cross was generally traced on the forehead again in the course of the final sacraments of initiation. It was often described as a 'seal'.[13] Some confusion can be caused by the fact that the term 'seal' is also sometimes used to describe the whole rite of initiation.

(ii)   The symbolism of the salt is explained by John the Deacon writing from Rome probably early in the sixth century:

> Now that he is a catechumen he will receive blessed salt, with which he is signed, because just as all flesh is seasoned

---

[10] *Sermon* 215.5; PL 38.1075. The forehead is the home of shame because it is there that a blush reveals shame. The sign of the cross on the catechumen's forehead should teach him never to be ashamed of the cross.

[11] 'Slaves are marked with their master's sign, soldiers with the name of the Emperor' (St Ambrose, *De Obitu Valentiniani*, 58; PL 16. 1376-7). This mark seems to have been a brand or a tattoo. Cf. H. Rondet, S.J., 'La Croix sur le Front', *Recherches de Science Religieuse* 42 (1954) 388ff. See SL, plate 6.

[12] *Sermon* 317.4.5; PL 38.1437.

[13] See below, p. 29.

and preserved by salt, so too the mind, sodden and soft as it is from the waves of the world, is seasoned by the salt of wisdom and of the preaching of the word of God.[14]

There is some evidence for the use of salt as an anti-demonic rite in pre-Christian Rome.[15] The salt continued to be given throughout the catechumenate, and was regarded as in some sense the catechumen's substitute for the Eucharist.[16] The rite survived in the Roman liturgy as part of the baptismal service until 1969, but does not appear in eastern liturgies.

(iii)   The imposition of hands is the traditional sign of the dedication of an offering to God[17] and a gesture of blessing. By this sign a person is often consecrated for a particular task like Joshua,[18] and Saul and Barnabas.[19] It could also be a ceremony for the forgiveness of sins[20] but that does not seem to be its significance in the rite of the enrolment of a catechumen in the early Church. In the modern rite the celebrant prays with hands stretched out over the candidates but not placed on their heads.

(iv)   Exorcism. In the early church pagans were thought to be possessed by the devil. The second-century writer who uses the pseudonym 'Barnabas' states: 'Before we believed in God the dwelling-place of our heart was corrupt and weak … because it was full of idolatry and was the home of demons, since we did everything that was opposed to God'.[21]

---

[14]*Ad Senarium*, 3; PL 59.402 (Whitaker, p. 155).

[15]See H. A. Kelly, *The Devil at Baptism* (Ithaca and London, 1985), p. 111.

[16]*De Peccatorum Meritis et Remissione, loc. cit.* This seems also to be implied by the use of the imperfect tense in the sentence quoted from *Confessions* i.11.17, which perhaps should be translated: '… I began to be signed'. The same would then be true of the tracing of the sign of the cross.

[17]Levi 1.4. The rite is mentioned by St Augustine in the same passage in *De Peccatorum Meritis et Remissione.*

[18]Num. 27.23.

[19]Acts 13.3; 1 Tim. 4.14; 2 Tim. 1.6.

[20]1 Tim. 5.22.

[21]*Epistle* 16.7.

Two elements were involved in the ceremony of exorcism: a form of words by which the devil was bidden to go out from the person; and the gesture of blowing.[22] This act of breathing signifies that the devil is, so to speak, blown away. It was a conventional gesture to express contempt: for example to breathe on the emperor's statue constituted treason.[23] The abbot Anthony told his monks that when devils appeared to him he blew at them to drive them away.[24]

In the RCIA exorcisms are not introduced until the Period of the Catechumenate.

SECOND PERIOD: CATECHUMENATE

The candidate thus enrolled was called a *catechumen* (that is, person under instruction) or a *hearer* (*audiens, auditor*).[25]

Hippolytus prescribed at least three years of catechumenate,[26] but it became customary to put off baptism for much longer, for it took the Church some time fully to realise her powers to forgive sins committed after baptism; consequently many who were convinced of the truth of Christianity preferred to postpone baptism at least until the passionate time of youth was over. Baptism involved such a radical change in life that one would not receive it until one felt completely ready.[27] St Ambrose himself, though coming from a devout Christian family, had not yet been baptized when the people chose him to be Bishop of Milan.[28] So too St Augustine's mother St

[22]Cf. Cyril of Jerusalem, *Procat.* 9; John the Deacon, *loc. cit.*
[23]St Augustine, *Op. Imperf. Contra Jul.* iii.199; PL 45.1333.
[24]Athanasius, *Vita Antonii*, 40; PG 26.901; cf. Tertullian, *Apologeticum*, 23.16; PL 1.415. In the Byzantine rite, the candidates themselves blow on the devil, and are told: 'If after you have blown upon the devil there is still anything evil in you, spit it out' (Whitaker, p. 70).
[25]St Augustine, *Serm.* 132.1 (PL 38.734); Tertullian, *de Paenitentia*, 6.14-15; St Ambrose, M 20.
[26]*Ap. Trad.* 17.1
[27]Cf. P. Brown, *Augustine of Hippo*, pp. 106-107.
[28]Paulinus, *Vita Ambrosii*, 7 (PL 14.29). However, he later preached against the practice of deferring baptism (S 3.13).

Monica decided that he should not be baptized when he was young because of the inevitability of sin.[29]

We know very little about the way this second period was conducted in the early Church. Chrysostom points out that the term 'catechumen' is derived from the Greek word 'echo';[30] the instruction the catechumens received was not only for their ears, but should resonate in their minds and find expression in their lives.

The RCIA suggests four means by which catechumens can be helped to mature as Christians: instruction, prayer, suitable liturgical rites, and active work in spreading the Gospel (n. 19). It contains a rite of Minor Exorcism; in the USA the Anointing with the Oil of Catechumens is also celebrated during this Period, rather than during the Vigil Service as part of the sacraments of initiation.

The catechumens were admitted only to the first part of the Mass, the Liturgy of the Word (Mass of the Catechumens); they were dismissed when, after the lessons and the sermon, they had been prayed for in the intercessions (bidding prayers).[31]

SECOND STEP: ELECTION OR ENROLMENT

By the fourth century Easter was accepted as the normal time for administering baptism; although St Siricius, who was Pope from 384-399, also allows Pentecost.[32] About the beginning of Lent those catechumens who wished to be baptized were urged to 'give in their names'. This phrase became a technical term for the request for baptism. St Ambrose as early as the Epiphany began to ask for names: preaching on the text 'We toiled all

---

[29] *Confessions*, i.11.17.

[30] *Baptismal Homily* (Montfaucon), 2.1; ACW p. 173. M. Dujarier sets out some of the evidence in his *A History of the Catchumenate*.

[31] The fourth-century *Apostolic Constitutions* is an early text in which the Eucharist contains an intercession for catechumens (viii.6). Cf. Ambrose, *Ep*. 20.4 (PL 16.995).

[32] *Letter to Himerius*, 2.3 (PL 13.1134). Cf. Tertullian, *de Baptismo*, 19; Whitaker, p.9.

night and took nothing',[33] he compares the lack of response to his request for names to the apostles' unsuccessful night's fishing.[34]

To request baptism was also called to 'petition'.[35] Candidates whose application was accepted were called 'applicants' (*competentes*), 'chosen' (*electi*) or 'destined for illumination' (*photizomenoi*).

In the RCIA, preferably on the first Sunday in Lent, the godparents and catechists present the candidates, and testify that they are ready for admission to baptism, while the candidates have to reaffirm their intention. It is on the basis of this evidence that the community 'elects' the candidates, whose names are then inscribed in a register. This modern rite is an adaptation of the practice of the early Church.

Egeria,[36] a nun from Southern Gaul or Spain, in the account she wrote to her religious sisters of her experience on her pilgrimage to Jerusalem at the end of the fourth century, describes how the process was performed there:

> I think I also ought to tell you how instruction is given to those who are baptized at Easter. Those who give in their names do so the day before Lent begins; the presbyter writes down the names of all of them. This takes place before the eight weeks during which, as I told you, Lent is observed here. When the presbyter has made a note of all the names, later on another day in Lent, the day on which the eight weeks begin, the bishop's chair is set up in the middle of the great church, the church of the Martyrium. The presbyters sit on either side on chairs and all the clerics stand. Then the candidates are brought in one by one, the men with their 'fathers', the women with their 'mothers'. Then the bishop one by one asks their neighbours: 'Is he a good-living man? Does he respect his

---

[33]Lk. 5.5.

[34]*In Expos. Ev. Luc.* 4.76 (PL 15.1634f.).

[35]'*Petere*'; cf. Augustine, *DeFid, et Op.*, 6.9 (PL 40.202); Serm. 216.1 (PL 38.1077).

[36]Her name is also given in other forms, such as 'Aetheria'. J. Wilkinson's translation of her account, *Egeria's Travels* (London, 1971), contains much valuable background material.

parents? Is he a drunkard or untrustworthy?' He asks them like this about every vice, at least the more serious ones. If the bishop finds that the candidate is free from all these faults about which he has questioned the witnesses, he writes down the candidate's name with his own hand.[37]

THIRD PERIOD: ENLIGHTENMENT

The RCIA regards the six-week period of Purification and Enlightenment as a time of spiritual preparation rather than of instruction. In the fourth century the instruction was more emphasised; in the second part of Lent this instruction centred on a series of expositions of the Creed. Then, as now, the period contained a number of rites which were designed to contribute to the process of illumination.

(1) Exorcisms

One of the most important elements in the final preparation for baptism was the rite of exorcism, by which the candidate was released from the power of the devil. These exorcisms seem to have formed part of almost daily meetings of the candidates.[38]

Theodore of Mopsuestia also gives an account of the ceremony; he compares it with a lawsuit in which the candidate is the defendant, the devil is the plaintiff:

> Anyone who wishes to have recourse to the gift of baptism should present himself to the Church of God. He is received by the appointed official and his name is recorded in the customary way for candidates seeking baptism. The official inquires into the candidate's way of life from his 'sponsor'. He then writes down in the Church's book the witness's name beside the candidate's ... The candidate

---

[37]Egeria, *Peregrinatio,* 45. The 'fathers' and 'mothers' are the godparents.
[38]Thus Cyril of Jerusalem: 'Come regularly to the exorcisms' (*Cat.* 1.5). Cf. Hippolytus, *Ap. Trad.* 20.3; Egeria, 46.1.

must then always have recourse to the 'exorcists'. You are, as it were, pleading a suit; you must stand in silence before your accuser. You stand with hands outstretched in the attitude of prayer and keep your eyes lowered. For the same reason you remove your outer garments and stand barefoot on sack-cloth.[39]

St John Chrysostom gives a similar account of the exorcism. The candidate stands unshod and half naked as a reminder that he was once in the devil's power.[40] St Cyril tells the candidate that when he is exorcised he will be breathed on and his face will be covered to secure for him peace of mind from the dangers of a roving eye.[41]

St Augustine's rite also used the symbolism of the sack-cloth made of goat's hair. After urging the candidates to do penance with hair-shirt and fasts, he continues:

It is true that, when you were scrutinised and the instigator of your flight and desertion was duly upbraided in the name of the omnipotence of the awesome Trinity, you did not wear goat's hair, but your feet stood on it as a symbol. You must tread underfoot your vices and the goat's fleece. You must tear the rags of the goats that are placed on the left.[42]

The symbolism of the goat's fleece is fourfold:

(a)   Sack-cloth is the traditional sign of penitence;
(b)   It recalls the tunics of skin worn by Adam and Eve after the fall and so reminds the candidate of original sin (Theodore);

---

[39]BH 1(12), *Synopsis.* Sack-cloth is made of goat's-hair.
[40]BH 2.14; cf. ACW 10. 14-16.
[41]*Procat.* 9.
[42]Sermon 216. 10-11 (PL 38.1082). Cf. J. Quasten, 'Theodore of Mopsuestia on the Exorcism of the Cilicium', *Harvard Theological Review* 35 (1942) 209ff. Cf. also Quodvultdeus of Carthage, *Sermon on the Creed to the Catechumens*, 1.1 (PL 40.637, where it is found misplaced among St Augustine's works; Whitaker, p. 107); Augustine, *de Civ. Dei*, xv.20: 'Making confession we prostrate ourselves on sack-cloth'.

(c)   It is an acknowledgment of the candidate's former slavery to the devil (Theodore and Chrysostom);

(d)   The trampling of the goat's hair shows that the candidate wishes to be numbered among the sheep rather than the goats at the Last Judgment.

The fourth-century *Clementine Recognitions* explain that demons are generally expelled from a man only gradually; as faith grows, the area occupied by the devil contracts.[43]

(2) Scrutinies

In the modern rite the scrutinies are celebrated on the third, fourth and fifth Sundays of Lent. The purpose of these rites is 'self-searching and repentance'; they are intended 'to uncover, then heal all that is weak, defective, or sinful in the hearts of the elect; to bring out, then strengthen all that is upright, strong, and good' (nn. 25, 154). The scrutiny is exercised by the candidates on themselves, during a period of silent prayer (n. 162).

In the early Church the function of the rite was somewhat different. It was the community which scrutinised the candidates. Exorcism formed an integral part of the process; in the words of Pope Leo the Great, the elect were 'scrutinised by exorcisms'.[44] Hippolytus required the bishop himself to perform the last exorcism so that 'he may be certain that [the candidate] is purified'.[45] St Augustine, while expecting the elect to scrutinise their own hearts, saw the exorcisms as a means of testing whether they were free from the influence of unclean spirits.[46] Zeno of Verona lists some of the reactions which candidates could show to exorcism, such as turning pale, gnashing the teeth, foaming at the mouth, shaking, weeping;[47] presumably the bishop scrutinised the candidate to ascertain that none of

---

[43]4.17; PG 1.1321.

[44]Leo, Ep. 16.6; PL 54.702.

[45]*Ap. Trad.* 20.3.

[46]Serm. 216. 6, 10, 11; PL 38.1080, 1082.

[47]Zeno, *Tractatus*, (Löfstedt) i.2.6; PL 11.374. I owe this reference and those on p. 26 to Rev. Gordon Jeanes.

these phenomena were present, as they would indicate continuing diabolic influence.

(3) Lenten Liturgy and Instruction

St Ambrose speaks of the 'daily moral discourse when the history of the patriarchs or the precepts of the Proverbs were read'.[48] St Cyril urges his candidates to 'attend the catechism regularly and remember what you are told ... Be regular at the meetings [*synaxeis*], not only now, when you have to give an account of your regularity to the clergy, but also after you have received the grace [of baptism]'.[49]

Egeria describes the daily exorcisms and instruction on the fast-days of the first seven weeks of Lent. The candidates sit in a circle round the bishop, together with their godparents and any other of the baptized who wish to attend. Catechumens, of course, are excluded.[50]

Many of the teachings and practices of the Church were kept secret from outsiders; this cult of secrecy became known to later scholars as the *Disciplina Arcani*.[51] It was not until the Lent preceding baptism that a candidate would begin to receive systematic instruction about these secret matters. This course of instruction would normally conclude with an explanation of the ceremonies of the baptismal service itself, four examples of which form the main body of this book. But throughout Lent the candidate received instruction on other subjects including the scriptures.[52]

(4) Presentation and Recitation of the Creed

In the modern rite the Creed is presented to the candidates in

---

[48]M 1.

[49]*Cat.* 1.5, 6.

[50]*Peregrinatio*, 46.

[51]See Introduction, pp. 55-59.

[52]Examples of these Lenten instructions are St Ambrose's sermons *De Elia et Ieiunio* (PL 14.697ff.), *De Abraham* (PL 14.419ff.), *Explanatio Symboli (Sources Chrétiennes*, 25 bis); St Cyril's first eighteen catechetical sermons; Theodore's *Catechetical Homilies* (1-11); and St Augustine's Sermons 56-59 and 212-216 (PL 38.377ff. and 1058ff.). Cf. Egeria, 46, for Cyril's method of instruction.

the week after the first scrutiny, and recited by them on Holy Saturday. In the early Church the process was called the 'handing over' (*traditio*) and the 'giving back' (*redditio*) of the Creed. It had in those days a greater importance, because the words and meaning of the Creed were included among the secret subjects in which the candidates were instructed during Lent. Thirteen out of Cyril's eighteen Lenten Catecheses took the form of an exposition of the Creed clause by clause. The candidates had to learn the words by heart; to take them down in writing would risk betrayal of the secret.[53] The bishop or a deputy taught the Creed phrase by phrase; during the following week the godparents helped the candidates to learn the words. It was in the course of the sermon *Explanatio Symboli*, quoted above, that St Ambrose taught the candidates the Creed: 'Now is the time, now is the day for us to hand over the Creed'.[54] He wrote a dramatic letter giving an account of the Arian violence that took place on the Palm Sunday of the year 386 while 'I was handing over the Creed to some candidates in the baptisteries'.[55]

St Augustine shows his sympathy for the nervousness the candidates must have felt when faced with the task of learning the Creed:

> Today week you will have to repeat what you have learnt today. Your godparents are responsible for teaching you ... No one need be nervous and so fail to repeat the words. Do not worry, I am your father. I do not carry a strap or a cane like a schoolmaster.[56]

If they forgot the words, they would have another chance of repeating them on the day they were baptized.[57]

Egeria describes the ceremony as she saw it taking place in Jerusalem:

---

[53]'The creed should not be written down. You have to be able to repeat it, but no one must write it down' (Ambrose, *Explanatio Symboli*, 9).

[54]*Exp. Symb.* 1.

[55]Ep. 20.4 (PL 16.995).

[56]*De Symbolo*, 11 (*Miscellanea Agostiniana*, ed. Morin, Rome, 1930, i.449-50).

[57]Sermon 58.1 (PL 38.393).

When the seven weeks (of Lent) have passed and there only remains the paschal week, which is called here the great week, the bishop comes in the morning to the Martyrium in the Great Church. His throne is set at the back of the apse behind the altar, and the candidates approach him one by one, the men with their godfathers, the women with their godmothers, and repeat the Creed to him.[58]

(5) Presentation and Recitation of the Lord's Prayer

In the modern rite, in the course of the week after the third Scrutiny, a short rite is celebrated during Mass, during which the candidates listen to a reading of the passage in the sixth chapter of St Matthew's gospel in which Jesus teaches the apostles the Our Father. There is no later rite of recitation, as there is for the Creed.

In some parts of the fourth-century Church there took place both a handing over and a giving back of the Lord's Prayer, for outsiders were not allowed to learn the words of this most sacred and characteristic of Christian prayers. In St Augustine's church the Prayer was handed over on the same Sunday as the recitation of the Creed, and given back by the candidates a week later; in Jerusalem and Milan, however, it was not taught until after baptism.[59] Besides learning the words, the candidates were given an explanation of their meaning. The explanations given by Cyril and Ambrose formed part of *Mystagogic Catecheses* and *De Sacramentis*, but have been omitted from this book. Surprisingly, so intellectual a preacher as Theodore explained the Lord's Prayer as a prayer of moral instruction.[60]

(6) Lenten Penance

St Ambrose's work on *Elijah and Fasting* is a compilation of sermons on Lenten penance addressed, though not exclusively,

---

[58] *Peregrinatio*, 46.

[59] Augustine, Serm. 58.1 (PL 38.393); Whitaker, p. 103. Cyril of Jerusalem, MC 5.11-18. Ambrose, S 5.18-30; 6.24.

[60] *Cat.* 11.19.

to the baptismal candidates. In it, following St Paul, he compares himself and his congregation to athletes, and continues:

> Can an athlete enjoy leisure once he has given in his name for an event? No, he trains and is anointed every day. He is given special food; discipline is imposed on him; he has to keep himself chaste. You too have *given in your name* for Christ's contest; you have entered for an event, and its prize is a crown. Practise, train, anoint yourself with the oil of gladness, an ointment that is never used up. Your food should be frugal, without intemperance or self-indulgence. Your drink should be more sparing for fear drunkenness should catch you unawares. Keep your body chaste so as to be fit to wear the crown. Otherwise your reputation may lose you the favour of the spectators, and your supporters may see your negligence and abandon you. The Archangels, the Powers, the Dominions, the ten thousand times ten thousand Angels are all watching you. Before such spectators have some sense of shame and consider how dishonourable such conduct would be.[61]

St Augustine regards even the legitimate use of marriage during this pre-baptismal period as sufficient to disqualify a candidate.[62]

(7) Confession of Sins

In the RCIA the candidates, by the act of submitting to baptism, implicitly acknowledge their sinfulness and seek forgiveness. There are certain indications in the early documents, however, that some more explicit confession was required.

Tertullian derives the link between baptism and confession of sins from Mt. 3.6. 'They were baptized by him in the River

---

[61] *De Elia et Ieiunio*, 21.79 (PL 14.726). In this passage St Ambrose alludes to some of the ceremonies: the giving in of names, the participation of the sponsors. In Milan the Lenten Fast was not kept on Saturdays and Sundays, but in Rome one fasted on Saturdays also (*op. cit.* 10.34; PL 14.708. Augustine, Ep. 36. 14.32; PL 33.151).

[62] *De Fid. et Op.* 6.8 (PL 40.202).

Jordan, confessing their sins'.[63] Cyril of Jerusalem seems to have a detailed confession in mind;[64] St John Chrysostom, on the other hand, speaks of confession of sins to God alone, who does not require that they should be 'proclaimed in the presence of others'.[65] St Ambrose says that acceptance of baptism is in itself so explicit an acknowledgment of sin that no express confession is necessary.[66] However the extraordinary rites which Emperor Constantine underwent when he was baptized shortly before his death were preceded by a confession of sins, made on his knees, followed by a laying on of hands.[67]

(8) Prebaptismal Bath

'Let those who are to be baptized be instructed to wash and cleanse themselves on the fifth day of the week [Maundy Thursday]'.[68] The context suggests that the purpose of this regulation in Hippolytus' liturgy is hygienic. St Augustine notes that the practice of the Maundy Thursday bath, though originally adopted 'because the candidates' bodies had become dirty through Lenten observance and could not be handled at the font without offending the senses', was also followed by some of the baptized, who allowed themselves the indulgence of a day's interruption of fast.[69] In Roman life, a bath was a luxury not so much because of its rarity as because of its elaborateness.

There is of course no equivalent of this rite in the RCIA.

(9) Preparation Rites on Holy Saturday

The RCIA gives several rites which may be celebrated on Holy Saturday morning as a last preparation for the sacraments of initiation. They are: the Presentation of the Lord's Prayer (if

---

[63]*De Baptismo*, 20.1; Whitaker, p. 9.

[64]'Now is the time for confession. Confess the sins you have committed by word and deed, by night by day' (*Cat.* 1.5).

[65]ACW 12.36.

[66]S 3.12. Cf. *Expos. Evang Luc.* vi.3 (PL 15.1669).

[67]Eusebius, *Vit. Const.* iv.61.

[68]*Ap. Trad.* 20.5.

[69]Ep. 54.7.10 (PL 33.204).

this has been postponed), the Recitation of the Creed, the Ephphetha, and the choosing of a baptismal name. The Anointing with Oil of the Catechumens may be conferred at this point, rather than in the Vigil Service, or earlier during the Period of Catechumenate, as is the custom in the USA.

In some parts of the early Church, such as Antioch in Chrysostom's time,[70] there was a break between the last preliminary rites celebrated on Holy Saturday and the Vigil Service itself. However, since practice varied so widely, it seemed simplest to include them all in the following section under the Sacraments of Initiation.

THIRD STEP: THE SACRAMENTS OF INITIATION

A. BAPTISM

In Hippolytus' liturgy an all-night vigil, beginning on Saturday night, is laid down, at which there were to be scriptural readings and homilies.[71] The seven baptismal readings of the Roman liturgy or the Paschal vigil are a survival from this practice. 'May God speak to us in his readings; let us speak to God in our prayers,' says St Augustine in a sermon preached during the vigil.[72] In Rome it was presumably still dark when the ceremonies began at cockcrow.[73] The ceremonies described by Cyril and Ambrose begin in a vestibule to the baptistery.[74]

(1) The Ephphetha (Opening)[75]

This is a ceremony known only in the west. Our Lord restored the deaf and dumb man by touching his mouth and ears with saliva, saying 'Ephphetha ... Be opened'.[76] In the modern rite,

---

[70]See p. 150.

[71]*Ap. Trad.* 20.9.

[72]Sermon 219, (PL 38.1088).

[73]*Ap. Trad.* 21.1.

[74]MC 1.2; S 1.4.

[75]S 1. 2-3. This name Opening was also given later to a totally different ceremony in which the candidate received the book of the gospels into his hands. Cf. B. Botte, 'Apertio Aurium', *RAC* 1.487ff.

[76]Mk. 7.34.

after the reading of the gospel episode in the seventh chapter of St Mark, the celebrant touches the candidate's ears and lips, and repeats our Lord's words.

In the early Church it was the nostrils rather than the lips which were touched. St Ambrose takes the ceremony to mean that the candidate becomes capable of understanding what he will hear during the ceremony and sensitive to the 'aroma of Christ'.[77] Later Roman liturgical books prescribed that the minister should use saliva to touch the candidate's ears and nose,[78] and it is in fact only very recently that this unhygienic rubric has disappeared from the Roman rite. John the Deacon, on the other hand, describes a rite in which the ears and nostrils are touched with oil.[79] St Ambrose, however, mentions neither spittle nor oil, and Hippolytus is also silent on this point.[80] In the *Apostolic Tradition* a similar rite formed part of a ceremony of exorcism.[81] It seems likely that St Ambrose has lost sight of its original purpose.

After this ceremony, according to St Ambrose's rite (though not in St Cyril's) the candidate entered the baptistery proper.

(2) The Renunciation of Sin

The RCIA prescribes no actions in connection with this rite, contenting itself with giving the words. The early Church, by contrast, performed the rite very dramatically: the candidate faced Satan and renounced him to his face. This rite is described by all four of our preachers, though the details vary. Chrysostom and Theodore[82] say that the candidate kneels in adoration and in humble acknowledgment of his fall and slavery to sin. The hands are stretched out in the attitude of prayer that is commonly depicted in early art and is still adopted by the priest

---

[77] 2 Cor. 2.15.

[78] '*Gelasian Sacramentary*' (Mohlberg, p. 68; Whitaker, p. 183).

[79] *Ad Senarium*, 4 (PL 59.402); Whitaker, p. 156.

[80] 'Let him breathe on their faces and seal their foreheads and ears and noses, and then let him raise them up' (*Ap. Trad.* 20.8). It is possible, however, that saliva was used in Milan in St Ambrose's time, and that his silence is prompted by delicacy, for he omits all mention of spittle in his account of two of our Lord's miracles (S 1.2; 3.11ff.).

[81] *Ap. Trad.* 20.8.

[82] Chrysostom, BH 2.18 and ACW 11.22; Theodore, BH 2.3.

at Mass. Cyril describes how the candidate is made to face west to address the devil. He explains that the west is the source of darkness, and stands for the devil's abode.[83]

It is commonly suggested that the westward-facing stance for the Renunciation did not feature in Latin liturgies.[84] It may, however, be inferred from Ambrose's *de Mysteriis*: 'So after you enter to behold your adversary, whom you consider you had to renounce to his face, you turn to the east'.[85]

More dramatic gestures were subsequently added to the ceremony. By the end of the fifth century in Syria the candidate was required to breathe upon the devil, thus blowing him away with the common rite of exorcism.[86] Some liturgists detect evidence in St Ambrose for an even more picturesque ceremony: the candidate has to spit in the devil's face. They argue from the passage in *de Mysteriis* quoted above: 'Whom you consider you had to renounce to his face'. By emending one word in the awkward Latin phrase (*cui renuntiandum in os putaris*) and accepting a MS variant in another word, they produce the startling statement 'into whose face you spat in renunciation' (*cui renuntiando in os sputaris*).[87] However, this practice is elsewhere unknown in the west, though it is practised in some oriental rites today.[88] We should not therefore attribute to St Ambrose a practice against all textual and liturgical probability.

The list of what is renounced is different in each liturgy: Satan, service, works (Hippolytus); Satan, works, pomp and worship (Cyril); Satan, pomp, worship, works (Chrysostom); Satan, angels, works, worship, vanity and worldly enticements (Theodore); devil, works and world and its pleasures (Ambrose).[89] When explaining the list, preachers customarily allowed themselves time to develop a detailed catalogue of the

---

[83]MC 1.2, 4.

[84]Cf. J. M. Hanssens, *La Liturgie d'Hippolyte*, pp. 459-460; and M. Righetti, *Storia Liturgica*, iv, p. 86.

[85]M 7.

[86]Pseudo-Dionysius, *De Ecclesiastica Hierarchia*, 2.5; PG 3.420.

[87]Cf. Botte, *De Sacramentis*, p. 27, and the other references given there.

[88]Cf. H. Leclercq, DACL 15. 1651-1652. For the Byzantine Rite, cf. Whitaker, p. 70.

[89]In other places Ambrose (*Hexameron* 1. 14; PL 14.129) and Chrysostom (ACW 12.48) quote different formulas.

devil's works and pomps. The theatre and the turf feature regularly.[90] The RCIA gives alternative lists.

(3) The Profession of Faith

In the RCIA the Renunciation of Sin is followed by a triple profession of faith in the Father, Son and Holy Spirit. This rite has developed from what in the early Church was called an act of Adhesion to Christ, by which the candidate, after rejecting the service of Satan, now pledged his allegiance to Christ. Chrysostom gives this declaration explicitly: 'I enter into your service, O Christ'.[91] In Cyril the formula of acceptance takes the form of a profession of faith: 'I believe in the Father, the Son and the Holy Spirit, and in one baptism of repentance'.[92] Theodore's profession also includes a declaration of faith: 'I pledge myself by vow, I believe and I am baptized in the name of the Father, of the Son and of the Holy Spirit.[93] Cyril describes how the candidate turns away from the devil in the west to face Christ, the source of light, in the east before making this act of adhesion.[94] It is only after this ceremony in Cyril's liturgy that the candidate enters the baptistery proper.

The early Christians adopted the eastward direction of prayer generally, and not only for the Rite of Adhesion; churches were normally built with an east-west axis. The Fathers give a variety of explanations: Paradise lay in the east;[95] the Ascension took place to the east of Jerusalem;[96] the second coming was expected from the east.[97] Tertullian remarks that the practice led pagans to accuse Christians of sun-worship.[98]

---

[90]Cyril, MC 1.6; Chrysostom ACW 11.25. Theodore includes organs (BH 2.12).

[91]BH 2.21; ACW 11.24.

[92]MC 1.9.

[93]BH 2, *synopsis.* The formula of adhesion is less evident in western liturgies than in liturgies of the East, though Ambrose does perhaps allude to it indirectly when he refers to the agreement to 'take on your opponent', and to the 'note of hand' and the 'guarantee' (S 1.4,5,6).

[94]MC 1.9. Cf. Ambrose M 7: 'You turn to the east'.

[95]*Ap. Const.* ii.57; Basil, *de Spir. Sanct.* 27.66 (PG 32.189-192).

[96]*Ap. Const.* loc. cit.

[97]Origen, *Hom. in Lev.* ix.10 (Baehrens, p. 438). Cf. Mt 24.27; Acts 1.11.

[98]*Apologeticum,* 16.

The east was already connected with worship in the Old Testament.[99]

(4) Stripping

At some point in a rite which included anointing of the whole body and total immersion, the candidates had to remove their clothes. (This is not required in the RCIA, in which it is not necessary for the whole body to come in contact with the oil and water.) Ambrose with his usual delicacy makes no mention of the stripping in S or M, though he does speak of it in another place; the Christian's descent into the Jordan (i.e. the font) recalls his naked entry into life and his naked departure from it, and reminds him to avoid superfluities.[100] Cyril, on the contrary, has no inhibitions against speaking about nakedness: he sees in it an imitation of Christ's nakedness on the cross and a sign that the old man and the devil have been discarded.[101] He is confident that this is the one occasion when hearers will have experienced no shame in nakedness: in this they resembled Adam's innocence in Paradise M. Righetti, with less simplicity, reminds us that the sexes were sometimes separated for baptism,[102] that deaconesses in some places attended to the women,[103] that the ancients were used to mixed bathing, and that anyhow baptisteries were discreetly dark. Some early baptisteries had curtains round them.[104]

(5) Anointing with Oil

In both the modern and the early rites the candidate was anointed with oil more than once. The RCIA, reflecting ancient practice, contains three different rites: a prebaptismal anointing with oil of catechumens, a postbaptismal anointing with chrism,

---

[99]Ezek. 43.2; 47.1. Cf. J. G. Davies, 'Orientation', in *DLW.*

[100]*In Ps. 61 Enarr.* 32 (PL 14.1180).

[101]MC 2.2; cf. Chrysostom, ACW 11.28-9; Theodore, BH 3.8.

[102]*Op. cit.* iv, p. 106; cf. *Ap. Trad.* 21.5.

[103]*Didascalia,* (Connolly) xvi, p. 146; Whitaker, p. 13. The deaconesses' duties included the pre-baptismal anointing of the whole body.

[104]Cf. H. Leclercq, DACL 2.398-9.

and a further anointing with chrism as a sign of the gift of the Holy Spirit.

The first anointing is best understood as a sign of the candidates' release from the power of the devil in preparation for baptism, and their strengthening for the conflict that lies ahead. In the RCIA the candidate is anointed on the breast, hands and other parts of the body, with the words:

> We anoint you with the oil of salvation in the name of Christ our Saviour. May he strengthen you with his power.

This anointing may be conferred at one of three different points: it can form part of the sacraments of initiation themselves, or be one of the final preparatory rites celebrated on Holy Saturday before the vigil, or be included among the rites of the Period of Catechumenate. The bishops of the USA have chosen the third position.

In the early Church the whole body was rubbed with oil, so as to recall the preparation of a wrestler's body for the contest. As St Ambrose explained:

> You were rubbed with oil like an athlete, Christ's athlete, as though in preparation for an earthly wrestling-match, and you agreed to take on your opponent (S 1.4).

In the *Apostolic Tradition* the rite is explicitly exorcistic: the presbyter anoints the candidate with 'oil of exorcism', saying, 'Let all evil spirits depart from you'.[105]

Cyril's explanation is quite different. The oil suggests to him the symbolism of the olive-tree: anointing confers a share in the richness of Christ, the true olive. It also serves as an exorcism to scare away the devil and remove the traces of sin.[106]

(6) Prayer over the Water

Although theologians today are agreed that in an emergency ordinary water may be used for baptism, in the fourth century

---

[105] *Ap. Trad.* xxi.10.
[106] MC 2.3.

it was held, at least in theory, that the water must first be consecrated if it was to have its effect. 'Not all waters have a curative power; only that water has it which has the grace of Christ ... The water does not heal unless the Spirit descends and consecrates the water.'[107]

In the RCIA this blessing of the water is described under the heading of 'Prayer over the Water'. This prayer consists of two parts: God's saving actions worked through water (e.g. in the Flood) are gratefully recalled; and the Holy Spirit is called down on the water in an Epiclesis.[108] This rite is performed at every baptism, except during the Easter Season, when the water consecrated at the Paschal Vigil is still used; in that case the prayer said over the blessed Easter water is regarded simply as an act of thanksgiving. At the Vigil the dipping of the Paschal candle into the water denotes the presence and power of the risen Christ. We recall also Cyril of Jerusalem's belief that all baptismal water owes its efficacy to the power imparted by Jesus when he went down into the Jordan.[109] Moreover, as he rose in the power of the Holy Spirit, the immersion of the candle is a symbol of the coming of the Holy Spirit upon the water.

For the early Christians first the devil had to be driven out of the water by an exorcism, then the bishop invoked the Trinity to become present in the water.[110] This belief that the sacramental effect is conditional upon the invocation of God's presence also applies to the other sacraments. 'The bread and wine of the Eucharist is merely bread and wine before the invocation of the sacred and adorable Trinity, but after the invocation the bread becomes the body of Christ and wine his blood'.[111] 'Just as the bread of the Eucharist after the invocation of the Holy Spirit is no longer just bread, but the body of Christ, so the holy chrism after the invocation is no longer merely ordinary ointment but Christ's grace, which through the

---

[107]Ambrose, S i.15. Cf. Theodore, BH 3.9; Tertullian, *de Bapt.* 4 (Whitaker, p. 7).

[108]See pp. 48-49 for a discussion of the later Epiclesis which forms part of the Eucharist.

[109]MC 3.1.

[110]Ambrose, S i.18.

[111]Cyril, MC 1.7.

presence of the Holy Spirit instils his divinity into us'.[112] So too for Theodore a transformation takes place when the Holy Spirit is called down on the baptismal water.[113]

The invocation is not always addressed to the same person: sometimes the whole Trinity is invoked:[114] sometimes God (the Father) is asked to impart the Holy Spirit;[115] sometimes the Holy Spirit himself is said to be called upon.[116] There is even one text, the Sacramentary of Sarapion of Thmuis in Egypt, in which the Father is invited to send his Son on the water so that it may be filled with the Spirit.[117] St Ambrose gives an explanation of this variety of language: 'In everything we have done, the mystery of the Trinity has been preserved. The Father, the Son and the Holy Spirit are present everywhere; they exercise a joint causality, a single sanctifying action, although some aspects do seem to be peculiar to the individual persons'.[118] In baptism, for example, one is called by the Father, dies with the Son and receives the seal of the Holy Spirit.

The doctrine of the presence of the Holy Spirit in the baptismal water received further elaboration. Theodore saw the font as a womb into which the candidate descended to receive second birth from the Holy Spirit, whose presence impregnates the water.[119] St Leo the Great compared the Spirit's action of filling the font with his other action of filling our Lady's womb.[120]

St Ambrose in several places implies that the symbolism of the cross features in the ceremony of the blessing of the font. 'What is the water without the cross of Christ?'[121] Perhaps he is alluding to a sign of the cross which the bishop traces with his

---

[112]*Ibid.* 3.3. Concerning the *epiclesis*, cf. Cyril MC 1.7 with note 13.

[113]BH 3.9.

[114]Ambrose, S 1.18; Cyril, MC 1.7.

[115]Cyril, MC 5.7.

[116]Cyril, MC 3.3.

[117]*Euchologion*, 7; Whitaker, p. 83.

[118]S 6.5; cf. 6.6-8.

[119]BH 3.9.

[120]*Sermon* 24 (On Christmas, iv) 3; PL 54.206. Cf. Cyril, MC 2.4: 'The water of salvation became both tomb and mother for you'.

[121]M 20. Cf. S 2.13, 23; M 14.

hand. But it is quite possible that the cross is the one the bishop carries in his hand. In some Coptic rites the bishop uses this cross to bless the font.[122] In the *Apostolic Constitutions* the epiclesis over the water includes the prayer that the baptized may be crucified and die with Christ.[123]

(7) Baptism

The early accounts of this rite suggest that the candidate stood about waist-deep in water, and was immersed by bowing forward with the bishop's hand pressing on his head. Theodore regards the candidate's gesture of bending his body beneath the surface as a sign of humble acceptance.[124] (In those days the font was a real pool let into the floor.) However, a different impression is given by the fonts belonging to the period that have been discovered and the pictures of the ceremony that have survived, particularly representations of the baptism of Christ which are apparently modelled on contemporary liturgical practice. In many places it seems that the font was too small for the candidate to immerse his whole body, even if he bent. He must have stood in water that came scarcely above his knees while the minister poured water on to his head.[125]

It seems to have been the general practice in the early Church to immerse the candidate three times in the water. The obvious significance of the triple immersion is trinitarian, especially as the mention of the name of a Person of the Trinity often accompanied each immersion. According to the fourth-century Alexandrian Didymus, Eunomian heretics, who did not believe in the Trinity, administered baptism by a single immersion in the name not of the Trinity but of the death of Christ.[126] Cyril, however, departs from tradition and takes the

---

[122]Cf. Denzinger, *Ritus Orientalium*, i.204, 229. I am grateful to Dr W. Macomber for this suggestion. In early representations of the Baptism of Christ, the Baptist (= the bishop) is sometimes shown carrying a cross.

[123]*Ap. Const.* vii. 43; Whitaker, p. 34.

[124]BH 3.19.

[125]Cf. J. G. Davies, *The Architectural Setting of Baptism*, pp. 25-26.

[126]*De Trinitate*, ii.15; cf. ii.12; (PG 39.720, 672).

three immersions to represent Christ's three days in the tomb.[127] John the Deacon gave both explanations.[128]

As St Paul saw, immersion signifies not only washing, but also the burial of the old man which must come before the new birth.[129] With this symbolism in mind, Ambrose points out that the font is tomb-shaped.[130] This seems to suggest a rectangular shape. However the archaeological evidence indicates that in Milan both fonts and one of the baptisteries were octagonal; this shape could perhaps be seen to recall the appearance of a mausoleum, as well as symbolising the eighth day. In some instances the fonts were fed by running water. There is even an indication that the water was sometimes comfortably heated.[131]

Our Lord's words, '... make disciples of all nations, baptizing them in the name of the Father and of the Son and of the Holy Spirit',[132] might make us expect to find in all baptismal liturgies the modern Roman formula: 'N., I baptize you in the name of the Father and of the Son and of the Holy Spirit'. The formula in use at Antioch in the fourth century was very like this: 'N. is baptized in the name of the Father and of the Son and of the Holy Spirit'.[133] But in Milan and Jerusalem the act of baptism was linked instead with a profession of faith. St Ambrose describes the ceremony as follows: 'You were asked: "Do you believe in God the Father almighty?" You replied: "I believe," and you were immersed.' The ceremony continues with similar acts of faith in the Son and the Holy Spirit.[134] Hippolytus had earlier recommended a longer triple profession of faith for use in Rome;[135] the ceremony Tertullian knew in Africa seems to have taken a similar form,[136] which continued to be used in

[127]MC 2.4.
[128]*Ad Senarium,* 6 (PL 59.403); Whitaker, p. 157.
[129]Rom. 6.3-4. Cf. Ambrose, S 2.20.
[130]S 3.1.
[131]Zeno of Verona, (Löfstedt) i.23; i.32 (PL 11.480-481, 476).
[132]Mt. 28.19.
[133]Theodore, BH 3, *synopsis*; Chrysostom, BH 2.26.
[134]S 2.20; cf. Cyril, MC 2.4.
[135]*Ap. Trad.* 21.12-18.
[136]*De Pudicitia,* 9.16; *De Corona,* 3.3. Both passages contain hints that the words used at baptism are a dialogue between minister and candidate.

Rome about the sixth century.[137] Evidently the early Church did not believe that fidelity to Mt 28.19 required the minister to quote Christ's words as we do today at the moment of baptism.[138]

In explaining the symbolism of baptism and the way in which it confers grace, all four Fathers refer to Christ's baptism in the Jordan. Theodore believes Christ's baptism 'foreshadowed your baptism in sign'.[139] Chrysostom takes it to be a paradigm of Christian baptism: just as Jesus was baptized by the Word (which led his body down into the Jordan), by the Father (who spoke from heaven) and by the Holy Spirit (who descended), so too we are baptized by the Trinity.[140] Cyril and Ambrose believe that Christ's entry into the Jordan gave the baptismal water its sanctifying power.[141] The Emperor Constantine delayed his baptism in the hope of being baptized in the Jordan. It has been suggested that the sacrament of baptism originally arose from the desire that a Christian should share in Jesus' Jordan experience.[142]

(8) Anointing with Chrism

In the text of the RCIA baptism is immediately followed by an anointing of the head with chrism, preceded by the words:

> He [God the Father] now anoints you with the chrism of salvation, so that, united with his people, you may remain for ever a member of Christ who is Priest, Prophet and King.

---

[137]Cf. *'Gelasian Sacramentary'*, Mohlberg, p. 74; Whitaker, p. 195.

[138]Some liturgists have thought that a formula like, 'I baptize thee in the name ...' must always have been used; but their view cannot claim the support of the majority of modern scholars, and puts a strain upon the evidence.

[139]BH 3.24.

[140]ACW 11.13. The Christology has an Apollinarian ring. Theodore has a similar, but less suspect, passage: BH 3.24.

[141]MC 3.1; S 1.15-19. Cf. Sarapion, *Euchologium*, 7; Whitaker, p. 83.

[142]G. Winkler, 'The Original Meaning of the Prebaptismal Anointing and Its Implications', in *Worship*, 52 (1978), pp. 24-45.

We have seen above how Christian baptism was linked in the early Church with that of Jesus. The Father's words, 'This is [*or* You are] my beloved Son', quoting as they do a coronation psalm, suggested to the first disciples that Jesus' baptism was the moment when he was proclaimed the Messiah or Christ, the anointed King whose coming was prophesied.[143] Thus it was a short step from seeing Christian baptism as a participation in that of Jesus, to seeing it as the Christian's share in Jesus' messianic anointing, and then to expressing this insight by the introduction of a literal anointing of the candidate's head, modelled on the anointing of kings and priests.[144]

It is evident from St Ambrose's account that the chrism was not dabbed on with the thumb, as it is today, but poured over the head so that it ran down like the oil which the psalmist describes running down Aaron's beard.[145] He sees the ceremony as a symbol of eternal life and the Christian's royal and priestly powers.[146] Tertullian takes a similar view of the symbolism of the ceremony.[147] John the Deacon in sixth-century Rome explains the post-baptismal anointing of the head with chrism in the same way.[148] Cyril's liturgy, however, does not include an anointing at this point.

Chrysostom and Theodore surprisingly place the rite before the anointing of the whole body with oil. Theodore sees it as the placing of a mark of ownership. He uses a military metaphor: the rite makes the Christian a 'soldier of the King of Heaven'; but he confuses the imagery by saying that the anointing also brands the candidate as a 'sheep of Christ'.[149] Chrysostom and

---

[143]Cf. Mt. 3.17; Mk. 1.11; Lk. 3.22. St Peter's sermon (Acts 10.37-38) links Jesus' baptism with his messianic anointing.

[144]This is G. Winkler's argument in the article quoted in note 142. I have discussed this view myself in two articles: 'Initiation: Sacrament and Experience', in *Liturgy Reshaped*, ed. K. Stevenson, London, 1982, pp. 17-31; and 'Anointing at Baptism', in *Living Stones*, 1 (1987), pp. 27-31.

[145]S 3.1; M 29-30. Cf. Tertullian, *de Bapt.* 7: 'the oil runs'. See Ps. 133.2.

[146]Eternal life: S 2.24. Royal and priestly powers: S 4.3; M 30 (Whitaker, p. 132). There is an allusion to 1 Pet. 2.9.

[147]*De Baptismo*, 7.1; Whitaker, p. 8. Cf. *De Resurrectione Mortuorum*, 8.3: 'The flesh is anointed in order that the soul may be *consecrated*' (Whitaker, p. 10).

[148]*Ad Senarium*, 6; Whitaker, p. 157.

[149]BH 2.17.

Theodore both regard the rite as a protection against the devil: by the anointing the sign of the cross is fixed on the candidate's forehead to make the devil turn away his eyes.[150]

As early as the time of Hippolytus two kinds of oil were used for baptismal ceremonies, 'Oil of Exorcism' and 'Oil of Thanksgiving'. The former is used for the first anointing, the latter for the second and third.[151] Hippolytus does not let us see if the two kinds consist of different materials or whether the difference lies simply in the different prayers that are said over them. Ambrose, Cyril and Chrysostom, however, distinguish the olive-oil from the chrism or '*myron*', which is olive-oil mixed with a perfume, sometimes at least balsam.

In antiquity balsam was used for both medical and cosmetic purposes. Oddly, the earliest mention of the use of chrism in a baptismal ceremony occurs in an account by St Irenaeus of the liturgical practices of a heretical gnostic sect: 'They also anoint with balsam-juice the person who was been initiated, for they say that this myron is a sign of the universal good odour.'[152] There is no evidence for its liturgical use in orthodox circles until the fourth century. For St Ambrose the chrism symbolizes the attraction of Christ: 'We shall run following the perfume of your robes'.[153] At about the same time in Syria the *Apostolic Constitutions* took the chrism as the sign of 'the scent of the knowledge of the Gospel' and 'the aroma of Christ'.[154] Chrysostom explains that 'the myron is for the bride, the oil for the athlete'.[155] For a ninth-century bishop, on the other hand, the myron symbolizes Christ's divinity, the oil his humanity.[156]

This anointing with chrism, constituting as it does a mark of ownership, is often described as a 'seal'. The term was doubly appropriate, because it was also applied to the Jewish rite of

[150]Chrysostom, BH 2.22-23; ACW 11.27; Theodore, BH 3.18. For an explanation of the symbolism of 'sealing' cf. p. 36f., and G. W. H. Lampe, *The Seal of the Spirit*, pp. 7-18.

[151]*Ap. Trad.* 21.6-8.

[152]*Adversus Haereses*, i.21.3; PG 7.664 (Harvey i.185).

[153]M 29, translating a text probably based on the LXX version of Cant 1.4.

[154]vii. 44; Whitaker, p. 34. Cf. 2 Cor. 2.15.

[155]ACW 11.27; Whitaker, p. 37.

[156]Moses Bar Kipho, *On Myrrh*, 7, mentioned by G. Khouri-Sarkis, 'Prières et Cérémonies du Baptême', *L'Orient Syrien* 1 (1956) 180, n.22.

circumcision, of which baptism was the Christian equivalent.[157] Zeno of Verona, apparently referring to a post-baptismal anointing, speaks of a sacrament by which women as well as men are circumcised.[158] The fifth-century Syriac poet Narsai, referring to a prebaptismal anointing, compares the oil with the iron of the circumcision-knife which the bishop sharpens with words; he also sees it as the 'drug' which administers the Holy Spirit.[159]

This 'messianic' anointing of the Christian is rich in symbolism. However the RCIA states that it should be conferred only in those rare cases where confirmation is deferred to a later date (n. 224). Evidently the reason is that the anointing at confirmation takes the place of the 'messianic' anointing; but in that case, it is a pity that all reference to the Christian's union with Christ the Priest, Prophet and King is lost.

(9) The Washing of the Feet

The next rite which Ambrose describes has no counterpart in the RCIA, or in the accounts of Cyril, Chrysostom, Theodore or Hippolytus: the bishop, assisted by the clergy, washes the neophytes' feet.[160] It was, however, practised in Turin, in Gaul, in North Africa and possibly even in Syria.[161] St Ambrose says explicitly it was not practised in Rome.[162] Its use was forbidden at the Council of Elvira early in the fourth century; it must therefore have been practised in Spain.[163]

---

[157]Cf. S. P. Brock, 'The Transition to a Post-baptismal Anointing in the Antiochene Rite', in *The Sacrifice of Praise*, ed. B. D. Spinks, pp. 215-225.

[158](Löfstedt) 1.3.21; PL 1.352.

[159]Homily 22, *On Baptism*: Whitaker, p. 52. See below, p. 37.

[160]S 3.4-7.

[161]Turin: Maximus, *De Baptismo*, iii (PL 57.779-780). Gaul: Caesarius of Arles, *Sermons* (CCSL, ed. Morin), 64.2 and 204.3. N. Africa: Augustine, *Ad Januarium*, ii.33 (PL 33.220). Syria: Aphrahat, *Homily* 12, *On the Pasch*, TU III.iii-iv, p. 192 (where the Washing of the Feet is connected with baptism). In Aquileia the rite was performed *before* baptism, as Ambrose's contemporary Chromatius testifies (Serm. 15.6, Corpus Christianorum 9A.69; I owe this reference to G. Jeanes).

[162]S 3. 5-6.

[163]Canon 48; Hefele-Leclercq, I.i.249.

Several early baptisteries that archaeologists have discovered contain a second, much smaller, font beside the main one. It has been suggested that this small font was used, at least in some cases, for the foot-washing.[164] However, it seems possible that these little basins had a different purpose, perhaps the baptism of children, who were too small to stand comfortably in the main font.

St Ambrose is aware of an attempt to explain the ceremony as an injunction upon the neophyte to perform humble service to others in the spirit of our Lord's words, 'If I then, your Lord and Teacher, have washed your feet you also ought to wash one another's feet'.[165] He insists, however, that the ceremony is principally a sacramental rite; its effect is to afford protection against the liability to sin inherited from Adam.[166] However, St Ambrose's interpretation of the washing of the feet never won general support in the Church.

(10) The Baptismal Garment

In the RCIA the newly baptized may be given a baptismal garment of white, or any other appropriate colour; the godparents help the neophyte to put the garment on. This symbolises the fact that the baptized have 'put on' Christ.[167] The celebrant urges them to bring the baptismal garment 'unstained to the judgment seat of our Lord Jesus Christ'.

In the early Church, after baptism the naked neophyte was dressed, not in the clothes he wore before, but in white. These white robes were a symbol of the life of the resurrection to which the new Christians had now passed, and of the innocence that should now distinguish them.[168] A variety of Old Testament

[164]Cf. J. G. Davies, *Architectural Setting*, p. 26. T. C. Akeley, *Christian Initiation in Spain c. 300-1100*, p. 54 and Plate 1, gives a further example.

[165]Jn. 13.14; S. 3.5. Maximus, Caesarius and Augustine all gave the ceremony this interpretation in the passages quoted above.

[166]S 3.7; see note 19, there. So too Chromatius, Serm. 15.6.

[167]Cf. Gal. 3.27.

[168]Theodòre, BH 3.26; Chrysostom, ACW 4.3ff., especially 18; Cyril, MC 4.8; Ambrose, M 34. In S. Ambrose alludes to the white garment only indirectly: S 4.5-6; 5.14.

texts was quoted in explanation of the symbolism; Cyril, for example, quotes Isaiah: 'He has clothed me with the garment of salvation, and with the robe of gladness he has covered me'.[169]

Chrysostom compares the white robe to a uniform which should be an external sign of Christ, whom they have, in St Paul's phrase, 'put on' internally.[170]

> Men who have undertaken temporal duties often wear on their clothes an imperial badge as a sign to the public of their trustworthiness. They would not permit themselves to do anything unworthy of their uniform; and even if they attempted it, there are many people to stop them. If others wish them harm, the clothes they wear afford sufficient protection. Now the neophytes carry Christ himself, not on their clothes, but dwelling in their souls with his Father, and the Holy Spirit has descended on them there. They are even more obliged, then, to prove themselves reliable, and show everyone by their scrupulous conduct and careful lives that they wear the imperial badge.[171]

The white garment reminds Ambrose of the shining garments of the transfigured Christ.[172] John the Deacon also sees a connection with the wedding-garment.[173] Zeno likened it to the fleece of Christ the Lamb.[174]

It became customary in the west for the new Christians to wear their white garments throughout the octave of Easter until the Saturday before Low Sunday (*'in depositis albis'*), when they took their place among the faithful. The newly baptized

---

[169]61.10 (LXX). Other texts quoted are Ps. 51.2; Cant 1.5; 8.5 (LXX); Is. 1.18; Eccles. 9.8; Mt. 5.16; 13.43.

[170]ACW 4.18. 'As many of you as were baptized into Christ have put on Christ' (ACW 4.4, quoting Gal. 3.27).

[171]ACW 4.17.

[172]M 34, quoting Mt. 17.2.

[173]*Ad Senarium*, 6; Whitaker, p. 157.

[174](Löfstedt) *Tractatus* i. 38; PL 11.494.

Emperor Constantine went one better: in addition to his white garments, he had his throne draped in white.[175] In the sermons of Asterius the Sophist, delivered in the second quarter of the fourth century, the whole of Easter week is called 'the shining (*phaidra*) week'.[176] Chrysostom speaks of the garment as a wedding-robe which is worn for a marriage-feast that lasts seven days.[177]

In some places a white linen cloth was also spread over the candidate's head. Theodore took this to be a mark of freedom: slaves have to uncover their heads.[178] John the Deacon believed it to be a symbol of the priesthood: 'for the priests of that time always wore on their heads a mystic veil'.[179] St Augustine in a Low Sunday sermon takes the opposite view to Theodore: it is unveiling that symbolizes freedom:

> Today is called the octave of the infants.[180] The veils are due to be removed from their heads and this is a sign of freedom ... Today, as you see, our infants mingle with the faithful and fly as it were from the nest.[181]

(11) The Lighted Candle

In the modern liturgy the neophytes are each given a lighted candle as a sign that they have been enlightened by Christ. There is also apparently an allusion to the lamps of the bridesmaids of the parable.[182] There is no reference to this ceremony in any of the sermons quoted in this book. However,

[175]Eusebius, *Vita Constantini*, 4.62.

[176]'Asterii Sophistae Commentariorum in Psalmos', ed. M. Richard, *Symbolae Osloenses Fasc. Supplet.* xvi (1956). Apart from Asterius, the earliest evidence that the neophytes wore their white robes for a week seems to be a (fifth-century?) sermon by pseudo-Athanasius (PG 28.1086) and another by pseudo-Augustine (Caesarius of Arles?) (PL 39.2075).

[177]ACW 6.23-24.

[178]BH 2.19.

[179]*Ad Senarium*, 6; Whitaker, p. 157. But what does he mean by 'of that time'?

[180]A common name for the newly baptized. It referred to their second birth by baptism and does not imply that they were young in years.

[181]*Sermon* 376 (PL 39.1669f.).

[182]Mt. 25.1-13.

in a work which used to be attributed to St Ambrose but is now generally considered the work of another, there is a reference to 'the shining lights' of the neophytes, the 'white-robed members of the heavenly kingdom'.[183] The use of lights must in any event have been necessary in a dawn ceremony. Gregory of Nazianzus, preaching at Constantinople in 381, connects the lights with the symbolism of the parable of the bridesmaids.

> The lamps which you will light symbolize the torchlight procession in the next world, in which our shining, virgin souls will meet the bridegroom with the shining lights of faith.[184]

The symbol is appropriate for a sacrament which is called 'Enlightenment'.[185]

B. CONFIRMATION

(1) The Gift of the Spirit: Confirmation

The third anointing is connected with the rite for the giving of the Holy Spirit, which in the West evolved into the sacrament of confirmation. Originally the Christian was baptized and confirmed in a single ceremony. In the Orthodox Church, and in Eastern Rite Catholic Churches, this has remained true; baptism and confirmation are conferred together, normally by a priest. In the West, however, the two sacraments became separated.[186] For although it became first permissible and then normal for a priest to baptize, confirmation remained the prerogative of the bishop. Early in the fifth century, for example, Pope Innocent I maintained there was scriptural warrant for this arrangement:

---

[183]*De Lapsu Virginis*, 5.19 (PL 16.372).

[184]*Oratio* 40.46; cf. 45.2 (PG 36.425, 624).

[185]E.g. Heb. 6.4; Justin, 1 *Apol.* 61; Cyril, *Procat.* 1 (Whitaker, pp. 2, 24).

[186]See J. D. C. Fisher and E. J. Yarnold, 'Initiation: the West from about A.D. 500 to the Reformation', in SL, pp. 144-152.

Concerning the signing of children, it is clear that this may not be performed by anyone except the bishop ... This is evident not only from the Church's practice but from the passage in the Acts of the Apostles which states that Peter and John were sent to confer the Holy Spirit on those who were already baptized.[187]

Although the RCIA has reunited baptism and confirmation, confirmation is not normally conferred at the baptism of babies.

Once baptism and confirmation are regarded as distinct sacraments, whether celebrated on the same occasion or not, the question arises how their effects differ. Since the baptized already share the life of the risen Christ, and therefore have received the grace of the Holy Spirit, the difficulty is to explain the sense in which the Holy Spirit is conferred again at confirmation. The answer given in the Rite of Confirmation, promulgated by Paul VI in 1971, the year before the first publication of the RCIA, is that the sacrament 'conforms believers more fully to Christ and strengthens them so that they may bear witness to Christ for the building up of his Body in faith and love' (n.2). The implication seems to be that baptism is the first sacrament of entry into the Church, by which the Holy Spirit, who is the living power of the risen Christ, becomes the Christian's source of life; confirmation is the second sacrament of entry into the Church, by which the baptized Christians are appointed to be witnesses of Christ, so that the Holy Spirit they have already received now strengthens them for their new responsibilities. The candidate is 'sealed with the Gift of the Holy Spirit' (RCIA n.270).

The name, the rites and the significance of what we now call the sacrament of confirmation were all surprisingly fluid in the early Church. Many of the terms applied to confirmation occur in a passage in St Paul, which in fact concerns the saint's apostolic status and not the sacrament at all:

---

[187]*Ep. 25, Ad Decentium,* 3.6 (PL 20.554-555); cf. Acts 8.14-17. 'Children' again is a liturgical word meaning 'candidate for baptism' of whatever age.

But it is God who establishes us with you in Christ, and has commissioned [literally 'anointed'] us; he has put his seal upon us and given us his Spirit in our hearts as a guarantee.[188]

This text gives us five elements that were believed to be connected with the sacrament: (1) confirmation or strengthening ('establishes'); (2) anointing ('commissioned'); (3) the seal or sign; (4) the giving of the Holy Spirit; (5) the Spirit's guarantee. A sixth element is indicated by the passage from the Acts to which Innocent I referred: the apostles conferred the Holy Spirit through the 'laying on of hands'.[189]

Another name given to the ceremony was 'perfecting' (*teleiosis, perfectio*);[190] confirmation, in other words, was seen to complete the rites of initiation and the candidate's spiritual endowment.[191] Indeed, the original meaning of the term 'confirmation' seems to have been 'completion'; the gift of the Holy Spirit at confirmation completed or sealed the effect of baptism.[192]

In the *Apostolic Tradition* the ceremonial action has three main stages: the bishop's hands are laid on the candidates while he asks the Father to fill them with the Holy Spirit; oil is poured on them, and they are 'sealed' on the forehead.[193] There is no indication of the nature of the 'sealing'. We are not told whether oil was used or whether the sign of the cross was traced on the candidate's forehead. In some rites, however, it is the earlier 'messianic' anointing which is described as a 'sealing'.

Cyril devotes a whole sermon to the explanation of the ceremony. The candidate is anointed with chrism or myron after baptism and so receives the Holy Spirit, just as Our Lord's

[188]2 Cor 1.21-22.
[189]Acts 8.18. This gesture has already been discussed in connection with the rite of admission to the catechumenate, p. 5.
[190]Cf. Ambrose, S 3.8; Theodore, BH 3.19.
[191]The Greek verb meaning 'to perfect' (*teleioo*) means also 'to initiate'; but it is not implied that only confirmation, not baptism, can properly be described as an initiation.
[192]See the note "'Confirmation" as a Liturgical Term' in *The Study of Liturgy*, pp. 149-150.
[193]22.1-3.

baptism, at which the Spirit came upon him, was called figuratively an anointing.[194] The myron is applied to the forehead and the organs of sensation.[195] The effect is to 'instil divinity into us',[196] to give the candidate sensitivity to spiritual things,[197] to arm him against the devil and save him from the shame of original sin.[198]

In Theodore's rite after the immersion the bishop signs or seals the candidate on the forehead, apparently with some form of oil. Theodore links the action with the presence of the Holy Spirit and compares it to Jesus' 'anointing' with the Spirit after his baptism. Alluding to St Paul's phrase 'the first-fruits of the Spirit',[199] he concludes that the sacrament gives the candidate an anticipation of the blessings of immortality. It is argued below that Theodore means that this postbaptismal anointing is the sign, not of a new gift of the Spirit, but of the original gift of the Holy Spirit at baptism.[200] If so, Theodore is at one with Chrysostom, who, while not speaking of any post-baptismal anointing, explains that the Holy Spirit is conferred by the hand of the bishop that is laid on the candidate in the act of baptism.[201]

In giving no rite for the imparting of the Holy Spirit after baptism, Chrysostom is at one with many of the early Syrian sources.[202] In some of these rites, though not in Chrysostom, the gift of the Holy Spirit is explicitly connected with a single, 'messianic' anointing conferred before baptism. Chrysostom himself takes Holy Communion to be a further cause of the presence of the Holy Spirit.[203]

---

[194]MC 3. 1-2, quoting Acts 10.38.

[195]MC 3.4.

[196]MC 3.3.

[197]MC 3.4, 7.

[198]MC 3.4, 7.

[199]Rom. 8.23.

[200]BH 3.27 with note 65.

[201]BH 2.25-26.

[202]E.g., *Didascalia* (ed. Connolly) ch. 16, pp. 146-147; cf. ch. 26, pp. 242, 246; Narsai (ed. Connolly) *Homilies*, 21-22. Cf. A. F. J. Klijn, *The Acts of Thomas* (E. J. Brill, Leiden, 1962), pp. 54-57; R. H. Connolly, *The Liturgical Homilies of Narsai*, pp. xlii-xlix. Cf. E. J. Yarnold, 'The Early Syrian Rites'.

[203]BH 2.27.

St Ambrose speaks of a 'spiritual sealing' after baptism through which the neophyte receives the Holy Spirit with his seven gifts.[204] He gives no detail of this rite of sealing here but in another passage he seems to imply that a sign of the cross was made and an anointing took place. Wishing to show that all three Persons of the Trinity are operative together, but each in a different way, he says:

> God the Father anointed you, the Lord sealed you and placed the Holy Spirit in your heart ... Christ sealed you. You were sealed in the likeness of his cross and passion.[205]

In the parallel passage in *De Mysteriis*, 42, Ambrose uses the word 'confirm' to describe the effect of the sacrament.

In all these rites, therefore, the purpose is to confer the Holy Spirit. But the effects of the gift of the Holy Spirit are described in many different ways: perfecting, confirming, giving divinity and spiritual perception, an anticipation of heaven, strength against the devil. The image of the sealing is explained sometimes as a mark that the neophyte belongs to Christ.[206]

(2) Entry into the Church and Greeting

The candidate has now received the first two sacraments of initiation, and joins the rest of the community in the celebration of the Eucharist. This first holy communion of the newly baptized constitutes the third sacrament of their initiation.

In the early centuries the baptistery was set apart from the body of the church, so that the congregation would not witness the celebration of baptism and confirmation. Consequently the solemn entry of the baptized, clothed in their white robes, and dispelling the darkness with the light of their baptismal

---

[204]S 3.8-10.

[205]S 6.6-7.

[206]It is like the brand on cattle or slaves, or the tattoo on a soldier's hand or forehead. Plate 6 of *The Study of Liturgy* shows a sarcophagus figure representing a Roman commander with an X-shaped mark on his forehead.

candles, must have been a spectacular moment.[207] Then they were greeted by the rest of the congregation with a Kiss of Peace, which is described by Hippolytus and Chrysostom.[208] This kiss of greeting seems to be distinct from the kiss of reconciliation exchanged before communion.[209]

(3) Milk and Honey

Hippolytus states that at his first Mass the neophyte is offered not only the customary chalice of eucharistic wine, but two other chalices, one containing water, the other a mixture of milk and honey. This third chalice symbolized Christ's flesh under three images: the promised land flowing with milk and honey, the baby-food on which the faithful feed, and the sweetness of Christ's word.[210] Tertullian mentions the ceremony early in the third century,[211] and it was still practised in Rome in the sixth century.[212] It is possible that St Ambrose alluded to the ceremony when he quoted the Song of Songs: 'I have come down to my garden, I have gathered myrrh with my perfumes. I have eaten bread with my honey. I have drunk wine with my milk'.[213] St Jerome also mentions the drink of milk and honey 'to signify infancy.[214]

There remained, however, one ceremony in the Mass in which, according to Ambrose, the newly baptized were not

---

[207]Gregory of Nazianzus, *Or.* 40.46 (PG 36.425); Ambrose, S 3.11, 15; 4.5, 8; M 43; Chrysostom, BH 2.27. Hippolytus however places the entry before the rite of confirmation (*Ap. Trad.* 21.20).

[208]*Ap. Trad.* 22.3-4; Chrysostom, BH 2.27.

[209]Chrysostom, ACW 11.32; Theodore, BH 4.40; Justin 1 *Apol.* 65.2.

[210]*Ap. Trad.* 23.1-3. J. Daniélou, *The Theology of Jewish Christianity*, pp. 333-334, gives other evidence for the use of milk and honey in the Eucharist, and suggests that this practice was preserved by Jewish Christians and arose from the original setting of the Eucharist within a meal.

[211]*Adv. Marc.* i, 14.3

[212]John the Deacon, *Ad Senarium*, 12 (Whitaker, pp. 157-158). *Leonine Sacramentary* (Feltoe), p. 25 (Whitaker, pp. 153-154).

[213]S 5.15, quoting Cant 5.1 according to the Septuagint text. Ambrose seems to intend this verse to refer to various rites: anointing (perfumes); communion (bread and wine). There remains the mention of milk and honey. Ambrose refers to the ceremony in another work: *de Cain*, i.5.19 (PL 14.326).

[214]*Adv. Lucif.* 8; PL 23.164.

allowed to share: it was not until Low Sunday that they could join the offertory procession and bring their gifts to the altar. It is hard to imagine why the neophytes who had been initiated into many more precious mysteries should be debarred from this far more commonplace rite. The reason St Ambrose gives is that this ceremony can be performed only by people who know its meaning and have become established as Christians; he recalls that eight days is the Jewish period for purification; circumcision, for example, took place eight days after birth.[215]

C. EUCHARIST

The third of the three sacraments of initiation in the RCIA is the Eucharist. The newly baptized will probably have been encouraged to become familiar with the Mass during the periods of Catechumenate and Enlightenment; but they have never yet been fully one with the congregation there, because they have not been able to receive holy communion. Now, as they receive the Lord's Body for the first time, they become full members of his body, the Church. In the early church, because of the discipline of secrecy (which it is neither possible nor desirable to reintroduce in modern circumstances), the neophytes had been obliged to leave after the Liturgy of the Word; consequently the Mass at the Easter Vigil was not only the occasion of their first communion, but their first Mass. For this reason three of the four examples of mystagogic catechesis contained in this book end with a description of the Eucharist. At Milan and Jerusalem the candidates had received no more than hints at what went on; it was not until after their first Communion that they were judged ready to receive a full explanation. At Antioch, too, though the catechumens learnt of the mysteries of baptism in the days before they were baptized, instruction on the Eucharist was given only after the Easter Vigil. Theodore, like Cyril and Ambrose, in the course

---

[215] *In Ps. 118 Expos.*, Prologue, 2; (PL 15.1198-1199). However, the difficulty remains: why does participation in the offertory require more careful preparation than communion?

of his baptismal instruction gives a detailed account of the eucharistic liturgy. Sermons on the Eucharist are also included among Chrysostom's baptismal instructions; but as they are devotional rather than descriptive or theological, it has not been thought worthwhile lengthening this book in order to include them. They can be read in the ACW edition of the Baptismal Homilies.

The instructions of Cyril, Ambrose and Theodore are of first-rate importance for our knowledge of the eucharistic practice of the fourth century. It may help the reader to follow their descriptions if an outline is given of the principal parts of the Mass. I have, of course, been greatly helped by the two great works on the Mass that appeared in the 1940s: *The Shape of the Liturgy*, by the Anglican Benedictine liturgist, Gregory Dix; and *Missarum Sollemnia*, by J. A. Jungmann S.J., as also by the insights of L. Bouyer's later work *The Eucharist.* One of the great contributions of Dix and Bouyer has been to show the extent of the Mass's indebtedness to its Jewish origins. The reader may find further help in J. D. Crichton's valuable and concise survey *A Short History of the Mass.*

The catechetical preacher had no need to explain the Mass of the Catechumens (Liturgy of the Word), because, as the name implies, his hearers had long frequented it. It consisted of Scriptural readings, psalms, sermon and prayers, after which the catechumens were dismissed. Then began the Eucharist proper, the principal parts of which were:

(1) The Preparation of the Gifts

As early as the end of the first century the act of setting the bread and wine on the altar was seen to have a significance of its own.[216] We have seen how by St Ambrose's time the Offertory had achieved such importance that it was the one function that the newly-baptized were not qualified to perform.[217]

---

[216]The bishop's main duty is to 'offer the gifts' (*prospherein*) (Clement of Rome, *First Epistle*, 44.4).

[217]Cf. p.40.

There is no evidence of the ceremonial details of the Offertory in the fourth century. Later evidence shows that one deacon stood in front of the altar holding a dish or cloth, while another stood with a large cup or bowl; each member of the congregation came forward and placed some bread in the dish or cloth, and poured wine from a little flask into the bowl. No prayer was said aloud.

The 1970 Missal refers to this rite as the 'Preparation of the Gifts', rather than by its traditional name of the 'Offertory'. The reason is that the true offering in the Mass is that of the sacrifice of Christ which takes place during the Eucharistic Prayer, when the congregation's gifts of bread and wine are caught up into the sacrifice of Christ. This is not to say, however, that the placing of the bread and wine on the altar, perhaps preceded by an offertory procession, has no significance; the General Instruction to the Missal regards the rite as 'meaningful and of spiritual value' (n.49).

The Fathers frequently saw the Offertory as the expression of the congregation's offering of themselves.[218] Irenaeus compares the Offertory to the widow contributing her mite, which was 'all the living that she had',[219] and Augustine tells the first communicants that they are themselves on the altar and in the chalice.[220] In the Eucharistic Prayer of some Egyptian rites, the use of the past tense, 'We *have* offered', before the words of institution suggests that the offering takes place when the gifts are set on the altar.[221] All sacramental rites are elaborations of an essential core. That the Offertory should anticipate some features of the Canon should arouse opposition only from the liturgical pedant. The Offertory prayers of the 1970 Roman rite are something of a compromise; they speak of the offering of the bread and wine, but not in terms which should only be applied to the offering of Christ.

The description and interpretation of the Offertory given by Theodore is somewhat different from anything found earlier.

---

[218]Cf. Dix, *op. cit.*, pp. 110-118.

[219]*Adv. Haer.*, iv.18.2 (Harvey ii. 201; PG 7.1025), quoting Lk 21.4. The context shows that the author is writing about the Offertory, not the eucharistic sacrifice.

[220]Sermon 229; PL 38.1103.

[221]These liturgies can be conveniently studied in R. C. D. Jasper and G. J. Cuming, *Prayers of the Eucharist, Early and Reformed.*

The people are not given a particular function; the deacons lay the offerings on the altar, but we are not told where they get them. Cloths are first spread on the altar, and when the offerings are placed there they are attended with considerable pomp. The Eucharistic Prayer itself is the only act of offering.[222]

If Theodore's Offertory bears peculiar features, his explanation of the meaning of the ceremonies is far more peculiar. The Offertory procession represents our Lord as he is led out to the Passion; when the offerings have been placed on the altar, they stand for his body in the tomb. It can already be described as the 'sacred, dread and incorruptible body'.[223] Later in the Mass, when the Holy Spirit is invoked, the offerings on the altar become Jesus' risen body.[224]

In the evolved Byzantine rite the practice and symbolism of the Offertory were developed. In a ceremony called the Prothesis that takes place before the Liturgy of the Word, the offerings are prepared on a table apart. With the 'Sacred Lance' the priest makes five incisions in the bread to signify the sacred wounds. At one point he gives the order: 'Perform the sacrifice, deacon', whereupon the deacon makes a cross-shaped cut in the bread. After the Liturgy of the Word, the ceremonious Great Entry takes place while the priest says prayers recalling our Lord's burial.

In Theodore's rite the Offertory concludes with a prayer over the offerings. Ambrose possibly alludes to this prayer.[225]

(2) The Lavabo

It is sometimes said that the origin of the ceremony was the deacons' need to wash their hands after they had been handling the people's offerings. This explanation was unknown in patristic times; in fact the deacons, who handled the offerings,

---

[222]BH 4.44-45 with note 83.

[223]BH 4.24-29.

[224]BH 5.11-12. The mode of Christ's presence before and after the invocation of the Spirit appears to be different. Before the invocation, the presence is symbolic ('You must imagine that Christ our Lord is being led out' — 4.25; 'We should consider that Christ ... is now placed on the altar as if in a tomb' — 4.26). After the Epiclesis the offering 'is *truly* the body and blood of our Lord' (5.12).

[225]S 4.14. See note 30, there.

did not wash their hands, but the bishop and priests did. As the Lavabo-psalm 26 suggests, the origin of the ceremony is more probably Jewish. Its meaning is the purity of heart needed by those who approach God. Cyril's account of the rite suggests that this psalm already formed part of the ceremony.[226]

(3) The Kiss of Peace

St Justin's brief description of the Mass as celebrated in Rome in the middle of the second century includes a description of this rite. Its position, however, varies in different liturgies. Justin places it before the Offertory, Cyril after the Lavabo, Theodore between the Offertory and the Lavabo, while the Roman rite puts it before communion. It was commonly seen as the fulfilment of our Lord's command: 'First be reconciled with your brother, and then come and offer your gift.[227]

(4) The Eucharistic Prayer

At the Last Supper Jesus 'gave thanks' over the bread and the wine. In doing this he was following the Jewish practice of saying grace (i.e. giving thanks) before individual parts of the meal. The Church took our Lord's thanksgiving to be an essential part of the action he told them to imitate in his memory.

In *Eucharist* L. Bouyer proposes the thesis that the Eucharistic Prayer incorporates also elements of another Jewish type of blessing, namely the blessings to be found in the synagogue service. He shows that both at table and in the synagogue there are two main classes of benefit for which God is thanked: the good things of creation, and God's special action on behalf of his chosen people. Bouyer then traces the adaptation of these two categories to the Christian Eucharistic Prayer.

More recent studies have shown that the Jewish prayers make a further distinction between 'blessing' or 'praising' God and 'thanking' him.[228] In the Christian liturgy, however, it was

---

[226]MC 5.2. On the origin of the ceremony, see Dix, *op. cit.* pp. 124-125.
[227]Mt. 5.24. See Justin, 1 *Apol.* 65.
[228]See T.J. Talley, 'From Berakah to Eucharistia', in *Worship*, 50 (1976), pp. 115-137.

the concept of 'thanksgiving' which became predominant, although St Ambrose retains the description 'praise' for a section of the Mass, most probably the Preface.[229] Hence the name 'thanksgiving' (Eucharist) came to be given to the whole rite of the Mass; and the central part of the Mass took the form of a prolonged prayer of thanksgiving beginning with such a phrase as: 'It is indeed right and fitting that we should give thanks to thee, Father'. This prayer of thanksgiving was generally, but not always, addressed to the Father. It consisted of several parts.

(a) *Introductory Dialogue.* In the early centuries it seems to have been the universal practice to introduce the Eucharistic Prayer with a dialogue between priest and people such as is still included in the Roman Mass:

'Lift up your hearts'
'We have raised them up to the Lord'
'Let us give thanks to the Lord our God'
'It is right and fitting'.

Some of these formulas go back to Jewish ceremonial.[230]

(b) *Preface and Sanctus.* Although as early as the fourth century the Sanctus separates the Preface from the rest of the Eucharistic Prayer, these two prayers actually form a single prayer of thanksgiving. The hymn 'Holy, holy, holy', introduced by a reference to the angelic choirs inspired by Is 6.2-3, became an appropriate way for the people to share in the priest's prayer of thanksgiving and praise. A shorter form of the Sanctus formed part of the Jewish synagogue blessings.[231]

(c) *Narration of God's Good Deeds* for which he is being thanked. In some liturgies the list of these benefits is long, and includes the whole history of salvation; but in practically every example the recital culminates in the narration of our Lord's words and actions at the Last Supper.[232] However, two of the

---

[229]S 4.14, with note 30.
[230]See G. Dix, *Shape*, pp. 126-128.
[231]See Jasper and Cuming, *Prayers of the Eucharist*, p. 12.
[232]The very early East Syrian Liturgy of SS. Addai and Mari has come down to us in a form which contains no supper-narrative, but originally it may have

sets of homilies in this book do not include an explicit mention of such a narrative in their accounts of the Eucharistic Prayer. That Cyril of Jerusalem's omits it, however, is not decisive, for his account is selective.[233] The same may be true of Theodore of Mopsuestia, who, though not quoting the words of institution, does paraphrase them.[234]

(d) *Anamnesis.* Our Lord's words, 'Do this in remembrance of me', have always been seen to imply that the Mass is a calling to mind of his passion. St Paul says in explanation of them: 'As often as you eat this bread and drink the cup, you proclaim the Lord's death until he comes'.[235] Justin shows us that this interpretation of the Mass was current in Rome in the middle of the second century, when he speaks of 'the bread of the Eucharist which Jesus Christ our Lord ordered to be performed in commemoration of his passion'.[236]

However, Jesus showed that he intended the Eucharist to point beyond the passion to the time when his Father's kingdom would come: 'I tell you I shall not drink again of the fruit of the vine until that day when I drink it new with you in my Father's kingdom'.[237] Accordingly the Church soon began to regard the Mass also as a commemoration of the Resurrection. In the liturgy that Hippolytus prescribed for Roman use in the third century, immediately after the Supper-narrative, the eucharistic prayer continues: '"When you do this you make commemoration of me". Now, therefore, making commemoration of his death

---

contained one. For a survey of recent studies of this puzzling liturgy, see the Introduction B.C. Spinks, *Addai and Mari — the Anaphora.* The absence of a written record of the words of institution might have been due to respect for the *disciplina arcani.* Liturgical MSS did not need to include passages which the celebrant could be presumed to know by heart. H. Lietzmann (*Mass and the Lord's Supper*) proposed that the early eucharistic liturgies fell into two classes: those without any institution narrative, which were intended to continue the meals of fellowship which Jesus ate with his disciples; and those which contained the narrative, and therefore commemorated the Last Supper and the sacrifice of Calvary. This theory, once influential, seems to have fallen from scholarly favour.

[233]Cf. MC 5.8 below, with note 14.
[234]BH 5.10.
[235]1 Cor. 11.24-26.
[236]*Dialogue,* 41.
[237]Mt. 26.29.

and resurrection, we offer you the bread and chalice, giving you thanks …'.[238] This act of commemorating is known to liturgists under its Greek name of 'Anamnesis'.

When Jesus told his apostles to 'commemorate' him, we should not suppose that he simply intended that his life should not be allowed to fall into oblivion. In the Bible to recall an event means to bring it to mind so that it becomes effective. Darius too, the Persian king who ordered a slave to say to him three times every day, 'Sire, remember the Athenians', was not simply wanting a memory to be revived; he wanted to be prodded into action. Our Lord's commission, therefore, means that by the imitation of his actions at the Last Supper his memory was to be made operative. This might be thought to mean that the memory of Jesus was to be a source of inspiration to the apostles and those for whom they celebrated the Eucharist. Taking a more sacramental view, we could say that each celebration of the Eucharist was to make available to the worshippers the fruits of our Lord's Passion. Several modern ecumenical dialogues have reached agreement along these lines.[239]

Some theologians think that Jesus' words also mean that his sacrifice is to be recalled to the Father. It is in this sense perhaps that Cyril speaks of 'the spiritual sacrifice, this worship without blood'.[240]

The Anamnesis of the Passion, Resurrection and Ascension is explicitly contained in Ambrose's liturgy. It is implicit in Theodore's rite ('we who all believe in Christ and continue to commemorate his death'[241]), and also perhaps in Cyril's ('when the spiritual sacrifice — this worship without blood — has been perfected'[242]).

---

[238]*Ap. Trad.* 4.10-11.

[239]For example, the *Final Report* of the Anglican-Roman Catholic International Commission, and the Faith and Order document *Baptism, Eucharist and Ministry*.

[240]MC 5.8. The phrase 'bloodless worship' was originally Jewish and referred to the heavenly liturgy, but by Cyril's time it had come to refer to the eucharistic sacrifice (cf. Lampe, *Greek Patristic Lexicon*, s.v. '*anaimaktos*'). For a justification of the foregoing explanation of *anamnesis*, see Dix, *Shape*, pp. 161-162; J. Jeremias, *The Eucharistic Words of Jesus*, pp. 237-255.

[241]BH 5.10.

[242]MC 5.8.

(e) *Prayer of Offering.* Many liturgies, both ancient and modern, have linked the *anamnesis* with a prayer of offering: it is in the act of offering the eucharistic sacrifice that the Church recalls the death and resurrection of Christ. What is offered now is not mere bread and wine, but these elements transformed by the presence of Christ. In the third Eucharistic Prayer of the Roman Missal, for example, the prayer runs:

> Father, calling to mind the death your Son endured for our salvation, his glorious resurrection and ascension into heaven, and ready to greet him when he comes again,
> we offer you in thanksgiving this holy and living sacrifice.

Hippolytus' prayer is equally explicit: 'making commemoration of his death and resurrection, we offer you the bread and the chalice'.[243]

(f) *Epiclesis over the Offerings*, the invocation of the Holy Spirit. According to Cyril and Theodore,[244] the prayer by which the Father is asked to send the Holy Spirit on the offerings is the moment when they are changed into the body and blood of Christ. The Egyptian Sarapion gives an unusual form of epiclesis over the eucharistic offerings as well as over the baptismal water: the Father is asked to send down the Word rather than the Holy Spirit.[245] For Ambrose, however, it is the 'word(s) of Christ' (i.e. the words of consecration) that brings about Christ's presence in the Eucharist.[246] The theology of Cyril and Theodore is more symmetrical here: for it is open to them to say that it is the invocation of the Holy Spirit that gives efficacy alike to the baptismal water, the holy oil and the eucharistic offerings. Ambrose takes this view of the water, but not of the bread and wine.[247] All the same, Ambrose's liturgy does include a prayer, presumably to the Father, that the bread and wine may become Christ's body and blood; but, as the logic of his system demands, this prayer occurs *before* the Supper-

---

[243] *Ap. Trad.* 4.11; cf. Ambrose, S 4.27.

[244] MC 5.7; BH 5.11-12. Such has remained the view of the Othodox.

[245] Eucharist: *Euchologion*, 1; Jasper and Cuming, *Prayers of the Eucharist*, pp. 77-78. Baptism: see above, pp. 23-24.

[246] S 4.14-23. This view gained general acceptance in the West.

[247] S 1.15. He alludes however to an Epiclesis in *de Spir. Sanct.* iii.16 (PL 16.803).

narrative, as in Sarapion's *Euchologion* and the modern Roman mass, not *after*, as in Theodore and Cyril, as well as the modern Byzantine liturgy.

There need, of course, be no inconsistency between the two views. The Holy Spirit effects the presence of Christ when we 'do this in remembrance of (him)'. A fully articulated liturgy should contain both a Supper-narrative and an Epiclesis. Disagreement comes only over the question, 'At what moment does the change take place?'; but perhaps that is a question that should not be asked. Just as the Offertory and Eucharistic Prayer are two separate expressions of a single offering, so too the Supper-narrative and Epiclesis are two expressions of the same transformation of the bread and wine into Christ's body and blood.

The extent to which the Epiclesis has coloured Orthodox thinking about the Eucharist is shown by the modern Byzantine liturgy. When the priest holds part of the consecrated Bread over the chalice, instead of speaking of the Body and Blood of Christ, he says: 'The fulness of the Chalice of Faith of the Holy Spirit'. Again, while the deacon pours the hot water into the chalice, the priest says: 'The hot water of faith full of the Holy Spirit.'

(g) *Epiclesis over the People*. 'The bishop also prays that the grace of the Holy Spirit may come upon all the assembly', according to Theodore's liturgy.[248] Hippolytus' epiclesis, as it stands in a defective text, is of this type:

> We pray that you may send your Holy Spirit upon the offering of the holy church; that, gathering them in one, you may grant to all your saints who receive for their filling with the Holy Spirit for the confirmation of the faith in truth.[249]

Ambrose and Cyril, however, have no prayer of this nature here.

(h) *Commemorations of the Living and Dead*. The inclusion

---

[248]BH 5.13; cf. 5.15.
[249]*Ap. Trad.* 4.12.

within the eucharistic prayer of petitions for the needs of the Church may derive from the Jewish practice of including petitions in both meal and synagogue blessings.[250] Cyril, for example, begins with prayers for peace among the Churches,[251] for good government, and for certain classes of individuals that need help. Then follows a twofold commemoration of the dead: first, the intercession of the saints is sought; secondly, prayer is offered on behalf of the dead. Theodore gives a prayer 'for all whom it is always customary to name in church', followed by a prayer for the dead.[252] Western liturgies seem to have been slower to adopt this practice than the liturgies of the East. The only petitions Ambrose refers to seem to correspond to the modern Bidding Prayers; he refers to them only in his brief list of prayers which precede the Canon.[253]

Theodore spoke of prayers 'for all whom it is customary to name'. This phrase implies a set formula, and even in the liturgies of Cyril and Ambrose we can detect its existence. Cyril mentions prayer 'for the kings, for soldiers and allies'; Ambrose, though placing them at a different point in the liturgy, refers to prayers 'for the people, for kings, for all others'. The striking coincidence lies in the plural 'kings', which is found also in the Liturgy of St James. It has led some liturgical scholars on a wild goose-chase looking for periods when there were two kings (i.e. emperors) in the Roman empire and thinking the liturgies must have been composed at such a time. In fact the phrase is most probably an echo of St Paul's words: 'First of all, then, I urge that supplications, prayers, intercessions and thanksgivings be made for all men, for kings and all who are in high positions'.[254]

---

[250]See Jasper and Cuming, *Prayers of the Eucharist*, p. 11 (meal blessing); L. Bouyer, *Eucharist*, pp. 70-78 (synagogue blessings).

[251]MC 5.8-9. A prayer against schism that was fully relevant to the age of the Arian controversy, when he and Athanasius and many more were driven into exile by their brother bishops.

[252]BH 5.14.

[253]S 4.14 with note 30.

[254]1 Tim. 2.1-2. An earlier echo of St Paul's words is to be found in Tertullian, *Apologeticum*, 39.2.

None of the three liturgies we are discussing mentions the doxology that concludes the Eucharistic Prayer and the people's response 'Amen', unless the doxology which Ambrose attaches to the Lord's Prayer serves also as the conclusion of the Canon.[255] Theodore does, however, discuss the Amen after the Prayer over the Offerings.[256] The doxology with its Amen must, nevertheless, be of very early origin, as they already feature in Hippolytus' liturgy, and the Amen rates inclusion even in Justin's very brief summary.[257] There is little doubt, then, that Cyril, Theodore and Ambrose also had them in their Masses.

(5) Communion

(a) The next stage that Cyril describes in the *Lord's Prayer*. It is sometimes suggested, in fact, that he was the first to introduce this prayer into the liturgy.[258] Ambrose seems to include it in his liturgy, though the position is less certain.[259] Theodore gives no indication of the use of the prayer during the Eucharist.

(b) *The Breaking of the Bread.* This action was considered an essential part of the eucharistic rite. Whatever the intention of St Luke, the Church came to read a eucharistic meaning into the disciples' recognition of our Lord at Emmaus in the breaking of bread;[260] and the daily meetings in the homes of the first Christians for 'the breaking of bread' after Pentecost

[255]S 6.24 (not included in this book).

[256]BH 4.33.

[257]'At the end of these prayers of thanksgiving, all present express their agreement by saying, "Amen"' (*Apology*, i.65). Cf. *Ap. Trad.* 4.13.

[258]Cf. Dix, *Shape*, pp. 108-109; 130-131. Cyprian seems to suggest that the prayer is already used in the liturgy, but he may not be referring to the use at Mass (*de Dominica Oratione*, 2). For a survey of the evidence, see R. Cabié, *The Church at Prayer, Volume II: the Eucharist*, pp. 107-109.

[259]It comes after the consecration: 'Before the words of Christ the offering is called bread ... Why then is it called 'our bread' in the Lord's Prayer which follows afterwards?' (S 5.24). It may even have come after communion; and at the end of the sixth century Pope Gregory the Great's ruling that the Lord's Prayer should be said 'over (Christ's) body and blood', suggests that he knew of places where the prayer was said either before the consecration or after communion (*Ep.* ix.12 (PL 77.956-957), quoted in Jungmann, *op. cit.*, ii.278).

[260]Lk. 24.30, 35.

seem to have been celebrations of the Eucharist.[261] Thus the practical requirement for the bread to be broken before it was distributed acquired a sacred significance; St Paul saw a sign of unity in the fact that all share the same loaf.[262]

Cyril and Ambrose give no account of a breaking of bread in their liturgy. Theodore does. He explains that it is an imitation of Christ's action, and is necessary for distribution. He sees it as the prelude to the mixing of the body and blood, which is the subject of the next section. Some Fathers connected it with the breaking of our Lord's body in the Passion, and a variant reading appeared at 1 Cor. 11.24 ('This is my Body which is broken for you'), which linked the two senses in which the body was broken.[263]

(c) *The Mingling of the Body and Blood.* Theodore describes two rites of mingling. First the bishop 'traces the sign of the cross over the blood with the bread and over the bread with the blood',[264] then he drops some pieces of consecrated bread into the chalice.[265] Theodore attaches the same meaning to the two ceremonies: they are to show that the body and blood have no efficacy by themselves, but derive their power from the one person to whom they belong.

The origin of the rite is probably quite different. As early as the second century, the bishops used to send to neighbouring churches a piece of the host from their Mass. This fragment was called the *fermentum* (leaven), and was dropped into the chalice during Mass in the local churches.[266] Later a further practice had developed: a fragment from an earlier Mass was dropped into the chalice as a sign of the continuity of the Eucharist.[267] By Theodore's time the rite had so lost its meaning that the

---

[261]Acts 2.42, 46.

[262]1 Cor. 10.17.

[263]Cf. Theodore, BH 5.15, note 33. T surprisingly links the fraction with Jesus' sharing out of himself in the resurrection-appearances (BH 5.17-18).

[264]BH 5.15.

[265]BH 5.17.

[266]Cf. Irenaeus in Eusebius, *Church History*, v.24 (PG 20.508), though this interpretation of the passage is not certain.

[267]Cf. Dix, *op. cit.*, p. 134; Jungmann, *op. cit.*, ii.312.

fragment dropped into the chalice came from the bread that had been consecrated at the same Mass.

(d) *Preparation for Communion.* In Theodore's liturgy the preparation takes the form of a prayer for the donor of the offering, which Theodore himself seems to interpret as a prayer for all the congregation, since they have all joined in making the offering. Then a blessing is given, to be followed by a dialogue that still occurs in very similar form in the Byzantine liturgy: Deacon: 'Let us attend'. Bishop: 'What is holy for the holy'.[268] Choir: 'One holy Father, one holy Son, one Holy Spirit'.

Cyril gives two similar ejaculations, adding the detail that the Cantor sings a Communion psalm.[269]

(e) *Communion.* The laity came forward to receive communion after the clergy. Cyril gives exact instructions. Presumably standing,[270] they received the Body in the palm of their right hand, which rested on the left, and consumed it, then moved across to the minister who held the chalice. Theodore and Cyril both show that the sacred species were not immediately consumed, but were applied to the other organs of sense.[271]

Ambrose, Theodore and (by implication) Cyril give the words that accompany communion: 'The Body of Christ',

[268]These words are also quoted by Cyril (MC 5.19). In the Byzantine liturgy they are spoken by the bishop while he shows the congregation the Body of Christ, and seem to derive from our Lord's warning: 'Do not give dogs what is holy' (Mt. 7.6), which appeared in a eucharistic context as early as the *Didache* (9). (The *Didache* is probably a mid-second-century compilation of earlier sources.)

[269]Ps. 34.8: 'Taste and see'. The same psalm is prescribed in *Apostolic Constitutions*, viii.13.16.

[270]This detail is confirmed by the east Syrian Father Aphrahat, who in 336 compared the communicants with those who stood to eat the Passover meal (Ex 12.11): 'And where it says "Eat it in haste", this is observed in the Church of God; for they eat the Lamb itself in haste, in fear and trembling, standing on their feet, because they are in haste, to eat "Life" by the gift of the Spirit which they have received' (*Demonstr.* xii, 'on the Pasch', Patr. Syr. 1, col. 528.15-21, trans. R. Murray, who pointed out the passage to me).

[271]BH 5.28; MC 5.21-22. Cf. Connolly, *Narsai*, p. 29 note; A. Raes, 'Attouchement des sens avec l'eucharistie', *L'Orient Syrien*, 3 (1958) 488-489. That it was the custom in the West also for the Body to be received on the palm of the hands is shown by Tertullian, *De Idololatria*, 7.

'Amen'. No explicit mention is made of words spoken over the chalice, though another fourth-century Syrian rite gives the words: 'The Blood of Christ, the chalice of life'.[272]

(f) *Post-communion*. Both Theodore and Cyril include a reference to a prayer of thanksgiving after Communion.[273] None of the sources studied in the book mentions a final blessing or words of dismissal.

---

[272]*Apostolic Constitutions*, viii.13.15 (Jasper and Cuming, p. 113).
[273]BH 5.29; MC 5.22.

2

The Awe-Inspiring Rites

A. THE DISCIPLINE OF SECRECY

Despite Jesus's words to Annas 'I have spoken openly to the world ... I have said nothing secretly',[1] there was an element of mystery and secrecy about his teaching. The apostles as well as evil spirits are told not to reveal the knowledge they have about Jesus' person.[2] He teaches in parables, not only to make his message more intelligible, but to conceal it from those who are not ready to receive it; 'to you has been given the secret of the Kingdom of God, but for those outside, everything is in parables; so that they may indeed see but not perceive and may indeed hear but not understand; lest they should turn again and be forgiven'.[3] His words in the Sermon on the Mount probably have the same meaning; 'Do not give dogs what is holy; do not throw your pearls before swine'.[4]

Although in the second century St Justin speaks freely to a pagan audience concerning the Eucharist,[5] by the third century a tradition of secrecy is apparent. Tertullian urges his wife not to remarry if he dies because her second husband is likely to be a pagan who will catch her giving herself Holy Communion in

---

[1]Jn. 18.20. F. Homes Dudden gives a valuable account of the practice of secrecy (*Disciplina Arcani*) (*The Life and Times of St Ambrose*, pp. 453ff.). The term *Disciplina Arcani* is a modern invention.

[2]Cf. e.g. Mk. 9.9 ('He charged them to tell no one what they had seen, until the Son of Man should have risen from the dead'); Mk. 3.12.

[3]Mk. 4.11-12.

[4]Mt. 7.6. The *Didache* applied this text to the Eucharist (9.5).

[5]1 *Apol.* 65-66.

the morning, according to the contemporary custom; Tertullian takes it for granted that the pagan will not otherwise know anything about the Eucharist.[6] Origen tries to answer the accusation of his opponent, Celsus, that Christianity is a religion of secrecy like the pagan mystery religions: Christian doctrine is not secret, he asserts, though he has to concede that some things are not for outsiders, not to reach the ear of the general public.[7] Hippolytus, at the end of his account of baptism, adds this note: 'If anything needs to be explained, let the bishop speak in private to those who have received baptism. Those who are not Christians are not to be told unless they first receive baptism. This is the white stone which John spoke of: "A new name is written on it which no one knows except him who receives the stone".'[8]

By the fourth century and the first half of the fifth, this practice of preserving the central elements of the faith as a secret from outsiders became universal. One can see it working at Rome;[9] Milan, in the writings of St Ambrose; Verona[10]; Jerusalem, in the writings of Cyril and Egeria; Egypt[11]; Constantinople[12]; Antioch[13]; North Africa[14]; Cappadocia[15]. The liturgy showed signs of the precautions taken to preserve this secrecy. Those who were not baptized had to leave the church before the eucharistic part of the liturgy; hence the division of the liturgy into the Mass of the Catechumens and the Mass of the Faithful. In the Byzantine liturgy the deacon has still to announce, 'The doors, the doors!' to show that, from this

---

[6]*Ad Uxorem*, ii.5. Cf. *de Praescript. Haer.*, 41, where Mt. 7.6 is applied to the exclusion of the unbaptized from the Eucharist and full instruction.

[7]*Contra Celsum*, i.7.

[8]*Ap. Trad.* 23.14, quoting Apoc. 2.17.

[9]Letter of Pope Innocent I to Decentius, A.D. 416 (PL 20.551ff.).

[10]Zeno (Löfstedt) *Tractatus* ii.7.14; PL 11.309.

[11]Sarapion, in the Anaphora (sec. 6; Jasper and Cuming, *Prayers of the Eucharist*, p. 76); Athanasius, *Apologia contra Arianos*, 11, 31 (PG 25.268, 300).

[12]Chrysostom, Letter to Innocent I, 3 (PG 52.533).

[13]*Apostolic Constitutions*, 2.57.10, 14; 7.25. Chrysostom, *In 1 Cor*, 40.1 (PG 61.347-348); *In Gen. Homily* 27.8 (PG 53.251).

[14]Augustine, *Sermon* 132. 1 (PL 38.734).

[15]Basil, *De Spiritu Sancto*, 66 (PG 32.188-189).

point, the doors have to be guarded to prevent the entry of the unbaptized.[16]

The secrecy of the Greek pagan mysteries had been very faithfully preserved,[17] probably for a variety of reasons.[18] There was the fear that outsiders might share with the initiates the means of gaining the god's favours. Besides, secrecy was felt to increase reverence and to attract the curious. Outsiders liked to think that secrecy was necessary in order to shelter ridiculous or sordid rites from contempt.[19] Although the Christian practice of secrecy goes back to the gospels, it seems likely that in the fourth century the desire to rival the pagan mysteries led to an elaboration of the practice of secrecy.[20] Chrysostom's phrase 'the holy and awesome rites of initiation'[21] seems to be worded in language borrowed from the Greek mysteries. He certainly parades the secrecy, hoping apparently that curiosity will lead catechumens to undergo instruction for baptism.[22] Cyril of Jerusalem is aware that some of the people who listen to his baptismal instructions will have come simply out of curiosity. From the very beginning he sets out to convert that curiosity into something more religious.[23]

Other motives for the secrecy are also apparent. It was felt that a Christian needed to experience the sacraments of baptism and the Eucharist before he was ready to receive instruction about them. Theological as well as pedagogical reasons are given for this practice.[24]

St Ambrose gives two other reasons which combine common sense with his characteristically quaint method of interpreting the Old Testament. He discusses Abraham's instructions to Sarah about making cakes,[25] in the Greek

---

[16]Cf. *Apostolic Constitutions*, 2.57.21: 'Let the doors be guarded'.
[17]Cf. Livy 31.14.
[18]Cf. O. Perler, *Reallexikon für Antike und Christentum*, i.667ff.
[19]Freemasons and Knights of St Columba still have to endure this suspicion.
[20]Cf. pp. 61-66.
[21]ACW 11.23. Cf. p. 60.
[22]*In Gen.*, 27.8: 'Those who are initiated understand what I mean'.
[23]*Procatechesis*, 2.
[24]Cf. Ambrose, S 1.1 with note 2; Cyril, MC 1.1 with note 2.
[25]Gen. 18.6.

version of which the word for cakes (*enkruphia*) can also mean 'hidden', presumably because the cakes were baked by being covered with hot ash. Ambrose deduces from this fact the lesson that 'every mystery ought to be hidden and, so to speak, concealed in a faithful silence so as not to be inconsiderately published to profane ears'.[26] In other words, the important truths of Christianity are too sacred for general publication. In another passage, he gives a different interpretation of the same text. The mysteries should be kept secret 'lest by premature speech you should commit them half-baked, so to speak, to faithless or weak ears and the hearer be repelled and feel repugnance and loathing; if he tasted them more fully baked, he would enjoy a taste of spiritual food'.[27] The aspirant to Christianity is not to be given knowledge until he is ready to receive it profitably.

The secrecy extended to the Creed and the Lord's Prayer,[28] the words, the sacred vessels and the species of the Eucharist,[29] baptism and the rites of initiation.

The secrecy surrounding the pagan mysteries had the reputation of being very scrupulously observed and this reputation seems to have been merited. Did the Christians succeed in keeping their secrets so well? Some were extremely scrupulous. Pope Innocent I, writing liturgical directives to a bishop, tells him that the Kiss of Peace should be given 'after everything which I am not entitled to make public'.[30] Zeno regards a breach of the secrecy as sacrilege.[31] Still, there must have been gossips even among the early Christians; and a sharp-witted catechumen could make much of the hints he picked up from sermons and from the scriptures. We can deduce from a remark of Ambrose's that the secrecy was not

---

[26]*De Abraham*, i.38 (PL 14.436).

[27]*De Cain*, i.35-37 (PL 14.334-5).

[28]Cf. pp. 12-14.

[29]Epiphanius, the Bishop of Salamis in Cyprus, is so cautious that he gives this cryptic description of the Last Supper: 'He stood up [*v.l.*, sat down] at the Supper, took these things and gave thanks, saying: "This is my this"' (*touto mou esti tode*) (*Ancoratus*, 57.3; PG 43.117).

[30]*Letter to Decentius*, 1.4 (PL 20.553).

[31](Löfstedt) *Tractatus* ii.7.14; PL 11.309.

perfectly observed;[32] but it would be a mistake to conclude that it was merely a liturgical fiction. Egeria gives a charming account of the enthusiasm with which the new Christians greeted the revelations made to them in the days after their baptism: 'while the bishop discusses and explains each point, the applause is so loud that it can be heard even outside the church'.[33]

It is a natural instinct to be reticent about something one holds precious. Publicity cheapens, *omne ignotum pro magnifico.* In the publication of everything we hold sacred, there has been a loss, not only for ourselves, but perhaps also for non-Christians, but the loss is irreparable. There is no way in which secrecy can be re-established.

B. MYSTERY RELIGIONS[34]

'The awesome mysteries about which it is forbidden to speak'; 'this awesome rite of initiation'; 'the awesome and holy rite of initiation'.[35] Chrysostom's descriptions of the ceremonies of the Easter vigil are not as far-fetched as they sound. Even before he gives in his name for baptism, the catechumen has heard mysterious hints of great secrets and privileges that lie before him. The almost daily fasts, the daily instructions and moral exhortations, the repeated exorcisms, the recurrent prayers, the constant attentions of his sponsor have all been focussed on his impending baptism, and have all conspired to tune him to a pitch of excited anticipation. Finally on Holy Saturday night he takes part in prolonged prayers; he hears the voice coming out of the darkness commanding him to renounce the devil to his face, to turn to Christ and swear allegiance; he remains only half-comprehending as he finds himself stripped, anointed, pushed down into the water; he is greeted with joy,

---

[32]*Exp. in Ps. 118*, 2.26 (PL 15.1219).

[33]47.2.

[34]I have treated of this subject at greater length in 'Baptism and the Pagan Mysteries', *Heythrop Journal*, 13 (1972), pp. 247-267.

[35]ACW 6.15; 10.2; 11.23.

dressed in white, led into the Church, shown for his first time the secret rites of the Mass; receives the sacred meal of bread and wine—often without a word of explanation. The procedure seems to be calculated explicitly to stir up emotions of spiritual exaltation and awe, which will help to make of baptism a life-long and profound conversion.[36]

Theodore indeed expressed very high hopes of the effect of this conversion:

> He has designed to deliver you from this slavery and to give you a share in the indescribable gifts of heaven, so that once you have received them you will be completely free from all evil.[37]
>
> You have been born again and have become a completely different man. You no longer belong to Adam, who was subject to change, because he was afflicted and overwhelmed by sin; you belong to Christ, who was entirely free from sin through his resurrection, and in fact had committed no sin from the beginning of his life.[38]

These high expectations of the effect of baptism on the Christian's life were in keeping with the Church's early uncertainty about the extent of her powers to forgive sins committed after baptism, and help to explain the practice of postponing baptism to a time when the catechumen felt prepared for a radically new life.[39]

The word 'awesome'[40] which Chrysostom used means literally 'causing a shiver' or 'making the hair stand on end'. How far the word had become a cliché is difficult to say; but it is significant that it formed part of the vocabulary of the pagan mystery-religions. The Athenian orator Aristides, for example, in the second century A.D., applied it to the Eleusinian

---

[36]In our own century the use of psychological devices to promote a lasting spiritual conversion was familiar to givers of old-style parish missions, and is still employed by the most up-to-date evangelists.

[37]BH 2.4.

[38]BH 3.25.

[39]Cf. P. Brown, *Augustine of Hippo*, pp. 106-107.

[40]*phriktos, phrikodes.*

mysteries.[41] Inevitably therefore a question arises: did the baptismal preachers of the fourth century self-consciously reshape the Christian ceremonies of initiation in imitation of the pagan mysteries?

Earlier in the twentieth century there was current in some scholarly circles the view that the influence of the mystery-religions on the development of Christianity went much further; St Paul, it was maintained, had radically altered the simple message of Christ by superimposing on it a theology of redemption and sacrament derived from the mystery-cults. This extreme view, which is associated especially with the names of Reitzenstein and Bousset, is now generally admitted to be unfounded, for there is no evidence that many of the ideas that St Paul is alleged to have borrowed from paganism were in fact current among the gentiles of his time. On the contrary pagan theology may have borrowed the ideas from Christianity.[42] The question we are now asking is a different one: was the process of Christian initiation modified in the fourth century in imitation of the rites of initiation into the pagan mysteries?

Forms of mystery religion had existed some thousand years or more before St Cyril preached his sermons. One of the most ancient was performed in honour of the corn-goddess Demeter at Eleusis, a shrine a few miles north-west of Athens. According to legend, Dis or Pluto, the god of the underworld, had fallen in love with Demeter's daughter Persephone and carried her off to his kingdom. While Demeter was mourning her loss she refused to let any corn grow; but through Zeus' intervention Persephone was allowed to return to the earth for eight months in the year, which symbolized the period when the corn is growing. Every year at the time of the autumn sowing the Athenians performed ceremonies at Eleusis in commemoration of Demeter's loss and recovery of her daughter. The ceremonies included an initiation. The candidates had first to be instructed by the hierophant (revealer

---

[41]*Eleusinios*, 256.
[42]Cf. H. Rahner, S.J., *Greek Myths and Christian Mystery*, pp. 3-45.

of the sacred objects) and purified by bathing in the sea; each
had to sacrifice a young pig. After a solemn procession
accompanied with hymns and dancing from Athens to Eleusis,
the rites of initiation were performed. As these rites were
celebrated in strict secrecy, we can only gather scattered hints
from a few written sources and artistic representations. The
candidate seems to have sat fasting and with veiled face on a
stool covered with a fleece, while a winnowing-fan was held
over his head; in this position he remained for a long time in
silent reflection. He was given a drink called *kykeon* made of
water, barley and herbs. These actions were imitations of
Demeter's mourning for her daughter. There seem to have
been other dramatic representations of the goddess's
bereavement and reunion with her daughter. A fourth-century
Christian writer describes them as follows:

> Proserpine [Persephone] is sought in the night by the
> light of torches. Once she is found the whole rite ends
> amid rejoicing and the waving of torches.[43]

An important stage of the initiation was the handling of certain
unspecified sacred objects. Clement of Alexandria records the
following profession made by the initiates:

> I fasted; I drank the *kykeon*; I took out of a box, handled
> and put away in a basket; I took out of the basket and put
> into the box.[44]

During these ceremonies the hierophant spoke enigmatic
words of comment.

The emotions of the candidate were continually excited.
After days of preparation and expectation, he found himself,
weak and exhausted as he was with fasting, sometimes in
darkness, sometimes surrounded by waving torches, a receptive
subject to the suggestive powers of mysterious objects, rites and

---

[43]Lactantius, *Divinarum Institutionum Epitome*, 18 (23).

[44]*Protrepticus* 2.21 (PG 8.88). It is possible that the basket was introduced by the
Alexandrians into a simpler Eleusinian rite.

utterances. The crowning experience in these and indeed all mysteries seems to have been the contemplation (*epopteia*) of a sacred object. 'Blessed is he who has seen' is a phrase often applied to the Eleusinian initiate.[45] In the decadent period of the pagan mysteries, when they were already beginning to be eclipsed by Christianity, there is evidence that mechanical trickery was resorted to in some shrines.[46] But originally the object of contemplation seems to have been extremely ordinary. According to Hippolytus it was an ear of corn, the obvious symbol of Demeter.[47]

This last ceremony can hardly have been such an anticlimax as it sounds, for the rites of initiation were commonly said to work a profound moral change in the initiates' lives. Cicero, who was as sophisticated as any Roman, was himself initiated at Eleusis and declared:

> Your Athens was the source of many great and wonderful benefits to the human race, but I think that none is greater than those mysteries which refined our uncouth rustic lives and made us humane and gentle.[48]

Was the moral improvement the consequence of a sense of *noblesse oblige* on the part of the initiates, or was it the result of a lasting and profound psychological experience which might be described as a conversion? We are fortunate that a contemporary answer has been preserved: a fifth-century bishop records a saying of Aristotle to the effect that 'those undergoing initiation are not expected to gain knowledge (*mathein*) but an experience (*pathein*) and a disposition'.[49] We in the century of

[45]E.g. Homeric *Hymn to Demeter*, 480.

[46]Cf. M. P. Nilsson, *Geschichte der Griechischen Religion*, ii.682.

[47]*Refutatio*, V.8.39ff. There are indications that in the decadent form of the rite the initiated watched while a priest and a priestess enacted the marriage of Demeter and Zeus; but as the evidence derives from Christian writers this detail may be an unfounded smear. Pagans had been just as sensational and inaccurate in their descriptions of cannibal rites at the Christian Eucharist.

[48]*De Legibus*, ii.36. However, Diogenes the Cynic complained against the unfairness of a system by which any initiated criminal could gain a happy after-life (Diogenes Laertius, vi.39).

[49]Aristotle, fragment 45 (15) (1483a19); *The Works of Aristotle*, tr. W. D. Ross, p. 87.

brain-washing and hidden persuasion should not doubt that the experiences in the hall of initiation could produce in the initiate a permanent and deep emotional change. One wonders nevertheless whether some initiates experienced the disappointment that St Ambrose fears new Christians may have felt at their first sight of the font from which they hoped for so much:

> You came into the baptistery, you saw the water, you saw the bishop, you saw the levite. And if anyone should perhaps be thinking of saying, 'Is that all?', I say, 'Indeed it is all'. There truly is all, where there is all innocence, all devotion, all grace, all sanctification. You saw all you could see with the eyes of the body, all that is open to human sight. You saw what is seen, but not what is done. What is unseen is much greater than what is seen.[50]

Of the many other mystery-cults, it must suffice to mention the cults of Isis and Mithras. Apuleius gives us a glimpse of the Egyptian rites in honour of Isis when, in his novel known to English readers as *The Golden Ass*, his hero Lucius is restored to human shape and is invited by the Goddess to undergo the initiation. After instruction from a priest, a bath of purification and a ten-day fast, he is brought into a secret part of the temple.

> After visiting the region of death and treading the threshold of Prosperine, I was conveyed back again through all the elements. In the middle of the night I saw the sun shining brightly. I came into the presence of the gods below and the gods above, and going up to them I worshipped.

Next day Lucius is set in public on a platform in embroidered vestments, with a garland on his head and a torch in his hand, and all the people feast in his honour.[51]

---

[50] S 1.10.
[51] *Metamorphoses*, xi.23-24.

The cult of Mithras originated in India and Iran. It gradually won great support among the Roman soldiers, who played a large part in its diffusion round the empire from the first century A.D. Mithras was a god of light, who in the final form of the cult became identified with the sun; his cult was the chief rival of Christianity in the fourth century. Apart from his slaying and carrying of a bull, little is known of his exploits. There seem to have been seven grades of initiates; the rites of initiation included some which resemble baptismal ceremonies, such as the administration of honey.[52] Tertullian describes one of the rites:

> When he is initiated in the cave (or rather in the camp of darkness) a garland is offered him while a sword is held in the way, to represent martyrdom. Then the garland is set on his head, and he is told to put up his hand and take it from his head and transfer it, if possible, to the god's shoulder, saying: 'Mithras is my crown'.[53]

Another rite, not directly connected with the worship of Mithras, was the *taurobolium*. As the ceremony is described by the fourth-century Christian poet Prudentius, the person undergoing the initiation goes down into a pit covered with perforated boards, over which a bull is slaughtered, so that its blood rains down on the votary below.

The mystery-rites appear to have been simple nature-rites which were to obtain from the gods the seasonal re-birth of the crops. Soon their aim was enlarged so as to include deliverance from natural disasters and from a miserable after-life. As Aristides said of the Eleusinian mysteries:

> The effect of the festival is not only immediate pleasure or release from past misfortunes; but with regard to death they have fairer hopes that they will enjoy a happier existence and not lie in the darkness and mud that are in store for the uninitiated.[54]

[52]Porphyry, *De Antro Nymphi*, 15.
[53]*De Corona*, 15.4
[54]*Eleusinios*, 259.

People were not content with a promise of such salvation; they felt the need of a 'sacrament' that would guarantee it.

This salvation was expressed in many ways. The initiate was 'born again for ever'; the initiation symbolized death followed by a resurrection; the day of his initiation was called his birthday; he was said to be 'like the gods'; he shares the divine potency.

Now we can at last return to our original question: were the rites of Christian initiation modified in the fourth century in imitation of the pagan mysteries? The answer perhaps is that the rites themselves were hardly influenced but the explanation given of them began to emphasize the element of mystery and fear. The custom of deferring an explanation until after the rites were completed may well be connected with this new tendency, though it is surprising that Ambrose and Cyril, who followed this practice, speak less of the awesome aspect of the rites than Chrysostom and Theodore, who did not.

One wonders whether Constantine was responsible for this development. In his gradual conversion from Sun-worship (presumably tinged with Mithraism) to Christianity, he seems to have wanted his temple at Jerusalem to be the Christian equivalent of a mystery-shrine.[55] Eusebius' account of Constantine's own baptism in 337, written shortly after the event, contains several terms borrowed from the vocabulary of the mysteries.[56] It was at Jerusalem that the veneration of the Christian sacred objects (the cross, Calvary, the tomb) began and apparently the practice of mystagogic catechesis began here too. Cyril applied to his sermons the name *mystagogia*, with all its pagan associations.

Was Christianity enriched or distorted by this new emphasis?

[55]See my article 'Who Planned the Churches at the Christian Holy Places in the Holy Land? *Studia Patristica* xviii, vol. 1, pp. 105-109.

[56]Eusebius, *Vita Constantini*, iv. 61-63.

3

Fourth-Century Baptismal Homilies

CYRIL OF JERUSALEM

St Cyril was probably born about 313, that critical year in the history of the Church when the Emperor Constantine, feeling an attraction to Christianity that to begin with, at least, seems to have been largely superstition, granted Christians the right to practise their religion. This toleration soon developed into favour as the Emperor began to see in Christianity, rather than paganism, the influence he needed to cement together his widespread and diverse subjects. Soon, in 325, he was convening the first Ecumenical Council at Nicaea to restore the unity which the Arian heresy had shattered. St Cyril grew up in the aftermath of this Council, when the Nicene definition that the Son was consubstantial with the Father was opposed for a variety of reasons by many different parties. St Cyril tried to steer a middle way through this controversy; but was driven out of Jerusalem three times by the Arians.

Soon after the Council of Nicaea, Constantine, with the fervour of a convert and with a propagandist's instinct for what would appeal to the people, decided to build a sumptuous church in Jerusalem on what was traditionally held to be the site of the tomb where Jesus had been buried. While the foundations were being excavated, some find was made which was interpreted as miraculous proof that here indeed was the site of the Lord's Passion. A tomb cut out from a rocky outcrop was discovered, which was identified as the tomb of Christ; also a rocky hillock, which was taken to be the hill of Calvary. By the end of the century there was to grow up the legend of the discovery of the true cross by Constantine's mother Helen. A sumptuous basilica was built, called the *Martyrion*, a term used to denote a chapel connected with a martyr's body or his relics. The tomb, elaborately decorated, dominated the open space behind the apse; a circular church was soon constructed round the tomb; this was called the *Anastasis* or Resurrection.[1] A door in the wall by the apse gave on to the rock of Calvary, standing in the same open space and pared down and built round with stone. On top of it a richly jewelled cross was set. It was in these buildings that Cyril preached his catechetical sermons, moving from site to site to gain the maximum effect.

The basilica was decorated in 335. Even before its dedication pilgrims began to make their way to Jerusalem. One pilgrim, a nun from Spain or the south of France, believed to have been called Egeria, came to Jerusalem a few years before Cyril's death.[2] The detailed and lively account she wrote helps us to recapture the atmosphere of the Holy Week ceremonies celebrated by Cyril on the scene of the original events, and the enthusiasm of the new Christians as they applauded each point of the mystagogic sermons as they were preached in front of the tomb of the risen Christ.

One of the chief sources of interest in these sermons lies in Cyril's theology of the Eucharist. The Eucharist is a sacrifice of propitiation (MC 5.8), in which Christ who has been slain is offered (MC 5.10); it can be offered for the living and the dead (5.8, 9); the bread and wine are 'transformed' into the body and blood of Christ (4.6, 9; 1.7; 5.7); the presence of Christ is brought about by the Epiclesis by which God the Father is asked to send down the Holy Spirit upon the offerings to transform them into the body and blood of Christ (1.7; 5.7); prayer in the presence of the body and blood of Christ has a special efficacy (5.9); each particle of the Host is precious as it is the body of Christ (5.21); the spiritual effect of Holy Communion is obtained through our bodies, which absorb Christ's body and blood (4.3-5).

---

[1] They are described by Eusebius, *Vita Constantini*, iii.25-40.
[2] See J. Wilkinson *Egeria's Travels*.

The best short introduction to Cyril's life and to various problems connected with the mystagogic catechesis is to be found in the introduction of the late Dr F. L. Cross's edition of *St Cyril of Jerusalem's Lectures on the Christian Sacraments* (S.P.C.K., 1966). His bibliography will prove of great use to any student who wishes to study the subject more deeply. A. A. Stephenson's introduction and notes to Cyril's works in *The Fathers of the Church* series, vols. 61 and 64, also contains much valuable information.

The following translation is based on a version made by Dr P. G. Walsh; he had indulgently allowed me to tinker with it here and there. The text followed has been the one used by F. L. Cross. A critical edition has since been made by A. Piédagnel in his edition of the Mystagogic Catecheses in the *Sources Chrétiennes* series. It does not, however, differ from Dr Cross's text in points of substance. Père Piédagnel's edition includes informative introduction and notes, with a full treatment of the problem of authenticity.

Cyril's sermons fall into two groups, separated by about thirty years. The first set consists of the *Procatechesis*, preached about 348 to those who had just been enrolled for baptism at the beginning of Lent, and the eighteen *Catecheses*, delivered during Lent in the same year, the last fourteen of which form a commentary on the Creed that was presented to the candidates at this time. The second group comprises the *Mystagogic Catecheses*, preached to the newly baptized in the week after Easter, probably not many years before Cyril's death in 387. Some scholars have attributed the Mystagogic Catecheses to John, Cyril's successor to the see of Jerusalem. I have attempted to vindicate Cyril's authorship in 'The Authorship of the Mystagogic Catecheses attributed to Cyril of Jerusalem', in *Heythrop Journal*, 19 (1978), pp. 143-161; in the present book I speak always of Cyril as the author. A convincing case for Cyril's authorship has been made by Alexis Doval in a so far unpublished thesis submitted to Oxford University entitled *The Authorship of the Mystagogic Catecheses attributed to St Cyril of Jerusalem* (1992).

SERMON I: THE PREBAPTISMAL RITES

The reading is from Peter's First Letter to the whole Church, from 'Brethren, be sober, be watchful' to the end.[1]

1. For some time now, true and beloved children of the Church, I have desired to discourse to you on these spiritual and celestial mysteries. But I well knew that visual testimony is more trustworthy than mere hearsay, and therefore I awaited this chance of finding you more amenable to my words, so that out of your personal experience I could lead you into the brighter and more fragrant meadow of Paradise on earth.[2] The moment is especially auspicious, since you became receptive to the more heavenly mysteries when you were accounted worthy of divine and vitalising baptism. It remains therefore to lay before you a feast of more perfect instruction; so let me give you careful schooling in this so that you may know the true significance of what happened to you on the evening of your baptism.

Renunciation of Sin

2. You began by entering the outer room of the baptistery. You faced westward, heard[3] a voice commanding you to stretch out your hand, and renounced Satan as though to his face. You should realise that the symbol harks back to the Old Testament. When Pharaoh, that most savage and cruel tyrant, afflicted the free and noble people of the Hebrews, God sent Moses to lead them out of their debasing slavery at the hands of the Egyptians. Their doorposts were smeared with the blood of a lamb so that the destroyer might avoid the houses bearing the bloodstain, and thus against all expectation the Hebrews gained their

---

[1] 1 Pet. 5.8ff.

[2] An allusion perhaps to 2 Cor. 12.3: 'I know that this man was caught up into Paradise'. St Cyril gives two reasons for not teaching the neophytes the meaning of baptism until after they are baptized: (1) it is sounder pedagogy to let the person experience baptism before learning its meaning; (2) baptism gives one the power to understand. Cf. Ambrose, S 1.1 and note 2.

[3] The words suggest that a disembodied voice came out of the darkness. On the use of darkness in the mystery religions to play on the emotions, cf. Introduction, pp. 62, 64.

freedom. But when they had been liberated they were pursued by the enemy, who saw the sea miraculously part to afford the Hebrews a path. Yet even so the Egyptians pressed on in their footsteps, and at once they were submerged and drowned in the Red Sea.[4]

3. Now turn your mind from past to present, from symbol to reality.[5] Of old Moses was sent into Egypt by God, but in our era Christ is sent into the world by the Father. As Moses was appointed to lead his afflicted people from Egypt, so Christ came to deliver the people of the world who were overcome by sin. As the blood of the lamb served to avert the destroyer, so the blood of Jesus Christ, the blameless lamb, had the effect of routing demons. That tyrant of old pursued the ancient Jewish people as far as the sea, and here and now the devil, bold and shameless, the source of all evil, followed you up to the waters of salvation. Pharaoh was submerged in the sea, and the devil disappears in the waters of salvation.

4. None the less, you are told to stretch out your hand, and to address the devil as if he were before you: *I renounce you, Satan.* I will tell you now, for you need to know, why you face westward. The west is the quarter from which darkness appears to us; now the devil is darkness, and wields his power in darkness. So we look to the west as a symbolic gesture, and renounce the leader of shadow and darkness.

So what each of you said as you stood there was: 'I renounce you, Satan, you wicked and most cruel tyrant',[6] and your meaning was 'I no longer fear your power'. For Christ has dissolved that power by sharing with me in blood and flesh, so that he might annihilate death by death and save me from subjection to eternal slavery.[7] I renounce you, you cunning and most vicious serpent. I renounce you, you plotter, who under the guise of friendship have worked all manner of wrong and

---

[4]Exod. 12.7, 13, 23; 14.21-29.

[5]On Cyril's use of the words 'symbol' (*tupos*) and 'reality' (*aletheia*) cf. 5.20 with note 23.

[5]The formula seems to be: 'I renounce you, Satan, and all your works, and all your pomp, and all your worship'. Cyril here expands the formula in order to explain it.

[7]Cf. Heb. 2.14-15.

caused our first parents to secede from God. I renounce you, Satan, author and associate in every evil.

5. The second phrase you are instructed to recite is: *and all your works.* The works of Satan are all wickedness; this you must also renounce, for when one escapes a tyrant, one surely escapes his weapons as well. So every form of sin is numbered amongst the devil's works. Now realise this: all that you say, especially at that most awesome moment, is written in God's books. So when you are found contravening your promise, you will be judged a transgressor.[8] When I say, then, that you renounce the works of Satan, I mean that you renounce all deeds and thoughts which are against your better judgment.

6. Next you say: *and all your pomp.* The devil's pomp is the mad world of the stage, horse-racing, hunting, and all such futility.[9] The holy man prays to be freed from this when he says to God: 'Turn my eyes from looking at vanities'.[10] Do not be keen to set eyes on the madness of the theatre, where you will witness actors indulging in obscenities and outrages and every kind of impropriety, and unsexed men dancing in abandoned fashion. Show no enthusiasm either for the stupid pursuits of huntsmen who expose themselves to wild beasts in order to titillate their wretched bellies. In seeking to indulge their own gluttony with food, they actually become food themselves for the bellies of the wild beasts; it would be fair to say that for the sake of their belly, that is their god,[11] they engage in hand-to-hand combat on the edge of a precipice to throw their lives away.[12] Avoid horse-racing as well, for it is a foolish spectacle which unseats the soul. All such sport is the pomp of the devil.

7. Also included in the pomp of the devil are the meat, loaves and other offerings suspended during the festivals in honour of idols, and polluted by the invocations of abominable demons.

---

[8]Cf. Gal. 2.18.

[9]It became traditional for preachers to give such a list of the objects that comprise the devil's works and pomp. Chrysostom gives a similar list (ACW 11.25); so too does Theodore (BH 2.10ff.).

[10]Ps. 119.37.

[11]Cf. Phil. 3.19.

[12]'Making the best of a bad text' – P.G.W.

For as the bread and wine of the Eucharist is merely bread and wine before the invocation of the sacred and adorable Trinity, but after the invocation the bread becomes the body of Christ and the wine his blood, so the foods attached to the pomp of Satan are in themselves merely food but become impure after the invocation of the devils.[13]

8. Your next words are: *and all your worship.* The devil's worship is prayer in pagan temples, honour paid to lifeless idols, kindling lamps and burning incense by fountains or rivers (for some are fooled by dreams or demons, and go to these waters expecting a cure for their bodily ailments), and similar rites. So do not practise them. Augury, divination, watching for omens, wearing amulets, writing on leaves, sorcery and other such evil practices are the worship of the devil. These, then, you must avoid, because if after renouncing the

---

[13]The argument of this paragraph is derived from 1 Cor. 10.14-21, where St Paul compared the Eucharist, which is a sharing with Christ, with the food of pagan sacrifices, which made those who eat it partners with demons. St Cyril is making two points about the Eucharist:

(a)   There is a change from bread and wine to the body and blood of Christ;

(b)   This change is brought about by the Invocation or *Epiclesis* (not by the words of consecration, 'This is my body . . . This is my blood'). Cf. 5.7, where it is seen that God (the Father) is called upon to send his Spirit on the bread and wine so as to make them into Christ's body and blood. Cf. also 3.3 and 5.19. St Ambrose, however, believes that it is the priest's repetition of Christ's words that brings about the change (S 4.14). See Introduction, pp. 48-49.

Later the question began to be debated whether it was the invocation of the Spirit or the recitation of Christ's words of consecration that brought about the change in the eucharistic elements, and this became one of the many subjects of bitter disagreement between the East and the West. But in the fourth century the difference, though present, seems not to have been felt. Moreover it did not have the later geographical basis, as in the East Chrysostom attributed the change to the recitation of Christ's words of consecration (e.g. *de prod. Judae* 1.6; PG 49.380).

C's words modify those of Irenaeus in the second century: 'For just as when bread from the earth receives the invocation of God, it is no longer ordinary bread, but the Eucharist, consisting of two elements . . .' (*Adv. Haer.* iv.18.5; PG 7.1028-1029).

Cyril believes that the presence of God (generally the Holy Spirit) in the sacramental elements is required not only in the Eucharist, but also in baptism (3.1) and confirmation (3.3).

devil and making your Act of Adhesion to Christ[14] you succumb to them, you will find Satan a harsher master in temptations, doubtless because he regarded you as his own before, treating you kindly and not subjecting you to cruel slavery, whereas now you have grievously embittered him. So you will both be deprived of Christ and become acquainted with the devil.

You will remember hearing in the Old Testament the account of Lot and his daughters.[15] He himself was saved together with his daughters, for he reached the mountain; but his wife was turned into a pillar of salt, pilloried[16] for ever to preserve a memorial of her wicked decision to turn back. So watch yourself, do not turn to what lies behind;[17] do not after putting your hand to the plough[18] revert to the bitter activity of the world. Flee to the mountain to Jesus Christ, the stone hewn without hands which has filled the world.[19]

The Profession of Faith

9. So when you renounce Satan, you trample underfoot your entire covenant with him, and abrogate your former treaty with Hell. The gates of God's Paradise are open to you, that garden which God planted in the east, and from which our first parent was expelled for his transgression. When you turned from west to east, the region of light, you symbolised this change of allegiance. Then you were told to say: *I believe in the Father, the*

---

[14]The Act of Adhesion to Christ is the Profession of Faith described in section 9. Cf. Introduction, pp. 20-21.

[15]Gen. 19.17ff.

[16]Pillar/pilloried (*stele/esteliteumene*): a typical play on words. So too *mneme* means both 'reminder' (grim irony) and 'memorial'; *halmura* ('bitter') means literally 'salty', and refers back to the pillar of salt. There may be a reference to Wis. 10.7, where reference is made to Lot's wife in these words: 'a pillar of salt standing as a monument to an unbelieving soul'.

[17]Cf. Phil. 3.13.

[18]Lk. 9.62.

[19]Cf. Dan. 2.34-35.

Son and the Holy Spirit, and in one baptism of repentance.[20] I spoke
to you at length about this in previous instructions,[21] as well as
God's grace permitted.

10. Now that these words have made you secure, 'be sober'.
'For our adversary the devil', in the words we have just read,
'prowls around like a roaring lion, seeking someone to devour'.[22]
In earlier times 'death was strong and devoured'[23] men, but at
the holy font of new birth, 'God wiped every tear from every
face'.[24] For now that you have cast off the old man you will no
longer mourn but keep holiday, clad in the saving garment
which is Jesus.[25]

Entry into the Baptistery

11. These rites were carried out in the forecourt. God
willing, when we enter the holy of holies at the next stage of our
initiation into the mysteries, we shall then become aware of the
symbolism of what was there performed. To God the Father be
glory, power and majesty, in company with the Son and the
Holy Spirit, for ever and ever. Amen.

[20]So too in the RCIA the Act of Adhesion takes the form of a Profession of Faith.
For the inclusion in a baptismal formula of a statement of belief in the remission
of sins, cf. Cyprian, Ep. 69.7; Whitaker, p.10.

[21]In the catechetical sermon St Cyril preached to them in Lent explaining the
Creed. See Introduction, p. 13.

[22]1 Pet. 5.8, part of the reading for the day.

[23]Is. 25.8 (LXX).

[24]Cf. Is. 25.8; Tit. 3.5; Apoc. 7.17.

[25]Cf. Col. 3.9-10.

SERMON 2: THE BAPTISMAL RITE

The reading is from the Epistle to the Romans, beginning 'Do you not know that all of us who have been baptized into Christ Jesus were baptized into his death?' as far as 'Since you are not under law but under grace'.[1]

1. These daily instructions on the mysteries, and these new teachings which proclaim new tidings, are useful to us all, but especially to you who have been granted new life from old age to rebirth.[2] Therefore I must describe to you the stage which follows on yesterday's instruction, so that you may know what was underlying the symbolic actions you performed in the inner baptistery.[3]

Stripping

2. Upon entering you took off your clothing, and this symbolised your stripping off of 'the old nature with its practices'.[4] Stripped naked, in this too you were imitating Christ naked on the cross, who in his darkness 'disarmed the principalities and powers' and on the wood of the cross publicly 'triumphed over them'.[5] Since hostile powers lurked in your limbs, you can no longer wear your former clothing; I do not of course refer to visible apparel but to 'your old nature which is corrupt through deceitful lusts'.[6] I pray that the soul which has once thrown off that old nature may never resume it, but rather speak the words of Christ's bride in the Song of Songs: 'I had put off my garment; how could I put it on?'[7] This was a remarkable occasion, for you stood naked in the sight of all and you were not ashamed. You truly mirrored our first-

---

[1]Rom. 6.3-14.

[2]Egeria also tells us that Christians of longer standing liked to join the neophytes to hear the mystagogic sermons (47).

[3]The rites described in Sermon 1 had taken place in the outer room (Sermon 1.2).

[4]Col. 3.9.

[5]Col. 2.15.

[6]Eph. 4.22.

[7]Cant 5.3. St Ambrose also attributes words in the Song of Songs to Christ's bride, the Church (e.g. S 5.14).

created parent Adam, who stood naked in Paradise and was not ashamed.[8]

Anointing with Oil [9]

3. Next, after removing your garments you were rubbed with exorcised oil from the hair of your head to your toes, and so you became sharers in Jesus Christ, who is the cultivated olive tree. For you have been separated from the wild olive tree and grafted on the cultivated tree,[10] and given a share in the richness of the true olive. The exorcised oil, then, symbolised your partaking of Christ's richness; it is the token which drives away every trace of the enemy's power. Just as the breath of the saints[11] and the invocation of God's name burn like a fierce flame and drive out devils, likewise the exorcised oil, through invocation of God and through prayer, is invested with such power as not merely to cleanse all traces of sin with its fire,[12] but also to pursue all the invisible powers of the wicked one out of our persons.

Baptism

4. Then you were conducted by the hand to the holy pool of sacred baptism, just as Christ was conveyed from the cross to the sepulchre which stands before us.[13] Each person was asked

---

[8]Cf. Gen. 2.25. For C the stripping symbolises: (1) putting off the old nature; (2) the stripping of Christ; (3) the innocence of Paradise.

[9]See Introduction, p. 21f. C takes this anointing to be a symbol of the neophyte's share in Christ's life, and also an exorcism.

[10]Cf. Rom. 11.24. The grafting of the wild shoot on to the cultivated tree is a bewildering horticultural process.

[11]Breathing on the candidate's face was one of the rites of exorcism; its purpose, C says, was to instil 'fear' (*Procat.* 9).

[12]The sacramental element of oil, like the bread and wine in the Eucharist, has no supernatural power unless God was first called down upon it. St Ambrose speaks in the same way of the baptismal water (S 1.15).

[13]According to Egeria (47.1), C delivered these sermons at the entrance of the tomb. C sees the baptismal rite as a re-enactment of Christ's passion (cf. 2.2, 5, 6); Theodore, on the other hand, sees similar symbolism in the Mass (BH 4.26).

if he believed in the name of the Father and of the Son and of the Holy Spirit.[14] You made the confession that brings salvation, and submerged yourselves three times in the water and emerged: by this symbolic gesture you were secretly re-enacting the burial of Christ three days in the tomb. For just as our Saviour spent three days and nights in the hollow bosom of the earth, so you upon first emerging were representing Christ's first day in the earth, and by your immersion his first night. For at night one can no longer see but during the day one has light; so you saw nothing when immersed as if it were night, but you emerged as if to the light of day. In one and the same action you died and were born; the water of salvation became both tomb and mother for you.[15] What Solomon said of others is apposite to you. On that occasion he said: 'There is a time to be born, and a time to die',[16] but the opposite is true in your case — there is a time to die and a time to be born. A single moment achieves both ends, and your begetting was simultaneous with your death.

Signs and Realities in Baptism

5. What a strange and astonishing situation! We did not really die, we were not really buried, we did not really hang from a cross and rise again. Our imitation was symbolic, but our salvation a reality.[17] Christ truly hung from a cross, was truly buried, and truly rose again. All this he did gratuitously for us, so that we might share his sufferings by imitating them, and gain salvation in actuality. What transcendent kindness! Christ endured nails in his innocent hands and feet, and suffered pain; and by letting me participate in the pain without anguish or sweat, he freely bestows salvation on me.

---

[14] This act of faith in the Trinity at the moment of baptism is distinct from the Profession of Faith (1.9). Ambrose (S 2.20) and Theodore (BH 3.18ff.) make it clear that at each mention of the name of one of the three Persons the candidate submerged.

[15] Ambrose compares the font with a tomb (S 3.1); Theodore compares it with a womb (BH 3.10).

[16] Eccles. 3.2.

[17] For the contrast between signs and reality, cf. 5.20 with note 23.

6. No one should think, then, that his baptism is merely for the remission of sins and for adoption in the way that John's baptism brought only remission of sins. We know well that not merely does it cleanse sins and bestow on us the gift of the Holy Spirit — it is also the sign of Christ's suffering.[18] This is why, as we heard just now, Paul cried out: 'Do you not know that all of us who have been baptized in Christ Jesus were baptized into his death? We were buried therefore with him by baptism into death'.[19] These words he said to those who had assented to the view that baptism confers remission of sins and adoption, but not that it further implies a share by imitation in the true suffering of Christ.

7. So in order that we may realise that Christ endured all his sufferings for us and our salvation actually and not in make-believe,[20] and that we share in his pains, Paul cried out the literal truth: 'If we have been planted together with him in a death like his death, we shall certainly be planted together with him in a resurrection like his'.[21] He does well to say 'planted together'. For since 'the true vine'[22] has been planted here in Jerusalem, we have been planted with him by partaking of the baptism of his death. Pay close attention to the words of the apostle. He did not say 'If we have been planted together with him in his death', but 'in a death like his death'. For Christ really died, his soul really was separated from his body; he really was buried, for his holy body was wrapped in pure linen. In his case all these events really occurred; but in your case there was a likeness of death and suffering, but the reality, not the likeness, of salvation.

8. Now that you have thus received instruction, I exhort you to keep it in your minds, so that I, your unworthy teacher, may

---

[18]It says much for the importance C attached to symbolism that the symbolic effect of baptism, i.e. the share in Christ's suffering, seems to him more important than the forgiveness of sins or adoption or even the gift of the Spirit.

[19]Rom. 6.3f. just read.

[20]St Cyril stresses the reality of Christ's sufferings, presumably in order to refute the Docetic heresy that Jesus was simply God masquerading as a man, while remaining free from human weakness.

[21]Rom. 6.5, just read (not the RSV version).

[22]Jn. 15.1.

say in your case: 'I love you, because at all times you are mindful of me and maintain the traditions which I have delivered to you'.[23] God, who has brought you from death to life, can grant you the power to walk in newness of life,[24] for his is the glory and the power, now and for ever. Amen.

[23] 1 Cor. 11.2 (paraphrased).
[24] Cf. Rom. 6.4, just read.

SERMON 3: THE ANOINTING AT BAPTISM

The reading is from John's First Epistle to the whole Church, beginning from 'You have been anointed by God, and know all things', as far as 'And not shrink from him in shame at his coming'.[1]

The Gift of the Spirit

1. Now that you have been 'baptized into Christ' and have 'put on Christ', you have become conformed to the Son of God.[2] For God 'destined us to be his sons',[3] so he has made us like to the 'glorious body of Christ'.[4] Hence, since you 'share in Christ',[5] it is right to call you Christs or anointed ones. As God said, referring to you: 'Touch not my anointed ones'.[6] You have become anointed ones by receiving the sign[7] of the Holy Spirit. Since you are images of Christ, all the rites carried out over you have a symbolic meaning.

Christ bathed in the river Jordan,[8] and having invested the waters with the divine presence of his body,[9] he emerged from them, and the Holy Spirit visited him in substantial[10] form, like

[1] Jn. 2.20-28 (paraphrased).
[2] Gal. 3.27; Rom. 8.29.
[3] Eph. 1.5.
[4] Cf. Phil. 3.21.
[5] Heb. 3.14.
[6] Ps. 105.15.
[7] For C's use of the antithesis between sign and reality, see 5.20 with note 23.
[8] Through the rites of initiation the candidate participates in Jesus' experience in the Jordan when he was proclaimed as the Messiah (the Christ, the Anointed one). See Introduction, pp. 27-28. C's rite does not include a separate 'messianic' anointing with chrism, distinct from the anointing for the gift of the Spirit.
[9] Literally, 'with the divinity of his skin'. Perhaps there is a reference to Moses, the 'skin' of whose face shone because he had been talking to God (Exod. 34.29). Ambrose also suggests that Christ's entry into the water of the Jordan gave all baptismal water its power to communicate his 'justice' (cf. S 1.15-19). One is reminded of the modern ceremony at the Paschal Vigil, in which the Paschal candle representing Christ is dipped into the baptismal water to give it power to communicate Christ's risen life.
[10] 'Substantial', in order to emphasize the equal status of the Holy Spirit within the Trinity against the Arians and the like.

coming to rest on like. In the same way, when you emerged from the pool of sacred waters you were anointed in a manner corresponding with Christ's anointing. That anointing is the Holy Spirit, of whom the blessed Isaiah spoke when he prophesied in the person of the Lord: 'The Spirit of the Lord is upon me because he has anointed me; he has sent me to bring good tidings to the poor'.[11]

2. For Christ was not anointed by human hand with any tangible oil or myron.[12] No, the Father chose him to be Saviour of the whole world, and anointed him with the Holy Spirit. As Peter says, 'Jesus of Nazareth whom God anointed with the Holy Spirit'.[13] Again, the prophet David cried out: 'Your Throne, O God, endures for ever and ever; your royal sceptre is a sceptre of equity. You love Righteousness and hate wickedness; therefore God, your God has anointed you with the oil of gladness above your fellows'.[14]

Just as Christ was truly crucified, buried, and raised again, and you are considered worthy to be crucified, buried and raised with him in likeness[15] by baptism, so too in the matter of anointing, Christ was anointed with the spiritual oil of gladness, that is, with the Holy Spirit, which is called the oil of gladness because the Holy Spirit is the author of spiritual joy; and you have been anointed with myron because you have become fellows and sharers of Christ.

3. But be sure not to regard the myron merely as ointment. Just as the bread of the Eucharist after the invocation of the Holy Spirit is no longer just bread, but the body of Christ,[16] so the holy myron after the invocation is no longer ordinary

---

[11]Is. 61.1. Cf. Lk. 4.18.

[12]This is perfumed oil or chrism; for its meaning, see Introduction, p. 29.

[13]Ac. 10.38 (paraphrased).

[14]Ps. 45.6-7.

[15]Again the language of typology. Cf. 5.20 with note 23.

[16]In 1.7 (cf. note 13 there) C explains that the bread and wine are changed into the body and blood of Christ through the invocation (Epiclesis) of the Trinity. Here and in 5.7 he states the theology more precisely: the Father is asked to send the Holy Spirit on the offerings so as to make them the body and blood of Christ. Cf. also 5.19.

Here C explains the consecration of the chrism in the same way: through the invocation of the Holy Spirit the chrism ceases to be ordinary chrism and becomes

ointment but Christ's grace, which through the presence of the Holy Spirit instils his divinity into us. It is applied to your forehead and organs of sense[17] with a symbolic meaning; the body is anointed with visible ointment, and the soul is sanctified by the holy, hidden Spirit.[18]

4. First you were anointed on the forehead so that you might lose the shame which Adam, the first transgressor, everywhere bore with him,[19] and so that you might 'with unveiled face behold the glory of the Lord'.[20] Next you were anointed on the ears, that you might acquire ears which will hear those divine mysteries of which Isaiah said: 'The Lord has given me an ear to hear with'.[21] Again, the Lord Jesus in the gospel said: 'He who has ears to hear, let him hear'.[22] Then you were anointed on the nostrils, so that after receiving the divine chrism you might say: 'We are the aroma of Christ to God among those who are being saved'.[23] After that, you were anointed on the chest, so that 'having put on the breast-plate of righteousness,

---

the 'grace of Christ', a share in his divinity. The Roman Mass for the blessing of chrism on Maundy Thursday has preserved such an Epiclesis: 'Send forth from heaven, we pray you, O Lord, your Holy Spirit the Paraclete on this rich produce of the olive . . .' Ambrose suggests that a similar process is at work at the consecration of the baptismal font: 'The priest comes, he says a prayer at the font, he invokes the name of the Father, the presence of the Son and the Holy Spirit' (S 2.14; cf. S 1.15).

This application of epiclesis-theology to baptism and confirmation has the advantage of emphasising the role of the Holy Spirit: the sacramental presence of Christ is the result of the action of the Holy Spirit. But this view obscures the different modes of Christ's presence in the Eucharist and the other two sacraments.

[17]C's rite for the anointing with chrism is unusual, in that it involves the anointing of the senses and not only of the forehead. The modern RCIA also contains a signing of the senses, not at this point however, but as an optional addition to the Rite of Acceptance into the Order of Catechumens (n.85).

[18]In the same way, according to C, the beneficial effect of the Eucharist on the soul comes about through assimilation by the body (MC 4.3).

[19]C seems to regard the forehead as the part of the countenance that shows the signs of shame. He may be thinking also of the mark God placed on Cain (Gen. 4.15). So too St Augustine, quoted on p. 4.

[20]2 Cor 3.18. St Paul is alluding to the glory of God which dazzled the Israelites when reflected on Moses' face (Ex. 34.29-35).

[21]Is. 50.4 (LXX). St Ambrose attributes a similar effect to the Opening (S 1.2).

[22]Mt. 11.15.

[23]2 Cor. 2.15, quoted by St Ambrose in explaining the Opening (S 1.3).

you might stand against the wiles of the devil'.[24] Just as Christ after his baptism and visitation by the Holy Spirit went out and successfully wrestled with the enemy, so you also, after your holy baptism and sacramental anointing, put on the armour of the Holy Spirit, confront the power of the enemy, and reduce it saying: 'I can do all things in Christ who strengthens me'.[25]

5. Now that you are reckoned worthy of this holy anointing, you are called Christians, and this title you substantiate by your new birth. For before being thought worthy of this grace you did not strictly merit such an address. You were still advancing along the path towards being Christians.

6. It is important for you to know that this anointing is foreshadowed in the Old Testament. When Moses entrusted to his brother the command of God and made him High Priest, after washing him with water he anointed him;[26] and his brother received the name 'anointed one', clearly because of this prefiguring anointing.[27] Likewise when the High Priest raised Solomon to the kingship, he anointed him after washing him in the waters of Gihon.[28] This happened to Aaron and Solomon by way of figure, but to you not in figure but in truth, for you were truly anointed by the Holy Spirit. Christ is the beginning of your salvation, for he is truly the firstfruit while you are the whole lump. If the firstfruit is holy, clearly the holiness will pass to the whole lump.[29]

7. Keep this anointing unspotted. For if it abides in you it will teach you all things, as you have just heard the blessed John say in his long discourse about the anointing.[30] For this sacrament

---

[24]Eph. 6.14, 11.

[25]Phil. 4.13. C in this paragraph lists a number of effects of the gift of the Holy Spirit. He does not distinguish clearly between the effects of the pre-baptismal and post-baptismal anointings.

[26]Ex. 40.12-13.

[27]In the translation 'prefiguring' and 'figure' represent the Greek word *tupikos*. Cf. 5.20 with note 23.

[28]1 Kg. 1.38-39. C seems to be relying on an extra-biblical tradition.

[29]Cf. Rom. 11.16; 1 Cor. 15.23.

[30]'But the anointing which you received from him abides in you, and you have no need that anyone should teach you; as his anointing teaches you about everything, and is true, and is no lie, just as it has taught you, abide in him' (1 Jn. 2.27, taken from the reading of the day).

is the spiritual preserver of the body, and the salvation of the soul. So the blessed Isaiah prophesied long ago: 'The Lord shall make provision for all nations on this mountain' (by mountain he means the Church, as elsewhere when he says, 'And it shall come to pass in the latter days that the mountain of the Lord will be made clear'[31]). 'They will drink of wine and gladness, and be anointed with myron'.[32] To convince you utterly, hear what he says about the sacramental nature of this myron: 'Give all these things to the nations, for the Lord's counsel is to all nations'.[33]

Now that you are anointed with this holy myron, keep it in yourself spotless and unsullied. Advance in good works, and be pleasing to the 'pioneer of your salvation',[34] Jesus Christ. To him be glory for ever and ever. Amen.

---

[31] Is. 2.2 (LXX).
[32] Is. 25.6-7 (LXX paraphrased).
[33] Is. 25.7 (LXX). Cyril takes these words as a prophecy that the Church will give her sacraments (wine and chrism) to the gentiles.
[34] Cf. Heb. 2.10; 12.2.

SERMON 4: THE EUCHARIST

The reading is from Paul's Epistle to the Corinthians: 'For I received from the Lord what I also delivered to you', and the verses which follow.[1]

The Bread and Wine are truly changed

1. This teaching of the blessed Paul is in itself sufficient to assure you fully on the divine mysteries, through being accounted worthy of which you are now 'of the same body'[2] and blood of Christ. As Paul proclaimed, in the passage just read: 'Our Lord Jesus Christ on the night when he was betrayed took bread, and when he had given thanks, he broke it and handed it to his disciples saying: "Take and eat; this is my body." And taking the cup, and giving thanks, he said: "Take and drink; this is my blood".'[3] Since, then, Christ himself clearly described the bread to us in the words 'This is my body', who will dare henceforward to dispute it? And since he has emphatically said, 'This is my blood', who will waver in the slightest and say it is not his blood?

2. By his own power on a previous occasion he turned the water into wine at Cana in Galilee; so it is surely credible that he has changed wine into blood.[4] If he performed that wonderful miracle just because he had been invited to a human marriage, we shall certainly be much more willing to admit that he has conferred on the wedding-guests[5] the savouring of his body and blood.

3. So let us partake with the fullest confidence that it is the body and blood of Christ. For his body has been bestowed on you in the form[6] of bread, and his blood in the form of wine, so that by partaking of Christ's body and blood you may share

---

[1] 1 Cor. 11.23ff.

[2] Cf. Eph. 3.6.

[3] 1 Cor. 11.23-25, with variations based on the Gospel narratives.

[4] St Ambrose argues similarly from other examples of Christ's miraculous power, without quoting this obvious example at Cana (S 4.14-23).

[5] Cf. Mk. 2.19: 'Can the wedding-guests fast while the bridegroom is with them?'

[6] *Tupos.* Cf. 5.20, note 23.

with him the same body and blood. This is how we become bearers of Christ,[7] since his body and blood spreads throughout our limbs; this is how, in the blessed Peter's words, 'we become partakers of the divine nature'.[8]

4. Christ once said in conversation with the Jews: 'Unless you eat my flesh and drink my blood, you have no life in you.'[9] They were scandalised because they did not interpret his words spiritually; they retreated from his presence, thinking he was exhorting them to cannibalism.

5. Even in the Old Testament there were 'Loaves of the Presence',[10] but since they belonged to the old dispensation they have come to fulfilment.[11] But in the New Testament the bread is of heaven and the chalice brings salvation,[12] and they sanctify the soul and the body; for as the bread relates to the body, so the word harmonises with the soul.

6. Do not, then, regard the bread and wine as nothing but bread and wine, for they are the body and blood of Christ as the Master himself has proclaimed. Though your senses suggest this to you, let faith reassure you. Do not judge the matter by taste but by faith, which brings you certainty without doubting, since you have been found worthy of Christ's body and blood.

Old Testament Prophecies of the Eucharist

7. The Blessed David will inform you of the meaning of the Eucharist when he says: 'Thou has laid a table before me against those who oppress me.'[13] What he means is this: Lord,

---

[7]The Greek is *Christophoroi* ('Christophers'). Cf. Ignatius, *Eph.* 9. C takes an extremely literal view of the Eucharist; our bodies assimilate Christ's body and blood, and so we share his divinity in our souls (cf. 4.5). C explains the working of the anointing in the same 'physical' way (3.3).

[8]2 Pet. 1.4.

[9]Jn. 6.53 (paraphrased).

[10]For the twelve Loaves of the Presence see Ex. 25.30; Lev. 24.5-9; 1 Sam. 21.2-6, etc.

[11]This seems another example of typology (cf. 5.20 with note 23). However, the Greek may simply mean, 'they have come to an end'.

[12]Cf. Ps. 116.13: 'I will lift up the cup of salvation and call on the name of the Lord.'

[13]Ps. 23.5 (LXX).

before your coming the diabolical spirits laid for me a table which was defiled, polluted, and filled with satanic power, but after your coming you laid a table before me. When man tells God: 'Thou has laid a table before me,' the only thing he can mean is that sacramental, spiritual table which God has made ready for us 'against' the evil spirits, that is, opposing and confronting them. And this quite naturally, for the one table was associated with devils, the other with God.

'Thou hast anointed my head with oil.'[14] With oil he anointed you on the forehead, imprinting there God's seal which you carry, so that you may become the impression of the seal, the holiness of God.[15]

'And the chalice which inebriates me, how godly it is.'[16] In that phrase you see mentioned the chalice which Jesus took in his hand, and giving thanks said: 'This is my blood which is poured out for many for the remission of sins.'[17]

The Baptismal Garment

8. It is for this reason, to hint at this gift, that Solomon says in Ecclesiastes:[18] 'Come then, eat your bread with enjoyment' — he means spiritual bread. 'Come then' — his invitation brings salvation and blessedness. 'And drink your wine with a merry heart' — the wine of the spirit. 'And let oil be poured over your head' — you see him here hinting also at the sacramental anointing. 'And let your garments be always white,[19] because the Lord has approved what you do.' For before you drew near to the gift, your works were 'vanity of vanities'.[20]

---

[14]*Ibid.* C applies these words to the post-baptismal anointing which he has already described in the preceding sermon. The wording of the psalm forces C to speak of olive-oil (*elaion*) rather than chrism or myron. The same is true of the passages quoted in sections 8 and 9.

[15]A reference to Ex. 28.36, which describes the engraved plate of gold bearing the words 'Holy to the Lord', which the Lord prescribed that Aaron should wear on his forehead.

[16]Ps. 23.5 (LXX).

[17]Mt. 26.28.

[18]Eccles 9.7-8. C allows himself to adapt the text to suit his purposes.

[19]C presumably sees in these words an allusion to the baptismal robe.

[20]Eccles. 1.2.

Once you have stripped off the old garments and put on those which are spiritually white, you must be clad in white always. I am not of course saying that you must always wear white clothing on your body, but that your spiritual dress must be truly white and shining, so that you may say, in the words of the blessed Isaiah: 'Let my soul rejoice in the Lord: he has clothed me with the garment of salvation, and with the robe of gladness he has covered me.'[21]

The Bread and Wine are changed

9. You have now been taught and fully instructed that what seems to be bread is not bread, though it appears to be such to the sense of taste, but the body of Christ; that what seems to be wine is not wine, though the taste would have it so, but the blood of Christ; that David was speaking of this long ago when he sang, 'Bread strengthens the heart of man, that he may make his face glad with oil'.[22] So strengthen your heart by partaking of that spiritual bread, and gladden the face of your soul. May you 'unveil' it 'with conscience undefiled', and 'reflect the glory of the Lord', and pass 'from glory to glory' in Christ Jesus our Lord.[23] To him be honour, power and glory for ever and ever. Amen.

---

[21] Is. 61.10 (LXX). It became customary for the newly-baptized to continue wearing their white garments until Low Sunday (see Introduction, pp. 31-33).

[22] Ps. 104.15 (LXX).

[23] Cf. 2 Cor. 3.18; 1 Tim. 3.9; 2 Tim. 1.3.

SERMON 5: THE EUCHARISTIC RITE

The reading is from Peter's Letter to the whole Church: 'So put away all filthiness, all guile, and all slander', and the following verses.[1]

1. At our earlier gatherings, you have received through God's kindness sufficient instruction on baptism, the anointing, and the reception of the body and blood of Christ. Now we must turn to the next topic, so that today we may put the topmost parapet on the spiritual building[2] of your instruction.

Lavabo

2. You saw the deacon offering water for washing to the priest[3] and to the presbyters encircling God's altar. Of course he did not do this because their bodies were dirty. Not at all; we did not enter the church with grimy bodies in the first place. No, the washing is a symbol of the need for you to be clean of all sins and transgressions. Since our hands symbolise action, by washing them we are clearly denoting the purity and blamelessness of our deeds. You have surely heard the blessed David interpreting this mystery when he says: 'I will wash my hands amongst the innocent, and go about thy altar, O Lord.'[4] So there is no doubt that the washing of the hands represents symbolically freedom from sins.

Kiss of Peace

3. Next the deacon says in a loud voice: *Receive one another, and let us kiss one another.* Do not assume that this is the customary kiss exchanged by friends in public. No, this kiss joins souls together in search of complete forgiveness from one another. So the kiss is a mark of fusion of souls, and of the

---

[1] 1 Pet. 2.1ff. C often quotes from memory; here he has introduced a phrase from Jas. 1.21 into the text.

[2] Language borrowed perhaps from Deut. 22.8.

[3] For C, as for Ambrose, the word 'priest' denotes the bishop.

[4] Ps. 26.6 (LXX).

expulsion of all resentment for wrongs. It is for this reason that Christ said: 'If you are offering your gift at the altar, and there remember that your brother has something against you, leave there your offering on the altar, and go first and be reconciled to your brother, and then come near and offer your gift.'[5] So the kiss is a reconciliation, and therefore holy. This is what I think St Paul meant when he said, 'Greet one another with a holy kiss', and St Peter when he says, 'Greet one another with the kiss of love'.[6]

Introductory Dialogue

4. Next the priest says in a loud voice: *Let us lift up our hearts.* For at that most awesome[7] moment we must indeed raise our hearts high to God, not keep them intent on the earth and on earthly matters. So the priest is virtually commanding you all at that moment to lay aside the cares of this life, your domestic worries, and to keep your heart in heaven on God who loves men.

Then you answer: *We have them lifted to the Lord.* By these words of assent you declare you are at one with him. Now no one should stand there saying with his lips, 'We have them lifted to the Lord', while in his mind he is preoccupied with worldly thoughts. We must be mindful of God at all times, but if human weakness makes this impossible we should try especially hard at this time.

5. The priest then says: *Let us give thanks to the Lord.* For we ought truly to give thanks, because he has called our unworthy persons to this great gift, because he has reconciled us though we were enemies, and because he has counted us worthy of the 'Spirit of sonship'.[8] Then you say: *It is right and just.* So our

---

[5]Mt. 5.23-24 (paraphrased).

[6]1 Cor. 16.20: 1 Pet. 5.14.

[7]'Awesome' (*phrikodestate*) is an adjective commonly applied to the sacraments of initiation (e.g. 1.5; cf. Introduction, p. 59); here C applies it also to the Eucharist. There was a widespread tendency in the 4th century to stress the mysterious aspect of worship. For the origins of the Introductory Dialogue, see Introduction, p. 45.

[8]Cf. Rom. 5.10; 8.15.

giving thanks is a right and just act, whereas God's action is not guided by what is just; his actions have gone beyond mere justice, for he has treated us generously and reckoned us worthy of such great blessings.

Preface

6. After that we make mention[9] of sky and earth and sea, sun and moon, stars and all creation — whether endowed with reason or not, whether seen or unseen. We recall Angels, Archangels, Virtues, Dominions, Principalities, Powers, Thrones, and the Cherubim of many faces.[10] In effect we bid them, in the words of David: 'Magnify the Lord with me.'[11] We recall also the Seraphim, whom Isaiah by the power of the Holy Spirit saw encircling God's throne. With two wings they covered the face, with two more the feet, and with two more they flew, saying: *Holy, holy, holy, is the Lord of Hosts.*[12] The reason why we utter this praise of God which the Seraphim have bequeathed to us is that we wish to join the heavenly armies as they sing their hymn.

Epicesis over the Offerings

7. Once we have sanctified ourselves with these spiritual hymns, we call upon the merciful God to send the Holy Spirit on our offerings, so that he may make the bread Christ's body, and the wine Christ's blood;[13] for clearly whatever the Holy Spirit touches is sanctified and transformed.

---

[9]We mention them in order to thank God for them.

[10]There are many points of resemblance between C's liturgy and the Egyptian Eucharist; cf. G. J. Cuming, 'Egyptian Elements in the Jerusalem Liturgy', JTS 25 (1974), pp. 117-124. One example is the mention of the choirs of angels, with the Seraphim using their wings to cover *the* face (cf. Sarapion, *Euchologion*, 1; Jasper and Cuming, p. 77). There was a tradition in Alexandria that the Seraphim described in Is. 6.2 covered *God's* face with their wings (cf. Origen, *de Principiis*, iv.3.14. For the connection between Christian worship and the heavenly liturgy, see Heb. 9. Cf. Ambrose's comparison of ministers with angels (S 1.6 with note 13).

[11]Ps. 34.3.

[12]Is. 6.2-3.

[13]For the Epiclesis (invocation of the Holy Spirit) cf. 3.3 with note 16.

Prayers for the Church

8. Then, when the spiritual sacrifice — this worship without blood — has been completed,[14] we beg God over the sacrifice of propitiation for general peace among the churches, for the right order of the world, for the kings,[15] for soldiers and allies, for the sick and the afflicted, and in short we all make entreaty and offer this sacrifice for all who need help.[16]

Commemoration of the Dead [17]

9. Next we recall those who have gone to rest before us, and first of all the patriarchs, prophets, apostles and martyrs, so that God may listen to our appeal through their prayers and representations. After that, we pray on behalf of the holy

[14]It is striking that C's account of the eucharistic prayer contains no explicit reference to the recital of the Supper-Narrative. Some early liturgies, notably that of SS. Addai and Mari, in the form in which they have come down to us contain no such narrative (see Introduction, p. 46). G. Dix (*Shape*, pp. 197-203) thinks that C's rite had no Supper-Narrative. A similar view is taken by E. J. Cutrone, 'Cyril's *Mystagogical Catecheses* and the Evolution of the Jerusalem Anaphora', *Orientalia Christiana Periodica*, 44 (1978), pp. 52-64; J. R. K. Fenwick, *Fourth Century Anaphoral Construction*, Bramcote Notts., 1986; and G. J. Cuming, 'The Shape of the Anaphora', *Studia Patristica*, 20.ii (1989), pp. 333-345. It seems to me more likely that his liturgy did include the Words of Institution; either C thought it unnecessary to quote them here because he had given an account of the Last Supper in MC 4, or he did quote them, but observance of the *disciplina arcani* has led to the omission of the words from the text. The phrase 'sacrifice . . . has been completed (*apartisthenai*)' may be a reference to the recital of words of institution, as in Chrysostom, *de Proditione Judae*, 1.6 (PG 49.380). If this conjecture is correct, C's liturgy, like several early liturgies from Alexandria, places the Epiclesis before the Supper Narrative.

[15]For the plural 'Kings', cf. Introduction, p. 50. For the epithet 'without blood', cf. Ambrose, S 4.27, and Introduction, p. 47.

[16]C applies sacrificial terminology to the Mass. The bread and wine are 'offerings' (*prokeimena*: sect. 7). The Eucharist is a 'sacrifice' (*thusia*), which is spiritual, bloodless and propitiatory (*hilasmou*: sect. 8). It is offered on behalf of the living (sect. 8) and the dead (sect. 10). We appease God on behalf of ourselves and of others by offering the slain Christ (*Christon esphagiasmenon . . . prospheromen*) (sect. 10). Prayer *over* (or 'at the time of', *epi tes thusias*: sect. 8) the sacrifice has a special efficacy (cf. the end of sect. 9).

[17]The commemoration has two parts: we ask the dead saints to pray for us, but also pray on behalf of the dead.

fathers and bishops and in general for all amongst us already gone to their rest, for we believe that these souls will obtain the greatest help if we make our prayers for them when the holy and most awesome sacrifice has been set on the altar.

10. I should like to use an illustration to persuade you of the truth of this, for I know that many of you are saying: 'How is a soul which has quitted this world, whether in sin or not, helped by being mentioned in the prayers?' Well, surely if a king had exiled some opponents, and their friends wove a garland and presented it to him on behalf of those who had been penalised, would he not relax their punishment? It is the same when we make our entreaties to God on behalf of the dead, even if they are sinners. But we do not weave a garland; we offer Christ who has been slain for our sins, and so we appease the merciful God both on their behalf and on ours.

The Lord's Prayer

11.   Immediately after this, we recite the prayer which the Saviour handed down to his own disciples. With a clear conscience[18] we call God Father in these words: 'Our Father, who art in heaven ...'[19]

Holy Communion

19. Next the celebrant says: *What is holy for the holy.*[20] The offerings are holy since they have received the descent of the Holy Spirit, and you are holy because you have been accounted worthy of the Holy Spirit.[21] The holy things therefore correspond

---

[18]Probably an allusion to a phrase like that of the Roman liturgy: 'Let us pray with confidence to the Father; *audemus dicere, Pater noster*'.

[19]There follows an explanation of each petition of the Lord's Prayer. St Ambrose also gives his explanation of the Our Father in his account of the baptismal mysteries (S 5.18ff.; 6.24 – not included in this collection). But Theodore and St Augustine give the explanation of the prayer during Lent in connection with the rite of the Presentation of the Lord's Prayer (see Introduction, p. 14).

[20]These words also feature in Theodore's liturgy (BH 5.23). Cf. Mt. 7.6: 'Do not give dogs what is holy'. See Introduction, p. 55.

[21]I.e. in the rite described in Sermon 3.

with the holy people. Then you say: *There is one holy, one Lord, Jesus Christ.* For in truth there is only one holy, in the sense of holy by nature. We are holy not by nature but by participation, practice and prayer.

20. After this you hear the Cantor inviting you in sacred song to participate in the holy mysteries. His words are: *Taste, and see that the Lord is good.*[22] Entrust this judgment not to your bodily palate, but to faith which knows no doubt. For those who taste are bidden to taste not bread and wine but the sign[23] of Christ's body and blood.

[22]Ps. 34.8, here evidently used as a communion chant. Ambrose also quotes this verse in connection with Communion (M. 58); its use at communion became common (cf. Jungmann, *op. cit.*, ii, 392).

[23]*Antitupon.* The word 'sign' should not be taken as evidence that C is denying the Real Presence, for Sermon 4 puts his belief in this beyond doubt. To describe something as a 'sign' does not imply the absence of the thing signified: it is the sacramental sign which makes present an aspect of Christ's incarnate life so that we share in it. Baptism symbolizes his sufferings and makes them present; the Eucharist does the same for his body and blood. Ambrose's liturgy uses the word *figura* in the same sense (S 4.21 with note 44).

Sign/reality in C. – C repeatedly contrasts signs with realities. A table of contrasting pairs of words can be drawn up as follows:

1.3	symbol (*tupos*)	reality (*aletheia*)
2.5	symbolic imitation	reality
	(*eikon, mimesis*)	truly (*ontos*)
2.6	sign (*antitupon*)	
	imitation	true (*alethinos*)
	share (*koinonia*)	
2.7	share	reality
	likeness (*homoioma*)	
3.1	sign, manner corresponding	
	with Christ's (*antitupon*)	Christ's life
	symbolic (*eikonikos*)	
3.2	likeness	
	fellows and sharers	truly (*alethos*)
	(*koinonoi, metochoi*)	
3.6	foreshadowing (*sumbolon*)	in truth (*alethos*)
	in figure (*tupikos*)	
4.3	form (*tupos*)	Christ
	sharing (*metalabon*)	
5.2	symbol (*sumbolon*)	spiritual state
5.20	sign (*antitupon*)	Christ

Another table of correspondences can be drawn up showing the application of these two sets of terms:

21. So when you come forward, do not come with arm extended or fingers parted. Make your left hand a throne for your right, since your right hand is about to welcome a king. Cup your palm and receive in it Christ's body, saying in response *Amen*. Then carefully bless your eyes with a touch of the holy body,[24] and consume it, being careful to drop not a particle of it. For to lose any of it is clearly like losing part of your own body.[25] Tell me, if anyone gave you some gold dust, would you not keep it with the greatest care, ensuring that you did not lose by dropping any of it? So you should surely take still greater care not to drop a fragment of what is more valuable than gold and precious stones.

22. After partaking of Christ's body, go to receive the chalice of his blood. Do not stretch out your hands for it.[26] Bow your

	Symbol	Reality
1.3	Old Testament event	Events in Christ's life
		Corresponding event in sacramental life of the Church
2.5, 3.2	Sacramental effect	Event in Christ's life
2.7	Symbolic imitation of Christ's passion	Salvific effect
3.6	Old Testament event	Sacramental grace
4.3	Appearance of bread and wine	Body and blood of Christ
5.2	Washing of hands	Freedom from sins
5.20	Sign of body and blood	Body and blood of Christ

Underlying this terminology is the Platonic assumption that the symbol is less real than the thing it symbolizes, but shares in its reality. Ambrose (S 2.15; cf. note 25) and Theodore (BH 2.15; cf. note 25) make similar use of the contrast between symbols and realities.

Tupos literally means a stamp or die; *antitupon* the impression it produces. In Cyril both type and antitype are distinct from the sacramental grace they signify. Later however in the eighth century St John Damascene sometimes used the type/antitype terminology in a different way. For him the antitype is the reality, in contrast with the type or symbol; thus Mary is the living ark, the antitype of Noah's (PG 96.649B; cf. 98.232A). The first traces of this usage can be seen as early as 1 Pet. 3.21 (baptism the antitype of Noah's ark). But at other times he used the term *antitype* in a sense more like Cyril's (PG 94.1151C, 1153B).

[24]Theodore (BH 5.28) also tells his congregation to apply Christ's body to their eyes, and also to kiss it.

[25]C's belief that Christ is present even in the crumbs leads him to make the exaggerated suggestion that we receive less of Christ if we lose a crumb.

[26]C's words seem to suggest that the chalice is not touched by the communicants but held to their lips by the minister.

head and say *Amen* to show your homage and reverence, and sanctify yourself by partaking also of Christ's blood. While your lips are still moist with his blood, touch it with your hands and bless your eyes, forehead, and other organs of sense. Then await the prayer,[27] and give thanks to God who has counted you worthy of such mysteries.

23. Maintain these traditions without stain, and keep yourselves free from faults. Do not cut yourselves off from communion, do not deprive yourselves of these holy and spiritual mysteries through stain of sins.[28] 'May the God of peace sanctify you wholly; and may your body and soul and spirit be kept sound at the coming of our Lord Jesus Christ.'[29] To him be glory, honour and power, in the company of the Father and the Holy Spirit, now and always, for ever and ever. Amen.

[27]The prayer now called the Post-Communion.

[28]Theodore shows that he does not regard every sin as an obstacle to Communion (cf. BH 5.33ff.).

[29]1 Thess. 5.23 (with modifications).

AMBROSE

Ambrose was born in Trier, the northern capital of the Roman Empire, about 339. When he was about thirty, he was given charge of the province of Aemilia-Liguria and took up residence at Milan. At that time the see was ruled by an Arian bishop named Auxentius. When Auxentius died in 373 or 374, a clash between the Catholics and the Arians was expected over the election of his successor. Ambrose accordingly was present in order to keep the peace, but to his surprise and embarrassment found himself elected even though he was not yet baptized. His rule of his diocese was long and tumultuous. He was not afraid to defy the royal family. He refused the Emperor's mother Justina the use of one of the basilicas in Milan for her fellow Arians; later, however, the Empress had to make use of his services as envoy to the usurper Maximus. Ambrose had another battle of wills with the Emperor Theodosius, making him do public penance for the massacre of thousands of citizens who had rioted at Thessalonika. He was equally fearless and insistent on his principles in his relations with Pope Damasus.

But it would be wrong to imagine him as simply a tough politician. He exercised considerable influence on the development of Western theological thought, for he studied the Greek Fathers eagerly and assimilated their ideas into his own works. He won the admiration of St Augustine and eventually baptized him.

The six sermons that comprise the *De Sacramentis* were probably preached in the week after Easter about 391. The liturgical detail they preserve is especially valuable, but perhaps the most striking thing about them is the bold use that Ambrose makes of the allegorical method of interpreting the scriptures. His methods, however, do not appeal to our present age with its more exacting critical standard. They were traditional among Alexandrian writers, and Ambrose had probably learnt them from his reading of Origen. Clement,[1] for example,

---

[1] *Stromateis*, 1.28 (PG 8.921-924). Origen speaks of three senses, referring respectively to body, soul and spirit (*de Princ.* iv. 2.4).

distinguished four senses of scripture — the literal, the mystic (or allegorical), the moral and the prophetic. In his treatise *On Abraham*,[2] Ambrose states that the same text may be assigned two meanings. One fights with both edges of a two-edged sword, and scripture is sharper than the sword. 'Therefore I think it reasonable to apply the meaning to higher things and through the history of various characters to explain a certain development in the form of virtue.' Accordingly he gives an allegorical interpretation to the story of the Fall. Adam stands for the mind, Eve for the senses, and the Fall stands for the mind surrendering to pleasure. The Flood is the correction of the mind by instruction. The presupposition of this exegetical method is that, as all truth comes from the Holy Spirit, the words of scripture can be used to illuminate any truth to which they can be made to apply.[3]

The translation of the first five books was made by the late James Walsh, S.J. He kindly allowed me to make numerous small changes. The translation follows the text of Bernard Botte, O.S.B., in the *Sources Chrétiennes* series with the exception of the second sentence of 4.29, which is discussed in note 60. I have omitted the last parts of the fifth and sixth sermons, which are not explanations of the sacraments of initiation, but treatises on prayer and in particular the Our Father.

Although for some time it was suspected that Ambrose was not the author of the *de Sacramentis*, his authorship is no longer in doubt, thanks to the work of O. Faller and R. H. Connolly.[4] Ambrose was also the author of the *de Mysteriis* (M), which seems to be a version of the *de Sacramentiis* (S) abridged for publication, omitting certain details out of respect for the *disciplina arcani*; also of the homily *Explanatio Symboli* preached at the Presentation of the Creed. These two works are included in Botte's edition of S.

---

[2] 2.1.

[3] Cf. R. H. Malden, JTS 16 (1915) pp. 509-522; R. P. C. Hanson, *Allegory and Event*.

[4] See the Introduction to Botte's edition, pp. 7-25, for discussion and further references.

SERMONS ON THE SACRAMENTS
I
DISCIPLINA ARCANI

1. I shall begin now to speak of the sacraments which you have received. It was not proper for me to do so before this, because, for the Christian, faith must come first. That is why, at Rome, the baptized are called the faithful;[1] and our father Abraham was made just not by his works but by faith.[2] So you were baptized and came to believe. It would be impious for me to conclude otherwise. You would never have been called to grace, had not Christ judged you worthy of his grace.[3]

The Ephphetha (Opening)

2. What was it that we did on Saturday?[4] We began with the Opening.[5] The mysteries of the Opening were performed

---

[1]The Roman Church was not alone in limiting the use of the term 'faithful' (*fideles, pistoi*) to the baptized. Cyril of Jerusalem (*Cat.* 1.4; 5.1), Augustine (*Serm.* 132.1; PL 38.734) and John Chrysostom (ACW 11.11ff.) all seem to use the word in the same sense. However, the text is not certain; another reading would give the translation: 'That is why the baptized are properly (*recto nomine*) called the faithful.' I have discussed this problem in my article 'Ideo et Romae . . . JTS 24 (1973), pp. 202-207. On A's attitude to Rome, see S 3.5-6.

[2]Cf. Gen. 15.6; Rom. 4.1-25. A is seeking to justify the practice of not explaining the rites of initiation until after they have been received. Faith is needed before the rites can be understood, and faith is not given until baptism. In M 2 he gives two other reasons: (1) because of the demands of the *disciplina arcani* (cf. Introduction, pp. 55ff.); (2) because one learns more easily if one has seen before learning. Cf. Cyril of Jerusalem, MC 1.1.

[3]This sentence seems at first sight to anticipate the semi-Pelagian heresy that we have to give the first proofs of worthiness without any supernatural help. But A's insistence on the need of grace before any Christian action is clear from S 5.10. In 1.1 he seems to mean that the grace of baptism (i.e. faith) comes to us simply because Christ has chosen us to receive it, not because of any preaching on our part. The formula 'judged you worthy' is probably a liturgical phrase without semi-Pelagian implications. Cf. Cyril, MC 1.1: 'you were accounted worthy of divine and vitalising baptism'.

[4]I.e. at the Paschal Vigil. The six books of this work are six sermons delivered from Monday to Saturday or Tuesday to Sunday of Easter week. Cf. 4.29 with note 60.

[5]Cf. Introduction, pp. 17-18. The rite seems to have been intended originally as an exorcism (cf. Hippolytus, *Ap. Trad.*, 20.8).

when the bishop touched your ears and your nostrils. What does this mean? In this gospel, when the deaf and dumb man was brought to our Lord Jesus Christ, he touched the man's ears and his mouth: his ears, because the man was deaf; his mouth because he was dumb. And he said: Ephphetha, a Hebrew word which means 'be opened'.[6] The reason why the priest[7] touched your ears was that they might be opened to the word and to the homily of the priest.

3. But why, you may ask, the nostrils?[8] In the gospel, our Lord touched the man's mouth because he was dumb. He was unable to speak of the heavenly mysteries: so he received from Christ the power of speech. Again, in the gospel, the subject was a man; here, women are baptized. Nor is there the same purity in the servant as there is in the Lord, since the latter forgives sins, whereas the former has his sins forgiven, so that there is no comparison between them. The bishop touches the nostrils and not the mouth out of respect for what is done and what is given. He touches the nostrils so that you may receive the sweet fragrance of eternal goodness; so that you can say as the holy apostle said: 'We are the aroma of Christ to God';[9] and so that the full fragrance of faith and devotion may dwell in you.

Anointing with Oil[10]

4. Then we arrived at the baptistery. You went in, and were anointed. Think whom you saw, think what you said: recall it

---

[6]Mk. 7.34.

[7]'Priest' is Ambrose's normal term for the bishop; 'presbyter' corresponds to the modern term 'priest' (1.4); the deacon is the 'levite' (1.4).

[8]The bishop does not touch the candidate's mouth because it would be unseemly for him to do this to a woman. But if not the mouth, why the nose? A's answer is a little confused; he implies that the candidate both receives and emits the fragrance of piety. In the RCIA it is the ears and the lips which are touched.

[9]2 Cor. 2.15.

[10]Cf. Introduction, p. 21f. Cyril of Jerusalem, Chrysostom and Theodore place the Renunciation and the Profession of Faith before the Anointing. The RCIA follows Ambrose's order. The candidate must have been stripped for this ceremony, but A, with his customary delicacy, does not comment on this circumstance as other preachers do (cf. Introduction, p.21).

carefully. A levite came to receive you, and a presbyter as well. You were rubbed with oil like an athlete, Christ's athlete, as though in preparation for an earthly wrestling-match, and you agreed to take on your opponent. The wrestler has something to hope for: every contest has its trophy. You wrestle in the world, but it is Christ's trophy you receive — the prize for your struggles in the world. And even though this prize is awarded in heaven, the right to the prize is achieved here below.

Renunciation of Sin

5. When the question was put to you, *Do you renounce the devil and his works?* what was your reply? *I do renounce them.* And: *Do you renounce the world and its pleasures?* What was your reply? *I do renounce them.* Keep what you said in mind. The terms of the guarantee you gave must never fade from your memory.[11] If you give a man your note of hand, you incur a liability, if you want to receive his money. You are held to your obligation; the money-lender holds you to it if you seek to escape from it. If you refuse to admit it, you go before a judge, and there you are convicted on the evidence of your note of hand.

6. Think of the place where you made your promise, think of those to whom you made it. You saw a levite: but he is a minister of Christ. You have seen him exercising his ministry at the altar. That is why your guarantee is binding, not on earth, but in heaven. Think where it was that you received the heavenly sacraments.[12] If the body of Christ is here, then here too are to be found his angels. You have read in the gospel that

[11]In Cyril, Chrysostom and Theodore, the Renunciation takes the form of a straightforward statement by the candidate, not the question and answer as here. A makes no explicit reference to the Profession of Faith, but he perhaps alludes to it in his insistence on the 'guarantee'. Nor in this work does he tell us that the candidate faces west to address the devil, but it is perhaps implied in M 7 (cf. Introduction, p. 20).

[12]A's thought has leapt to a later stage of the ceremonies. When you received Holy Communion ('the heavenly sacraments'), the deacon was minister at the altar. This sacred function of his makes your promise to him in the baptistery more binding.

where the body is, there the eagles gather.[13] Where the body of Christ is, there also are the eagles, whose nature it is to fly where they can avoid earthly things and attain to the heavenly. Why do I say this? Because the men who are Christ's heralds are also angels and seem destined to take the place of angels.

7. How? Listen. John was the Baptist, and he was born of man and woman. And yet he also was an angel. Listen to what it says: 'Behold I send my messenger (angel) before thy face; who shall prepare thy way before thee'.[14] Listen again to what the prophet Malachi has to say: 'The lips of a priest should guard knowledge, and men should seek law from his mouth, for he is the messenger (angel) of the almighty God'.[15] All this is said to give glory to the priesthood, not to attribute anything to our personal merits.

8. So you have renounced the world, you have renounced this age. Be on the alert. He who owes money is always thinking of his written guarantee. And you, who have a duty to keep faith with Christ, guard that faith, which is far more precious than money. Money is an ephemeral possession, but faith is your eternal patrimony. So always keep in mind what you have promised, and you will be more prudent. As long as you keep your promise, your guarantee is safe.[16]

Symbolism of Water

9. After this you drew nearer, you saw the font itself, and you saw the bishop presiding over it. The thought which came into

---

[13]Mt. 24.28; Lk. 17.37. A does not hesitate to change the meaning of the text to apply it to the Eucharist (cf. 4.7). The description of the ministers as angels is perhaps connected with the 'angels' hands' in the prayer *Ergo memores* of the Canon (4.27 with note 55) (*Unde et memores* in the Roman Canon I). The identification of a minister with an angel and eagle is a commonplace. It occurs again, for example, in the 21st Homily of the fifth-century Persian Narsai (*Texts and Studies*, Cambridge, 1909, pp. 55 and 57). Theodore, BH 4.21, 25, 27, also states that the the deacons represent the angels of the heavenly liturgy. Chrysostom (sec. 20) speaks of the angels carrying the words of the Renunciation up to heaven.

[14]Mt. 11.10, quoting Mal. 3.1 – R. Murray has pointed out to me that there is an eastern icon tradition which represents John the Baptist with wings.

[15]Mal. 2.7.

[16]A was an inveterate punster. There seem to be two puns in this paragraph: 'faith' (*fides*) is used in the two senses of keeping a promise and belief; 'prudent' (*cautior*) is almost the same word as 'guarantee' (*cautio*).

the mind of Naaman the Syrian,[17] I am certain, must have come into yours: for though he was afterwards cleansed, he began by doubting. Why am I certain? Listen and I will tell you why.

10. You came into the baptistery, you saw the water, you saw the bishop, you saw the levite. And if anyone should perhaps be thinking of saying: 'Is that all?', I say, indeed it is all. There truly is all, where there is all innocence, all devotion, all grace, all sanctification. You saw all you could see with the eyes of the body, all that is open to human sight. You saw what is seen, but not what is done. What is unseen is much greater than what is seen: 'because the things that are seen are transient, but the things that are unseen are eternal'.[18]

11. Let us say first of all — take up the promissory note[19] my words represent, and demand its execution — we marvel at the Jewish mysteries given to our fathers, because their sacraments are pre-eminent for their antiquity and for their holiness. But I promise you that the Christian sacraments are older and more godly than the Jewish.[20]

12. Consider baptism, for example. What could be more extraordinary than this, that the Jewish people passed through the midst of the sea? And yet all the Jews who made that passage died in the desert.[21] But he who passes through the waters of this font — that is, from earthly things to heavenly (for this is the meaning of this passage, this pasch:[22] it is the passage of the

---

[17]2 Kgs. 5.1-14. It does not become clear which thought the neophytes shared with Naaman until sect. 14. Naaman contemplating the Jordan and the neophytes contemplating the font both must have thought, 'Is that all?' (Cf. sect. 10). In these half-extempore sermons A often rambles away from the logical order.

[18]2 Cor. 4.18. A contrasts the commonplace sacramental sign ('what is seen') with the sublime sacramental effect ('what is done').

[19]*Cautio* again. A is digressing to make a statement which he will not have time to prove until later.

[20]The paradoxical statement that Christian sacraments are older than the Jewish is proved in 1.23; 4.10-11. That they are more godly he proves in 1.12, and again in 4.13. A has in mind OT 'sacraments' like the offering of Melchizedek (4.10), the passage of the Red Sea (1.12) and the manna (4.13).

[21]Cf. Jn. 6.49-51.

[22]Cf. Exod. 12.11, 27. Cyril also compared baptism with the crossing of the Red Sea (MC 1.3).

The Pasch commemorates how the Lord 'passed over' the Israelites' houses when he slew the Egyptian firstborn. A takes the word to mean also a 'transit' from

person who is baptized; it is a passage from sin to life, from guilt to grace, from vileness to holiness) — he who passes through these waters does not die: he rises again.

13. As I was saying, Naaman was a leper. One of his slave-girls said to his wife: 'If my lord wishes to be cured, he should go into the country of Israel, and there he will find someone who can cure his leprosy.' This is what she said to her mistress; and the wife told her husband Naaman, who told the King of Syria. The king sent him, as one of his most highly favoured subjects, to the King of Israel. When the King of Israel was told that a man had been sent to him to have his leprosy cured, he rent his garments. Then the prophet Elisha sent a message to him: 'What is this? Do you rend your garments as though there were no God powerful enough to heal leprosy? Send the man to me.' The king sent him. The moment Naaman came, the prophet told him: 'Go down to the river Jordan; bathe there and you will be cured.'

14. Then he began to reflect within himself and to say: 'Is that all? I come from Syria to the land of the Jews and someone says to me: "Go to the Jordan, bathe there and you will be cured." As though there were not better rivers in my own country!' Then his servants said to him: 'Lord, why not do what the prophet says? Do it and see what happens.' Then he went to the Jordan, bathed there and came out cured.

Prayer over the Water

15. What is the meaning of this? You saw the water, but not all waters have a curative power: only that water has it which has the grace of Christ. There is a difference between the matter and the consecration, between the action and its effect. The action belongs to the water, its effect to the Holy Spirit. The water does not heal unless the Spirit descends and consecrates the water.[23] So you have read that when our Lord Jesus Christ

---

the state of sin to one of grace. In the same sense St John (13.1) seems to attribute to our Lord, the true Paschal Lamb, a passover from this world to the Father.

[23]The *matter* is water; its *action* is simply to wash. The *consecration* of the water brings the Holy Spirit down on it, and gives it a supernatural *effect*. Cf. 1.18 and Introduction, p. 22. Presumably A would have held that baptism with unconsecrated water was invalid.

instituted the rite of baptism, he came to John and John said
to him: 'I need to be baptized by you, and do you come to me?'
Christ answered: 'Let it be so now: for thus it is fitting for us to
fulfil all righteousness.'[24] See how the righteousness is
established in baptism.

16. Why then did Christ go down into the water, if it was not
that his flesh might be purified — the flesh he took of our
human kind? Christ had no need to be purified from sin,
because 'he committed no sin';[25] but we need it, because we are
liable to sin. If then the rite of baptism was instituted on our
account, a model is proposed for our faith.[26]

17. Christ went down into the water and it was John who was
the minister and baptized him. And behold 'the Holy Spirit
descended as a dove'.[27] It was not a dove which descended —
but the appearance of a dove. Remember what I told you:
Christ took flesh; not the appearance of flesh but its reality; he
truly took flesh.[28] But the Holy Spirit descended from heaven
under the appearance of a dove: not in the reality of a dove, but
in its likeness. John saw and believed.

18. Christ came down, the Holy Spirit came down. Why did
Christ come down first, and the Holy Spirit afterwards, since
the normal rite of baptism follows this order: first the water is
consecrated and then the candidate for baptism comes into it?
For, when the bishop enters, he first performs the exorcism on
the creature which is the water,[29] and then utters invocation

[24]Mt. 3.14-15 The literal meaning of the words 'fulfil all righteousness' is not
clear, but is unlikely to be the meaning A adopts. He takes the episode of Christ's
baptism, when the ceremony is given power to confer righteousness, as the formal
institution of the sacrament. Cf. Cyril, MC 3.1; Theodore, BH 3.22.

[25]1 Pet. 2.22

[26]The Holy Spirit descended at Christ's baptism to show us that the efficacy of
baptismal water is also due to the Spirit's presence.

[27]Jn. 1.32. Early representations of the Baptism of Christ are influenced by the
attempt to depict the incident as a liturgical baptism. Christ is sometimes depicted
as a child. He stands up to his knees or waist in the water, as if in a font: the Baptist,
like the minister, stands on dry land, with his hand on our Lord's head.

[28]A warns the neophytes against the heresy of Docetism, which denied Christ's
true humanity.

[29]The periphrasis 'creature that is the water' (*creaturam aquae*) is often found
in liturgical formulae; cf. 4.8. It still occurs in the Roman liturgy in the blessing of
holy water: '*Suppliciter deprecamur ut hanc creaturam aquae benedicere dignetur*' –

and prayer that the water may be sanctified and the eternal Trinity may dwell there.[30] But Christ descended first, and the Spirit came after. Why was this? It was in order that the Lord Jesus might not appear to have need of this mystery of sanctification, but that he himself might sanctify, and that the Spirit might also sanctify.

19. So Christ came down into the water, and the Holy Spirit came down in the likeness of a dove. God the Father also spoke from heaven.[31] So there you have the Trinity present.[32]

20. The apostle tells us that in the Red Sea we have a figure of baptism when he says: 'Our fathers were all baptized in the cloud and in the sea'; and he adds: 'All these things happened to them in figure.'[33] To them in figure, to us in reality. Moses had his rod in his hand; the Jewish people were enclosed on every side. On one side stood the Egyptian with his armies, on the other the Hebrews were cut off by the sea. They could not cross the sea, nor could they move back against the enemy. They began to murmur.[34]

21. Do not let yourselves be influenced by the fact that the Jews received a hearing. Those who murmured were not

---

literally 'we humbly ask that he would graciously bless this creature that is water'. ICEL, jejeunely, translates: 'ask God to bless it'. A similar form of words is to be found in the Anglican Book of Common Prayer: 'creatures of bread and wine'.

[30]The blessing of the font contained two elements: an exorcism, to expel the devil, and an 'invocation' (corresponding to the Greek word *epiclesis*) to call down the Holy Spirit. For the tradition that water needed to be freed from the devil's influence, cf. Tertulian, *de Baptismo*, 4-5; Cyprian, *Ep.* 70.1. The sign of the Cross was connected with the consecration of the water: 'What is water without the Cross of Christ?' (Ambrose, M 20; cf. S 2.23; 3.14). The form in which this sign was made is uncertain: perhaps the bishop exorcised or blessed the water by breathing on it in the shape of a cross, as in the old Milanese (Whitaker, p. 143) and Roman rites; perhaps he traced the sign with his hand; or perhaps he immersed his processional cross in it.

[31]Mt. 3.17.

[32]A states that all three Persons of the Trinity act together; this was a stock way of refuting the Pneumatomachian heresy, which made the Spirit inferior to the other two Persons. But later (S 6.5) A allows that each Person has his distinctive effect in the sacraments of initiation.

[33]1 Cor. 10.1, 2, 11 (not RSV). For Cyril's similar distinction between figure and reality, cf. MC 5.20, with note 23. See also Theodore, BH 2.15 with note 25.

[34]Exod. 14.10-12.

without blame, even though the Lord listened to them. When you are in difficulties, yours is to believe that you will come out safely; yours is not to murmur, but to implore; to pray, not to make complaints.

22. Moses took his rod and led the Hebrews, by night in a column of fire, by day in a column of cloud.[35] What is this fire except truth, which gives a clear and visible light? What is this column of light except Christ the Lord, who has scattered the darkness of infidelity and poured into the hearts of men the light of truth and spiritual grace? But the column of cloud is the Holy Spirit. The people were in the sea and the column of light went before them; then came the column of cloud; the shadow, as it were, of the Holy Spirit.[36] You see then that we have in the water and the Holy Spirit the type of baptism.

23. In the flood, too, baptism was prefigured,[37] and this was certainly before the sacraments of the Jews existed. If, then, the rite of baptism came first, you can see how the Christian sacraments are more ancient than those of the Jews.

24. But now my voice grows weak and time is running out;[38] so let this brief account of the mysteries of the sacred font suffice for today. Tomorrow, if the Lord gives me the power of speech and sufficient abundance of words, I will give a fuller instruction. Holy people, your ears must be attentive and your hearts properly disposed, so that you can retain what I am able to gather from the holy scriptures and offer to you, to the end

---

[35]Exod. 13.21.

[36]Cloud is a conventional manifestation of the divine presence: cf. Dan. 7.13; Acts 1.9. In the Transfiguration the cloud takes the place of the dove of the Baptism, which was the sign of the presence of the Holy Spirit (Mk. 9.7 and par.). For A's use of an allegorical interpretation of Scripture to prove his points, cf. p. 99. But what are his grounds for describing the columns of fire and cloud *together* leading the Israelites?

[37]For the Flood as a type of baptism, cf. 1 Pet. 3.20-21. A is concluding the argument begun in 1.11 that Christian sacraments existed in their prefigurations before those of the Jews.

[38]A makes the same excuse for cutting a sermon short in *Apologia David* II.5.28; PL 14.897. St Augustine records that, at a time when silent reading was almost unknown, even in private, A used to read without vocalising the words 'to preserve his voice, which easily became strained' (*Confessions*, VI.3).

that you may have the grace of the Father, Son and Holy Spirit, that Trinity whose reign is from eternity, is now, and lasts for ever and ever. Amen.

SERMONS ON THE SACRAMENTS

II

PREFIGURATIONS OF BAPTISM

1. Yesterday I began to explain that baptism is also prefigured in the flood. What is the flood, except the situation in which sin dies, in which the righteous man[1] is preserved to be the seeding-ground for righteousness? So the Lord, when he saw the sins of men multiplying, preserved the righteous man alone with his progeny, and commanded the waters to flow even above the level of the mountain-tops. In the flood, then, all the corruption of the flesh perished, and only the race and the likeness of the righteous remained.[2] Is not this flood baptism, by which all sins are wiped out and only the spirit and the grace of the righteous are revived?

2. There are many kinds of baptism, but only 'one baptism',[3] exclaims the apostle. Why does he say this? There are baptisms among the pagans, but they are not baptisms, they are washings; they cannot be baptisms. The flesh is washed,[4] but guilt is not wiped out; rather, in that washing, new guilt is contracted. There were baptisms among the Jews;[5] some were superfluous, the rest were in figure. The figure itself profits us, because it is the messenger of truth.

3. What was read yesterday? An angel, the scripture said, descended at a certain moment into the pool, and whenever the angel descended, the waters moved; and whoever was first

[1] I.e. Noah, described as 'just' in Gen. 6.9. Elsewhere (*de Noe*, 1.2; PL 14.363) he explains mistakenly that the name Noah *means* 'the just man'; but the author of Gen. 5.29 seems to take the name to mean 'consolation' or 'rest'.

[2] Cf. Gen. 7.23.

[3] Eph. 4.5.

[4] Elsewhere (*In Ps.* 40.5; PL 14.1070) Ambrose contrasts Christian baptism with the pagan rite in which a candidate is initiated by being showered with the blood of a bull or ram (*taurobolium*; cf. Introduction, p. 65).

[5] The examples of Jewish baptisms Ambrose gives here are the bathing of Naaman and of the sick at the Sheep Gate, and the baptism administered by John. In M 23 he adds the ritual washing of pots and cups (cf. Mk. 7.4).

into the water was healed of whatever sickness he had.[6] That
was a figure of our Lord Jesus Christ who was to come.[7]

4. An angel: Why? Because he himself is the angel of great
counsel.[8] At a certain moment: because the angel used to wait
until the final hour, so that he might seize the day in its dying
moments, and put off its decline.[9] As often as the angel came
down, the waters moved. You may be thinking: 'Why does it not
move now?' Listen to the answer: signs are for the unbeliever,
the believer has his faith.[10]

5. Whoever went down into the water first was healed of all
his sickness. What does 'first' mean? Was it a priority of time or
of dignity? It carries both meanings. The one to go down first
in the order of time was healed first: that is, the Jews rather than
the gentiles. The one to go down first in the order of dignity was
healed first: that is, he who had the fear of God, zeal for

[6]Jn. 5.4, quoted inaccurately from memory. The whole verse is omitted in the
best Greek MSS of John. Tertullian alludes to this passage in connection with
baptism in *de Bapt.* 5.

[7]The angel at the pool is a 'figure of Christ': (1) the Old Testament spoke of
the Messiah as an angel; (2) his descent 'at a certain moment' refers to the coming
of Christ inaugurating the Last Times; (3) the paralytic's complaint, 'I have no
man' (Sect. 6-7), looks forward to Christ, *the* Man; (4) the descent of the angel
giving healing power to the waters is a figure of the Holy Spirit's descent on the
baptismal water giving it power to forgive sin. (This last point is made more
explicitly in the parallel passage in M 22.) The neophyte 'goes down' into the font
as the sick 'went down' into the healing pool.

The whole episode is applied allegorically to baptism in other ways: (1) the
water symbolism; (2) the 'first' are healed by water.

[8]Is. 9.5 (LXX): 'his name is called "The Angel of great counsel".' (The Hebrew
text gives a different sense which is followed by the RSV (9.6): 'His name will be
called "Wonderful Counsellor".')

[9]Ambrose seems to see in the angel's activity at sunset a figure of Christ's
heralding in of the eschatological age. The Gospel gives no indication that the
angel used to come down in the evening. Perhaps Ambrose is influenced by Jesus'
words on the occasion of another miracle at another pool: 'night comes, when no
one can work' (Jn. 9.4). In the parallel passage, M 22, Ambrose adds another detail,
namely that one man was cured every year.

[10]An adaptation of 1 Cor. 14.22. Ambrose does not regard the sacramental rite
as a sign, for its significance can only be recognised by one who has faith. For him
a sign is evidence of divine action that does *not* require faith for its recognition, like
the visibly miraculous movement of the waters at the pool. Ambrose resumes this
point in Sect. 15; see note 25.

righteousness, the grace of charity, the love of chastity. But in those days only one was saved. In those days, he alone was cured who went down first; and this was in figure. How much greater is the grace of the Church in which all those who go down into the water are saved.

6. See the mystery[11] here. Our Lord Jesus Christ came to the pool: many sick people were lying there. Yes, certainly there were many sick lying there, and only one was cured. Then he said to the man who was paralysed: 'Go down into the water'. He replied: 'I have no man to take me down'.[12] See where you are baptized, see the source of your baptism. It is none other than the cross of Christ, the death of Christ. Here is the whole mystery: he suffered for you. In him you are redeemed, in him you are saved.

7. 'I have no man', he said: that is to say, 'death came by a man, and the resurrection came by a man'.[13] A man could not go down, could not be saved, if he did not believe that our Lord Jesus took flesh of a virgin. But he who said, 'I have no man', was waiting for 'the mediator between God and man, the man Jesus'; he was expecting him of whom it is written: 'And the Lord will send a man to save them'.[14] And so he was found worthy to be healed, because he believed in Christ's coming. Yet he would have been better and more perfect had he believed that he whose coming he was hoping for had already come.

8. Let us now recapitulate. We said that there was a pre-figuring in the Jordan, when Naaman the leper was healed. That young slave girl from among the captives, what does she represent? She bore a certain resemblance to the Church, she represented the Church in figure.[15] The gentiles were held

[11]I.e., figurative meaning. He has begun seeking it in Sect. 4; he cannot believe that the literal sense is an adequate explanation of the details of the incident. For A's method of interpreting scripture, cf. pp. 98ff.

[12]Cf. Jn. 5.7. In this section Ambrose applies the words to our Saviour: we *have* a man to heal us.

[13]Cf. 1 Cor. 15.21.

[14]1 Tim. 2.5; Is. 19.20 (LXX). Ambrose now gives a second figurative interpretation to the words, 'I have no man'. The words are an act of faith in the coming of a human (non-Docetic) Saviour.

[15]Here and in M 18 the slave-girl's resemblance to the Church is said to be her captivity: members of the Church before baptism are in the power of sin. But

captive: but not in the sense of being under the domination of some enemy nation. I am speaking of a worse captivity, when the devil and his minions impose a savage domination, and subject sinners to the yoke of their captivity.

9. There you have one kind of baptism; the flood is another. You have a third kind when our fathers were baptized in the Red Sea. You have a fourth in the pool when the waters moved.

Presence of the Trinity in Baptism

Now I ask you whether you ought to believe that, in this baptism by which Christ baptizes in his Church, you have the presence of the Trinity.

10. Certainly the Lord Jesus speaks in this way to his apostles in his Gospel: 'Go, baptize the gentiles in the name of the Father, and of the Son and of the Holy Spirit'.[16] This is the word of the Saviour.

11. Tell me, someone: Elijah called down fire from heaven, and fire came down from heaven.[17] Elisha invoked the name of the Lord, and the iron head of the axe which was sunk floated to the surface. Here we have another kind of baptism. How so? Every man before his baptism is weighted down and submerged, like the iron. When he is baptized, he is no longer like the iron: he is raised up; he is lighter, like the wood of a fruitful tree. Here then is yet another figure: it was the axe that was used for felling timber. The wooden haft fell from the axe; that is to say, the iron was submerged. The son of the prophet did not know

---

Ambrose confuses the argument by saying that she stands for the gentiles; in fact she was an Israelite (2 Kgs. 5.2). One gets the impression that Ambrose is alluding from memory to an argument he put much more clearly in *Expos. Evang. Luc.*, 4.50 (PL 15.1627), where the girl, who is obeyed by Naaman, stands for the Church *which the gentiles must join.*

[16]Mt. 28.19 (adapted).

[17]1 Kgs. 18.36-38. The fire descending on the sacrifice which had been soaked in water at Elisha's prayer symbolises the Spirit who is invoked and comes down on the waters of the font. Ambrose then forgets he is proving the presence of the Trinity at baptism, and turns aside to enumerate more examples of OT miracles in which wood was put into water, and which thus prefigure the connection between the cross and baptism: Elisha and the axe (sect. 11: 2 Kgs. 6.5-7); Moses and the spring of Marah (sect. 12; Exod. 15.22-25).

what to do. This alone he knew, that he must ask the prophet Elisha for a remedy. He threw the wood into the water, and the iron became light. You see, then, that it is in the cross of Christ that every man's sickness is lightened.

12. I will mention another event — though out of order, for who can hold in his mind all that Christ did, as the apostles have said?[18] Moses came into the desert, and the people were thirsty. They came to the spring of Marah and would have drunk. But when the water was first drawn, it was found to have a bitter taste: it was not possible to drink it. Then Moses put the wood in the spring, and the water which before was bitter now began to taste sweet.

13. What does this mean except that every creature subject to corruption is water bitter to every taste? It may taste sweet for a time, it may be delightful for a time; but it is still bitter because it cannot take away sin. When you drink it, you become thirsty;[19] when you have tasted the sweetness of the draught, you come to experience its bitterness: it is bitter water. But once it has received the cross of Christ,[20] the heavenly sacrament, it begins to be sweet and agreeable to the taste. And it is right that it should be sweet, this water in which our guilt is remitted. If, then, these baptisms are so powerful in figure, how much more powerful is that true baptism?

14. Consider now. The priest comes, he says a prayer at the font, he invokes the name of the Father, the presence of the Son and the Holy Spirit; he uses heavenly words. They are heavenly words, because they are the words of Christ which say that we must baptize in the name of the Father and of the Son and of the Holy Spirit.[21] If at a word of men, at the invocation by one of the saints,[22] the Trinity was present, how much more

---

[18]Cf. Jn. 21.25.

[19]Cf. Jn. 4.14.

[20]A gives two interpretations of the incident at Marah: (1) moral: all created things can lead to sin; (2) sacramental: the baptismal water must be consecrated by the sign of the cross (cf. 1.18 with note 30).

[21]A has turned to his proof of the presence of the Trinity at baptism.

[22]I.e., if Elisha's prayer was able to call down fire which symbolises the presence of the Trinity, *a fortiori* the Trinity will be present at baptism in response to our Lord's words just quoted (cf. M 26, where the argument is more clearly stated).

efficacious this presence is where the eternal word is working! Do you wish to know for certain that the Spirit has come down? You have heard that he came down in the likeness of a dove. Why in the likeness of a dove?[23] To call the incredulous to faith. In the beginning there had to be a sign; in the ages which followed there has to be fulfilment.

15. Now another point. After the death of our Lord Jesus Christ, the apostles were dwelling together and were at prayer on the day of Pentecost, and suddenly there was a loud roaring as though a fierce wind were blowing, and parted tongues were seen, as of fire.[24] What does this signify, except the descent of the Holy Spirit? He wished to show himself corporally to unbelievers: corporally by a sign, but spiritually by the sacrament. This was an evident proof of his coming; but now in our case the privilege of faith is offered. In the beginning there were signs for the sake of unbelievers; but for us who live in the time of the Church's full growth the truth is to be grasped, not by signs, but by faith.[25]

The logic of the argument, if insisted upon, requires us to be able to regard the symbolic presence of the Trinity in the baptismal water as equivalent to a real presence. Cf. Cyril, MC 3.3 with note 16; 5.20 with note 23.

[23]Ambrose gives a different answer in M 24: the Spirit came in the form of a dove to recall Noah's dove and so symbolise baptism by recalling the Flood. Cf. Cyril, MC 3.1.

[24]Acts 2.1-3.

[25]Cf. 1 Cor. 14.22. A returns to the argument of sect. 4 (cf. note 10). He systematically contrasts typological sign with sacramental symbolism as follows:

Type	Sacrament
Corporally	Spiritually
to unbeliever	in the time of the Church's full growth
by a sign	by a sacrament
evident proof	privilege of faith
signs	the truth
by sign	by faith
sign	fulfilment (sect. 14)
likeness, sacrament	Christ's cross (sect. 23)

The necessity of faith for understanding the sacramental truth explains why the sacraments of initiation are explained only after they have been received.

The manifestations of the Holy Spirit by dove and fire at Christ's baptism and Pentecost are examples of evident proof by signs that even unbelievers can grasp.

The Effects of Baptism

16. We must now examine what it is we mean by baptism. You came to the font, you went down into it, you turned towards the high priest,[26] you saw, there at the font, the levites and the presbyter. What is baptism?

17. In the beginning our Lord made man so that he would never die, so long as he never tasted sin. But he committed sin; he became subject to death; he was cast out of paradise. But the Lord, who wished his gifts to last for ever and to destroy all the wiles of the serpent and to cancel out all harm it had done, first passed sentence on man: 'You are dust and to dust you shall return',[27] and so he made man subject to death. The sentence was divine, and it could not be remitted by human kind. The remedy was found. It was that man should die and rise again. Why? So that what had formerly served as a sentence, should now serve as a gift. And what is this but death? 'How can this be?', you ask. Because death, when it comes, puts an end to sin. When we die, we do indeed stop sinning.[28] It seemed, then, that the sentence was being served; because man, who had been created to live for ever as long as he did not sin, now became mortal. But in order that God's gift might continue for ever, man died but Christ invented the resurrection, in order to restore the heavenly gift which had been lost through the

---

[26]I.e., the bishop.

[27]Gen. 3.19.

[28]Cf. Rom. 6.7. It was a common belief among the Fathers that death was not only a punishment, but also a benefit. Death remains a punishment, but is followed by a resurrection which restores our nature to its sinlessness. Cf. Theodore, BH 3.11-13.

In this section A seems to be thinking both of Christ's resurrection and of the general resurrection from the dead: '*man* should die and rise again'. In sect. 18-19 he turns to baptism, in which a man dies to his life of sin and rises from the font to a new life.

A here adopts several complementary theories of the Atonement. (1) God's sentence condemning man to death and burial is fulfilled by the sacramental death and burial at baptism (sect. 19); (2) man is flawed, but is remade flawless at the general resurrection; (3) the effects of Christ's resurrection are communicated to us; (4) the sacrament of baptism applies Christ's saving work, which took place at a point of history, to every age (sect. 18-19).

deceit of the serpent. Both death and resurrection, therefore, are to our advantage: for death is the end of sin and the resurrection is the reformation of our nature.

18. But to prevent the deceit and tricks of the devil prevailing in this world, baptism has been invented. If you would know the source of baptism, listen to what Scripture, or rather the Son of God, says: the Pharisees refused the baptism of John; they 'rejected the purpose of God'.[29] Baptism is therefore God's purpose. What grace there must be when God's purpose is in operation!

19. Listen. To break the hold of the devil in this world as well, a means was found for making a living man die and a living man rise again.[30] What does 'living' mean? It means living by the life of the body, since the man can come to the font and be immersed in it. Where does water come from if not from the earth? The heavenly sentence is thus served, without the loss of consciousness involved in death. Because you are immersed, the sentence, 'You are dust and to dust you shall return', is served. With the sentence served there is room for the gift and the heavenly remedy. I said that water comes from the earth; the conditions of human life did not permit us to be covered by the earth and then rise again from it. Besides, it is not earth which washes, but water. So it is that the font is a kind of grave.[31]

---

[29]Cf. Lk. 7.30. Actually the phrase is not Christ's, but is an explanation by the evangelist of Christ's praise of John the Baptist.

[30]The purpose of a sacrament is to apply 'in this world as well' the grace which Christ has already won for us in heaven. Cf. sect. 17: 'The Lord . . . wished his gifts to last for ever.'

[31]Cf. Rom. 6.3-4. Baptism has a double symbolism: (1) it is a symbol of purification from sin; (2) it is a symbol of death and resurrection. The second meaning would be plainer if the candidate were covered with earth instead of water. But, A remarks, this would be a dangerous procedure, and besides earth could not represent purification. Water, which comes from the earth, can combine the two symbols. Fonts were often, like graves, rectangular. Cf. 3.1; Cyril MC 2.4-5 with note 15; J. G. Davies, *Architectural Setting*, pp. 19ff. However the two fourth-century fonts excavated in Milan under the cathedral are octagonal. The official guide-book suggests that St Ambrose himself was baptized in the earlier of the two, and later baptized St Augustine in the other. See Introduction, p. 26.

Baptism

20. You were asked: 'Do you believe in God the Father almighty? You replied: 'I believe', and you were immersed: that is, buried. You were asked for a second time: 'Do you believe in our Lord Jesus Christ and in his cross?'[32] You replied: 'I believe', and you were immersed: which means that you were buried with Christ. For one who is buried with Christ rises again with Christ.[33] You were asked a third time: 'Do you believe also in the Holy Spirit?' You replied: 'I believe', and you were immersed a third time, so that the threefold confession might absolve the manifold lapses of the past.

21. We can give you an illustration of this. The holy apostle Peter appeared to lapse through human weakness during the Lord's passion. To wipe out and absolve the fault of his denial, he was asked by Christ three times if he loved Christ. Peter replied: 'Lord, you know that I love you'.[34] He answered three times so as to be absolved three times.

22. Thus the Father forgives sin, so does the Son, and so does the Holy Spirit. Do not be surprised that we are baptized in one name: in the name, that is, of the Father and of the Son and of the Holy Spirit;[35] because Christ spoke of only one name[36] where there is one substance, one divinity, one majesty. This is the name of which it is written: 'In this must all find salvation'.[37] It is in this name that you have all been saved, that you have been restored to the grace of life.

[32]This addition of the words 'and in his cross' is unparalleled anywhere except A's Milan; but A provides further evidence for it in M 28 and perhaps *Expos. Evang. Luc.* 5.102-103.

[33]Rom. 6.4-5.

[34]In Jn. 21.15-17. With Peter, as with the baptized, a 'threefold confession' is a means to obtaining forgiveness for repeated lapses.

[35]Theodore (BH 3.16) argues in the same way that the unity of nature in the Trinity is shown by the fact that we are baptized, not in the three *names* of Father, Son and Spirit, but in their one *name*. A and T are concerned to refute the error of the Arians and Pneumatomachians, who denied that the Son and the Spirit were equal to the Father.

[36]Mt. 28.19. This need not imply that the minister quoted the Matthaean formula: cf. Introduction, p. 26.

[37]Cf. Acts 4.12.

23. So the apostle exclaims, as you have just heard in the reading, 'Whoever is baptized, is baptized in the death of Jesus'.[38] What does 'in the death' mean? It means that just as Christ died, so you will taste death; that just as Christ died to sin and lives to God, so through the sacrament of baptism you are dead to the old enticements of sin and have risen again through the grace of Christ. This is a death, then, not in the reality of bodily death, but in likeness. When you are immersed, you receive the likeness of death and burial, you receive the sacrament of his cross;[39] because Christ hung upon the cross and his body was fastened to it by the nails. So you are crucified with him, you are fastened to Christ, you are fastened by the nails of our Lord Jesus Christ lest the devil pull you away. May Christ's nail continue to hold you, for human weakness seeks to pull you away.

Anointing with Chrism[40]

24. So you were immersed, and you came to the priest. What did he say to you? *God the Father Almighty,* he said, *who has brought you to a new birth through water and the Holy Spirit and has forgiven your sins, himself anoints you into eternal life.* See where the anointing has brought you: 'to eternal life', he says. Do not prefer this present life to eternal life. For example, if an enemy should come against you, wishing to rob you of your faith, if he threatens you with death to make you go astray, consider what choice you should make. Do not choose the life in which you have not been anointed. Choose the one in which you have been anointed. Choose eternal life rather than this life.

---

[38]Rom. 6.3 (adapted).

[39]A reference probably to the sign of the cross made in the course of the ceremony, perhaps at the blessing of the font. Cf. 1.18 with note 30.

[40]See Introduction, p. 27. A says more about this anointing in 3.1. He gives it a messianic interpretation in 4.3 and M 30.

SERMONS ON THE SACRAMENTS
III

1. Yesterday the subject of our instruction was the font, which has the shape and appearance of a sort of tomb.[1] When we believe in the Father, the Son and the Holy Spirit,[2] we are received and immersed in it; then we rise up: that is, we are restored to life. You also receive the *myron*, that is, the chrism,[3] over your heads. Why over your heads? Because 'the faculties of the wise man are situated in his head',[4] says Solomon. Wisdom without grace is inert; but when wisdom receives grace, then its work begins to move toward fulfilment. This is called regeneration.

Regeneration

2. What is regeneration? You can read in the Acts of the Apostles that a verse from the second Psalm, 'You are my son, today I have begotten you',[5] seems to refer to the resurrection. The holy apostle Peter interprets it in this way in the Acts of the Apostles: when the Son rose from the dead the Father's voice was heard proclaiming: 'You are my son, today I have begotten you'. That is why he is also called 'The first-born from the dead'.[6] For what is resurrection except that we rise from death to life? So it is in baptism, which is an image of death: when you are immersed and rise up again, there, certainly, is an image of the resurrection. So as Christ's resurrection is interpreted by the apostle as a regeneration, so also this resurrection from the font is a regeneration.

3. But what conclusions do you draw from the fact that it is in water that you are immersed? Are you a little lost here? Does some doubt creep in? We read: "'Let the earth produce from

[1]Cf. 2.19 with note 31.

[2]A reference to the baptismal formula given in 2.20.

[3]Cf. Introduction, p. 29.

[4]Eccles. 2.14 (adapted).

[5]Ps. 2.7 quoted (by St Paul, not St Peter) in Acts 13.33. Despite what is said in sect. 1, A attributes regeneration to baptism itself, not only to anointing. The theme of regeneration is prompted by the reference to 'new birth' in the words which accompany the anointing (2.24).

[6]Col. 1.18.

herself vegetation:" and the earth produced vegetation yielding seed'. You have read the same about the waters: '"Let the waters produce living things:" and living things were born'.[7] These were born in the beginning, at the creation; but this gift was kept for you: that the waters should regenerate you into grace, even as those other waters generated into life. Imitate the fish; it received a lesser grace than you, but you should still consider it a marvel. It is in the sea and above the waves. It is in the sea and swims on the waters. On the sea the tempest rages, violent winds blow; but the fish swims on. It does not drown because it is used to swimming. In the same way, this world is the sea for you. It has various currents, huge waves, fierce storms. You too must be a fish,[8] so that the waves of this world do not drown you. Those are wonderfully apt words of the Father: 'Today I have begotten you'. It means 'when you redeemed my people, when you fulfilled my will, you proved that you are my son'.

The Washing Of The Feet [9]

4. You came up out of the font. What then? You listened to the reading.[10] The high priest put on an apron: for though the presbyters did the same, it belongs to the high priest to begin the liturgy. What does this mystery mean? You must have heard it read that when the Lord had washed the feet of the other disciples he came to Peter, and Peter said to him: 'Do you wash my feet?'[11] That is to say: Do you, the master, wash the feet of the servant? Do you, the spotless one, wash my feet? Do you, the

[7]Gen. 1.11, 20 (adapted). On the equivalence of the symbols of earth and water, cf. S 2.19 with note 31.

[8]The fish usually stands for Christ; cf. H. Leclercq, 'ICHTHYS', in DACL, vii. 1990-2086. A seems to think fish float on top of the water.

[9]Cf. Introduction, p. 30f. This ceremony in the modern Roman liturgy is performed on Maundy Thursday, where it has no connection with baptism, but is performed for the purpose A finds insufficient, namely as a host would do it for his guests (sect. 5) or a sign of humility (sect. 7).

[10]M 31 shows that the reading was the account of the Washing of the Feet (Jn. 13.1ff.). M, with its greater regard for secrecy, never actually says that the neophytes' feet were washed, but puts its remarks in the form of a commentary on the gospel incident.

[11]Jn. 13.6.

creator of the heavens, wash my feet? You have the same thing elsewhere. He came to John, and John said to him: 'I need to be baptized by you, and do you come to me?'[12] I am a sinner, and you have come to the sinner in order to make a pretence of putting away your sins: you who never committed sin. See all the righteousness,[13] see the humility, see the grace, see the holiness. 'If I do not wash your feet', he said, 'you have no part in me'.[14]

5. We are aware that the Roman Church does not follow this custom, although we take her as our prototype, and follow her rite in everything.[15] But she does not have this rite of the washing of the feet. Perhaps it is because of the large numbers that she has ceased to practise it. But there are those who try to excuse themselves by saying that it should not be performed as a mystery,[16] not as part of the baptismal rite, not for regeneration, but that this washing of the feet should be done as a host would do it for his guests. However, humility is one thing, sanctification another. You must know that this washing is a mystery and sanctification. 'If I do not wash your feet, you shall have no part with me'. I am not saying this as censuring others; I am simply

---

[12]Mt. 3.14.

[13]Cf. Mt. 3.15: 'It is fitting for us to fulfil all righteousness'.

[14]Jn. 13.8.

[15]On the regions in which this rite was practised, see Introduction, p. 30.

A, who had so little experience in ecclesiastical affairs when he became bishop of a city that had been for some time under Arian control, seems to have adopted Roman practice as a safe standard to follow in reforming the liturgy and doctrine of Milan. Cf. A. Archdale King, *Liturgies of Primatial Sees*, pp. 297-300. He seems to have adopted the Roman Canon of the Mass (*ibid.* p. 397), introduced Roman feasts, and adopted the Roman Creed (*Explanatio Symboli*, 4; cf. *Ep.* 42.5). But he retained some independence, observing different fasting regulations (St Augustine, *Ep.* 36.32), and making hymnological innovations (Paulinus, *Vita*, 13; PL 14.31). In matters of Church politics A seems to have regarded his see (the imperial capital after 381) as at least the equal to Rome (cf. H. Lietzmann, *A History of the Early Church*, IV. 63-67).

However, when Ambrose came to edit the *extempore* remarks of S for publication in the form of M, he thought it wiser to omit the criticism of Roman liturgical practice. But even in S he feels it necessary to apologise for criticizing Rome, and alleges in excuse of Rome's deviation the 'large numbers' (sect. 5).

[16]I.e. as a quasi-sacramental rite, in which the effect is symbolised by the ceremony.

recommending our own rite. I wish to follow the Roman Church in everything: but we too are not devoid of common sense. When a better custom is kept elsewhere, we are right to keep it here also.

6. We follow the apostle Peter himself; it is to his devotion that we cling. What does the Roman Church say to this? He indeed it is who is the source of our argument, and he was the priest of the Roman Church: Peter himself, who says, 'Lord not my feet only, but also my hands and my head'.[17] Consider his faith. When he refused at first, this was because of his humility. The submission he made afterwards came from devotion and faith.

7. The Lord answered him after he had spoken of hands and head: 'He who has washed, does not need to wash again, except his feet only'.[18] Why? Because in baptism all guilt is washed away. The guilt has disappeared; but Adam was tripped and thrown by the devil, so that the devil's poison infected his feet; so you have your feet washed, in order to receive the special help of sanctification in the place where the serpent lay in ambush so that he cannot trip you up again.[19] You have your feet washed to wash away the serpent's poison. It also profits our own humility, in that we are not ashamed to do as a mystery what we might refuse to do as an act of homage which is unworthy of our position.

[17]Jn. 13.9. This very neat *ad hominem* argument shows that it was a well-known belief, even in Milan, that the Bishop of Rome was the successor of St Peter, who was 'the priest (*sacerdos*, i.e. bishop) of the Roman Church'.

[18]Jn. 13.10 (adapted).

[19]The association of the heel with that innate tendency to sin that is the consequence of the Fall (strangely reminiscent of Achilles' vulnerable spot) is derived from two Old Testament texts. (1) God's curse of the serpent (Gen. 3.15): 'I will put enmity between you and the woman, and between your seed and her seed; he shall bruise your head and you shall bruise (LXX lie in ambush against) his heel'. (2) Ps. 48.6 (LXX): 'The iniquity of my heel will surround me'. (RSV 49.5: 'The iniquity of my persecutors surrounds me', following the Hebrew.) Ambrose explains his thought more fully in his commentary on the second text (*In Ps.* 48.8-9; PL 14.1158-1159). Christ is the stag whose heel is invulnerable to the snake-bite (*De Interpell.* ii(iv). 1.4; PL 14.812-813).

Many commentators (e.g. H. Dudden, *op. cit.*, p. 705ff.) have held that M's interpretation is different from that of S. There A explains that St Peter (and therefore presumably the neophyte) had his feet washed 'in order that his inherited sins might be destroyed; for our personal sins are remitted by baptism'

The Gift of the Spirit [20]

8. The spiritual sealing follows. You have heard about this in the reading today.[21] For after the ceremonies of the font, it still remains to bring the whole to perfect fulfilment.[22] This happens when the Holy Spirit is infused at the priest's invocation: 'the Spirit of wisdom and understanding, the Spirit of counsel and strength, the Spirit of knowledge and piety, the Spirit of holy fear'.[23] These might be called the seven 'virtues' of the Spirit.

9. It is true that all virtues belong to the Spirit; but these are, so to speak, the cardinal, the fundamental virtues. What is more fundamental than piety, what is more fundamental than the knowledge of God, what is more fundamental than strength, than God's counsel, than the fear of God? Just as fear of the world is weakness, so fear of God is great strength.

10. These are the seven virtues you receive when you are sealed. For, as the holy apostle says, the wisdom of our Lord has many forms, and 'the wisdom of God has many forms';[24] so also the Holy Spirit is multiform and has a whole variety of virtues. so he is also called the God of powers[25] — a title which can be

---

(M 32). Clearly in M as well as in S Ambrose teaches that the washing of the feet cancels an effect of the Fall, not personal sin. But whereas S refers explicitly to a tendency to future personal sin (i.e. 'concupiscence' in the technical sense), M seems to refer to man's share in Adam's guilt (i.e. loss of grace, in later theological terminology). But in fact M can be reconciled with S. For A elsewhere uses the word 'sin' to describe precisely the inherited tendency to sin which S describes (*De Jacob*, 1.13 and 16; PL 14.604-6). St Augustine quotes a lost commentary of Ambrose on Isaiah in which he says that foot-washing removes 'the stain of a guilty succession' (*Contr. Ep. Pelag.*, 4.29; PL 44.632).

[20]Referred to by Ambrose as 'sealing'. See Introduction, p. 38. Ambrose makes no mention here of the ceremony of the white garment, though he seems to hint at it in 4.5, and speaks of it explicitly in M 34. See Introduction, p. 31ff.

[21]M 42 suggests that the reading included that text of St Paul's which combines five of the traditional terms used to describe Confirmation: 'But it is God who *confirms* us with you in Christ and has *anointed* us; he has put his *seal* upon us and given us his *Spirit* in our hearts as a *guarantee*' (2 Cor 1.21-22) (not RSV).

[22]The Gift of the Spirit is the completion of initiation. Cf. Introduction, p. 36.

[23]Is. 11.2-3 (LXX). RSV, following the Hebrew, gives only six 'virtues' of the Spirit.

[24]Cf. Eph. 3.10.

[25]The same Latin word (*virtus*) stands for both 'virtues' and 'power'. Ambrose is referring to the title 'God of hosts' (e.g. Ps. 80.4), which is still contained in the *Sanctus*.

applied to Father, Son and Holy Spirit. But this is another matter altogether, and must be reserved for another occasion.

Admission to the Eucharist

11. What happens after this? You can approach the altar. When you have arrived, you can see what you could not see before. This is the mystery[26] of which you have read in the gospel, if indeed you have read it; you have certainly heard it read. The blind man was brought to the Saviour to be cured. He had cured others by his word and discourses alone: by his simple command he had restored the light to blind eyes. Yet in the book of the Gospel according to John — John, who with greater clarity than the others saw the great mysteries and recounted and explained them — the intention is to see in the blind man this mystery prefigured. Now all the evangelists are saints, and all the apostles, except the traitor, are saints. Yet it was St John, the last to write a gospel as the friend sought out and chosen by Christ — he it was who trumpeted forth the eternal mysteries in the clearest tones. Everything he has said is a mystery.[27] The others said that a blind man was cured: Matthew said it, so did Luke, so did Mark. What is it that John alone says? 'He took clay and anointed the man's eyes, and said to him: Go to Siloam'. Rising, 'he went and washed and came back seeing'.[28]

12. Now you too must think about your eyes; the eyes of your heart. With your bodily eye you saw bodily things, but you were not yet able to see sacramental things with the eyes of your

---

[26]The 'mystery' is the fact that after baptism one can see with the eye of faith what one was blind to before (sect. 12).

[27]I.e. everything has a second, deeper meaning in addition to its literal meaning.

[28]Jn. 9.6-7. The Synoptic passages which Ambrose regards as parallels are Mt. 9.27-30; 20.30-34; Mk. 8.22-25; 10.46-52; Lk. 18.35-43.

Ambrose omits all reference to Jesus' use of spittle in John's version of the incident. He showed the same delicate reticence in 1.2-3. However, in a letter (*Ep.* 80.5) he allows himself the freedom to mention this unsavoury detail.

heart.[29] So when you gave in your name,[30] he took mud and spread it over your eyes. What does this mean? It means that you had to confess your sins, examine your conscience, do penance for your faults, you had to acknowledge, that is to say, the lot of human kind. For even though the person who comes to baptism does not confess his sins, yet in the sacrament he does make a confession of all his sins by the very fact that he asks for baptism in order to be made righteous:[31] that is, to pass from guilt to grace.

13. Do not think that what I am saying is otiose. There are some people — certainly to my knowledge there has been one — who would reply to our invitation — 'At your age[32] you need all the more to be baptized' — thus: 'Why should I be baptized? I am not guilty of sin. What sin have I committed?' Such a one has never received the mud: Christ has not spread it over his eyes: he has not had his eyes opened. For there is no man without sin.[33]

14. So the one who seeks refuge in the baptism of Christ acknowledges himself to be a man. Christ has spread the mud on your eyes, that is, reverence, prudence and the awareness of your frailty; and he has said to you: 'Go to Siloam'. What does Siloam mean? 'It means', the evangelist says, 'Sent';[34] that is, go to the font where Christ's cross is preached;[35] go to the font in which all your errors are redeemed.

15. You went there, you washed, you came to the altar, you began to see[36] what you had not seen before: that is to say,

---

[29]The neophytes have now received not only access to the sight of the eucharistic species with bodily eyes, but also the spiritual perception to understand by faith what they see with their eyes.

[30]See Introduction, p. 7. There is no evidence that the candidate's eyes were anointed when he gave in his name. A must be speaking metaphorically. The clay which 'he' (Christ?) smeared on the eyes stands for the spiritual sight of faith.

[31]See Introduction, p. 15. A now gives another example of the new supernatural sight; the neophyte now recognises his sinfulness.

[32]I.e. in youth. For the practice of postponing baptism till the passions of youth had become less importune, see Introduction, p. 6f.

[33]Cf. Job 1.4. (LXX), Rom. 3.23.

[34]Jn. 9.7.

[35]A probable reference to the sign of the cross made on the water at the exorcism and consecration of the font. See Introduction, p. 24f.

[36]Cf. Jn. 9.7.

through the font of the Lord and the preaching of the Lord's passion, at that moment your eyes were opened. Before, you seemed to be blind of heart; but now you began to perceive the light of the sacraments.

So, my beloved brothers, we have reached the altar, a subject of even greater richness. Time does not permit us to begin a full explanation: for this subject calls for treatment at some length. What I have said is enough today. Tomorrow, if the Lord wills, we shall treat of the sacraments themselves.[37]

---

[37]Here he uses the word 'sacraments' in the restricted sense of the Eucharist.

SERMONS ON THE SACRAMENTS

IV

THE SYMBOLISM OF THE APPROACH TO THE ALTAR

1. In the Old Testament it was usual for the priests to enter the outer tabernacle on many occasions; but only the high priest entered the inner tabernacle, and that once a year. It is clear that the Apostle Paul is reminding the Hebrews of this custom when he explains the terms of the old dispensation. In the inner tabernacle was the manna, and also Aaron's rod which was dry and dead but afterwards burst into flower; there also was the altar of incense.[1]

2. What is the purpose of all this? To enable you to understand what this inner tabernacle is, into which the high priest led you, where the custom is for him to enter once a year:[2] it is the baptistery, where Aaron's rod has blossomed. It was dry and dead, and then it burst into flower[3]. You were dry, and you began to flower again in the abundant waters of the font. You were dried up because of sin, because of your errors and faults; but you began to bring forth fruit, once you were 'planted by streams of water'.[4]

3. You may say: 'What difference does it make to the people if the priestly rod blossomed after being dry?' Well, who is this people if not a priestly people? To whom were the words of the Apostle Peter addressed: 'You are a chosen race, a royal priesthood, a holy people'?[5] Each one is anointed for the priesthood, anointed for the Kingdom, a spiritual kingdom and a spiritual priesthood.

4. In the inner tabernacle is also the altar of incense. From this altar a sweet fragrance constantly ascended. In the same

[1]This list of the sacred objects in the Holy of Holies is taken from Heb. 9.4-5; cf. Ex. 16.32-33 (manna). Ex. 30.6 says the altar of incense was to be outside the inner tabernacle. There is no OT evidence that Aaron's rod was kept there. Ambrose compares the high priest's entry into the inner tabernacle with the neophyte's admission into the baptistery.

[2]But in some other Churches baptism was permitted at other times. See Introduction, p. 7.

[3]Num. 17.8.

[4]Ps. 1.3.

[5]1 Pet. 2.9, a text linked with the second anointing in M 30. See Introduction, p. 28.

way, you too are now the sweet fragrance of Christ;[6] there is no longer in you any stain of sin, any taint of serious error.

The Baptismal Garment

5. After this you were to approach the altar. You began to draw near. The angels looked down and saw you coming. They saw the natural human state, until recently soiled with the gloom and squalor of sin, suddenly shine out brilliantly. This led them to say: 'Who is this that is coming up from the wilderness in white?'[7] The angels, then, also stand and marvel. Do you want to know the extent of their marvelling? Listen to the Apostle Peter, who says that there is granted to you what even the angels long to see.[8] It is also written: 'What no eye has seen, nor ear heard, what God has prepared for those who love him.'[9]

6. So take stock of what you have received. The holy prophet David saw this grace prefigured, and longed for it. Would you know how much he longed for it? Listen again to what he says: 'Purge me with hyssop, and I shall be clean; wash me, and I shall be whiter than snow'.[10] Why? Because snow, although it is white, quickly grows black with dirt and loses its colour. The grace you have received, if you hold on to what you have received, will last for ever.

7. You were coming to the altar, then, with desire: for you had seen a very great grace.[11] You were coming to the altar with desire: for there you would receive the sacrament. 'Then I will go to the altar of my God', says your soul, 'to God who gives joy to my youth'.[12] You put off the old age of sin, and clothed yourself in the youthfulness of grace. And this the heavenly sacrament brought to you. Then listen again to what David says; 'Your youth will be renewed like the eagle's'.[13] You begin

---

[6]2 Cor. 2.5, already quoted in S 1.3.

[7]Cant 8.5 (LXX). A reference to the white garments of the neophytes. See Introduction, p. 31ff.

[8]1 Pet. 1.12.

[9]1 Cor. 2.9.

[10]Ps. 51.7. Grace is whiter than snow, because it does not become dirty.

[11]Presumably the grace of baptism.

[12]Ps. 43.4 (LXX).

[13]Ps. 103.5.

to be a true eagle, aiming for heaven and despising the things of earth. The true eagles are around the altar: 'For where the body is, there the eagles will be gathered together'.[14] The altar is an image of the body, and the body of Christ is on the altar.[15] You are the angels, rejuvenated by being cleansed of sin.

8. You came to the altar, you turned your gaze to the sacraments[16] on the altar; and you marvelled at the object there; though it is an object that is common and familiar.

God's Dealings with Christians and Israelites compared

9. Perhaps someone will say: 'God gave as great a grace as this to the Jews, when he rained down manna from heaven for them. What more has he given to his faithful? What more has he given to those whom he promised more?'

10. Listen now to what I say. The Christian mysteries are more ancient than the Jewish, and the Christian sacraments more godlike than the Jewish.[17] How? Listen. When did the Jews come into being? At the time, of course, of Judah, the great-grandson of Abraham: or, if you wish to take another interpretation, at the time of the law, when they were reckoned worthy to receive God's legislation.[18] So they received the name of Jew in Moses' time from Abraham's great-grandson. Now God rained down manna from heaven for the grumbling Jews, but these sacraments were prefigured for your benefit as early as Abraham's time. He had assembled three hundred and eighteen men born in his house,[19] and had gone in pursuit of his enemies to rescue his nephew from captivity. When he was returning victorious, the high priest Melchizedek came to meet him and offered bread and wine.[20] Who had the bread

---

[14]Mt. 24.28; Lk. 17.37. Cf. S 1.6 and note 13, where the eagle stands for the sacred minister, not as here for the neophyte.

[15]Cf. S 5.7.

[16]I.e. the bread and wine.

[17]Cf. S 1.11 and note 20.

[18]An outrageous pun. Ambrose suggests (but has the grace tacitly to reject the suggestion) that the Jews (*Iudaei*) were so called from their acceptance of God's legislation (*ius dei*) — as if in English we were to say God's jew-risdiction. The Romans were eager but wildly fanciful etymologists.

[19]Gen. 14.14.

[20]Gen. 14.18.

and wine? Not Abraham. Well, who? Melchizedek. Then he was the initiator of the sacraments. Who is this Melchizedek, whose title means king of justice, king of peace?[21] Who is the king of justice? Can a mere man be king of justice? Who is the king of justice, except the justice of God? Who is the peace of God, the wisdom of God?[22] He who could say: 'My peace I give you, my peace I bequeath to you'.[23]

11. You are to understand, then, first of all that these sacraments you receive are more ancient than any sacraments the Jews claim to have; and the Christian people were in existence before the Jewish people: we existed in God's advance plan, though the Jewish name existed first.

12. So Melchizedek offered bread and wine. Who is Melchizedek? 'He is without father', it says, 'or mother, or genealogy, and has neither beginning of days nor end of life, but resembles the Son of God'.[24] So reads the Epistle to the Hebrews. Without father, it says, and without mother. The Son of God is born without mother according to his heavenly generation, because he was born of God the Father alone. Again, he was born without father, when he was born of the virgin. He was not generated by human seed. He was born of the Holy Spirit and the virgin Mary from a virgin's womb.[25]

---

[21]Heb. 7.2.

[22]Cf. 1 Cor. 1.30.

[23]Jn. 14.27. A's argument is that the Jewish sacraments began when the Israelites were given the manna in the time of Moses, but the Christian sacraments date back to Abraham, because Melchizedek, the offerer of bread and wine, has a name which shows he represents Christ.

[24]Heb. 7.3. The author of this epistle anticipated A in giving a typological interpretation to Melchizedek. In Genesis no genealogy of this king was given. The author of Hebrews argues from this fact that his priesthood is of a different order from that of the descendants of Levi. A applies the words of Heb. 7.3 to Christ, who also, as he explains, had no father or mother. For further references to Melchizedek, cf. S 4.27 with note 56 and 5.1-2 with notes 2 and 3. A's method of interpreting the Bible, therefore, is a mixture of allegorism and fundamentalism: while seeking to attach a symbolic meaning to every detail, he also insists on the literal truth of individual phrases, regardless of their context.

[25]A puts the argument more succinctly in M 46: Jesus was 'without mother in his divinity, because he was begotten by God the Father and is of one substance with the Father; without father in the incarnation, because he was born of a virgin'. Such a formulation, though meant in an orthodox sense, is superficially similar to

Melchizedek, who 'resembles the Son of God' in all things, was also a priest; because Christ is a priest, and of him it is written: 'You are a priest for ever after the order of Melchizedek'.[26]

13. Who, then, is the author of the sacraments except the Lord Jesus? These sacraments came from heaven, for all God's purpose is from heaven.[27] Still, it remains true that when God rained down manna for the people from heaven, and the people ate without working for their food, this was a great and divine sign.[28]

The Bread and Wine are transformed by Christ's Words

14. Perhaps you say: 'The bread I have here is ordinary bread'. Yes, before the sacramental words are uttered this bread is nothing but bread. But at the consecration this bread becomes the body of Christ. Let us reason this out. How can something which is bread be the body of Christ? Well, by what words is the consecration effected, and whose words are they? The words of the Lord Jesus.[29] All that is said before are the words of the priest: praise is offered to God, the prayer is offered up, petitions are made[30] for the people, for kings,[31] for

---

the later Nestorian belief that there were two persons in Christ, and that the properties attributable to one person are not transferable to the other; it follows for a Nestorian that Mary may not be called the Mother of God.

[26]Heb. 7.3, 17; Ps. 110.4.

[27]Cf. S 2.18: 'Baptism is therefore God's purpose'. Cf. Lk. 7.30.

[28]The proof (cf. S 1.11) that the Christian sacraments are more godly than the Jewish. For the former were founded by Christ in person during his lifetime, and in the Old Testament in his prefiguration, Melchizedek.

[29]Here it is assumed that the bread and wine are changed when the words of institution ('This is my Body ...') are said. Cf. Introduction, p. 49.

[30]Punctuating with Botte: '*laus deo, defertur oratio, petitur pro populo ...*' With this reading 'praise' is the Preface, 'the prayer' is the Prayer over the Offerings, 'petitions' are the prayers for the various sections of the Church (Bidding Prayers). In that case, A has inverted the order. Chadwick punctuates '*laus deo defertur, oratio petitur pro populo*'. This reading eliminates the *oratio super oblata*. Cf. Jungmann, *op. cit.*, i.53. It is, however, possible that the 'praise' is not the Preface, but a special Easter prayer of rejoicing like the Alleluia; cf. *Apologia David*, 1.42 (PL 14.867); and *In Ps. 118*, prol., 3 (PL 15.1199), where A explains that Alleluia *means* 'laus dei'.

[31]The prayer for the emperor recurs often in various liturgies, e.g. Cyril, MC 5.8. The wording suggests a link with 1 Tim. 2.2. Cf. Introduction, p. 50f.

all others. But when the moment comes for bringing the most holy sacrament into being, the priest does not use his own words any longer: he uses the words of Christ. Therefore, it is Christ's word that brings this sacrament into being.

15. What is this word of Christ?[32] It is the word by which all things were made.[33] The Lord commanded and the heavens were made, the Lord commanded and the earth was made, the Lord commanded and the seas were made, the Lord commanded and all creatures came into being. See, then, how efficacious the word of Christ is. If, then, there is such power in the word of the Lord Jesus that things begin to exist which did not exist before, how much more powerful it is for changing what already existed into something else. There was no heaven, there was no sea, there was no earth. And yet, as David says: 'He spoke and it was made; he commanded and it was created'.[34]

16. To answer your question, then, before the consecration it was not the body of Christ, but after the consecration I tell you that it is now the body of Christ. He spoke and it was made, he commanded and it was created. You yourself were in existence, but you were a creature of the old order; after your consecration, you began to exist as a new creature. Do you wish to know how new this creature is? 'If any one is in Christ', it is written, 'he is a new creation'.[35]

17. Listen, then, and I will teach you how the word of Christ has a tendency to change every creature and changes at will the established course of nature. 'How?', you ask. Listen, and first of all I will give you an illustration from his birth. Normally a human being does not come into existence except by the instrumentality of man and woman in the material relationship.

---

[32]In sect. 15-20 A shows by examples how Christ's words can change the nature of things. Surprisingly he draws several examples from the Old Testament. (Heb 1 also sees Christ to have been active in the Old Testament.) This attribution to Christ of events before the Incarnation is in harmony with A's typological interpretation of the Old Testament.

[33]Cf. Is. 55.11: 'So shall my word be that goes forth from my mouth; it shall not return to me empty, but it shall accomplish that which I purpose'.

[34]Cf. Ps. 148.5; 33.9.

[35]2 Cor. 5.17. Just as the Christian becomes a new creature at baptism ('consecration'), so too the bread and wine are changed.

But because the Lord willed it so, because he chose this mystery, Christ was born of the Holy Spirit and of a virgin;[36] that is to say, 'the man Jesus Christ is the mediator between God and men'.[37] You see, then, it was against the established course and order of nature that a man was born of a virgin.

18. Here is another illustration: The Jewish people were pursued by the Egyptians and were cut off by the sea. At the divine command, Moses touched the waters with his staff and the water divided;[38] this certainly did not happen according to the normal course of their nature, but thanks to the heavenly command. Another illustration: the people were thirsty and came to the spring. The spring was bitter. Blessed Moses put a piece of wood into the spring; and the spring which before was bitter became sweet: that is to say, it changed its nature, and received the sweetness of grace.[39] Here is a fourth illustration. The iron head of an axe had fallen into the water, and the iron, according to its nature, sank. Elisha threw in a piece of wood; immediately the iron rose to the surface and floated on the water — which is indeed contrary to its nature.[40] For iron is a material heavier than the element water.

19. You see from all this, surely, the power that is contained in the heavenly word. If it is effective in the earthly spring, if the heavenly word is effective in the other cases, why should it not be so in the heavenly sacraments? So now you have learnt that the bread becomes the body of Christ, and that, though wine and water are poured into the chalice,[41] through the

---

[36]Cf. Lk 1.35: 'The Holy Spirit will come upon you ...; therefore the child to be born will be called holy, the Son of God.' A implies that Christ derived his humanity from Mary, his divinity from the Spirit, and only thus can he be the mediator between God and men. The Virgin Birth, according to A, was necessary for the Incarnation. Cf. 4.12.

[37]1 Tim. 2.5 (adapted).

[38]'Lift up your rod, and stretch out your hand over the sea and divide it' (Ex. 14.16). In making Moses touch the water with his rod, A is going beyond his source; he was more accurate in the corresponding passages in S 1.20 and M 51.

[39]Ex. 15.23-25.

[40]2 Kgs. 6.5-6. Irenaeus had earlier associated the word of God with Elisha's axe in *Adv. Haer.* v. 17.4. Ambrose quoted this miracle and the crossing of the Red Sea above in S 1.12, 20; 2.11-12 as symbols of baptism.

[41]On the symbolism of the mixing of the water with the wine, see S 5.2-4.

consecration effected by the heavenly word it becomes his blood.

20. But you may say: 'I do not see the appearance of blood'. No, but the likeness is there.[42] Just as you have taken on the likeness of death, so also you drink the likeness of the precious blood, in order that nothing of the horror of blood may be there and at the same time the price of our redemption may become operative. So now you have learnt that what you receive is the body of Christ.

The Eucharistic Prayer

21. Do you wish to know how the consecration takes place by the power of the heavenly words? Hear what the words are.

Epiclesis over the Offerings

The priest says:[43] *Make this offering for us approved, spiritual,*[44]

---

[42]A might have been expected to repeat his argument of S 2.15 that in the sacraments the believer does not need visible evidence. Instead he argues that it would not do for the eucharistic species to have the appearance of blood, because then it would be repulsive; it is enough for it to bear a partial resemblance. That there should be the 'likeness' of blood does not imply that the Blood itself is not present. Cf. note 45 on 'the *figure* of the body and blood'.

[43]The traditional Roman Canon, which remained in force after the revisions of 1969, is very close to A's. Translated more literally than in the ICEL version so as to facilitate comparison, this section of the Roman Canon runs: 'Vouchsafe, we beseech you, O God, to make this offering blessed, approved, recognised, spiritual and pleasing, so that it may become for us the body and blood of you beloved Son, our Lord Jesus Christ, who, the day before he suffered, took bread in his holy and venerable hands, and, looking up to heaven, to you, his almighty God and Father, and giving thanks to you, he blessed it and broke it and gave it to his disciples saying: Take and eat of this all of you, for this is my body. In the same way, after supper, taking this glorious chalice into his holy and venerable hands, and giving thanks to you, he blessed it and gave it to his disciples saying: Take and drink of this, all of you, for this is the chalice of my blood of the new and eternal covenant (the mystery of faith), which will be shed for you and for many for the forgiveness of sins. As often as you do these things, you should do them in memory of me.'
The Roman Canon and A's are compared by B. Botte, *Le Canon de la Messe Romaine.* A's version is less polished, contains fewer honorific adjectives, and at several points reveals Eastern influences.

[44]Cf. Rom. 12.1: 'Present your bodies as a living sacrifice, holy and acceptable [pleasing] to God, which is your spiritual worship'. St Paul's words are characteristic

pleasing; it is the figure[45] of the body and blood of our Lord Jesus Christ.

Last Supper Narrative

The day before he suffered, he took bread in his holy hands, looked up to heaven to you, holy Father, almighty, eternal God, and giving thanks blessed it and broke it, and gave what was broken to his apostles and disciples, saying: Take and eat of this, all of you, for this is my body which shall be broken for many.[46]
    22. Listen carefully. *In the same way, after supper on the day before he suffered, he took the chalice, and looked up to heaven to you, holy Father, almighty, eternal God, and giving thanks he blessed it and gave it to his apostles and disciples, saying: Take and drink of this, all of you, for this is my blood.[47]* Now, all these are the words of the evangelist as far as 'take' — the body or the blood. What follows are the words of

of a tendency in the early Church to reject circumcision and ritual, including animal sacrifices, in favour of 'circumcision made without hands' (Col. 2.11) and 'spiritual worship' — i.e. right interior dispositions. This insistence on the internal was not thought to be incompatible with the establishment of new Christian rites like baptism and the Eucharist.
    [45]Taken by itself, this description of the offerings as the 'figure' of Christ's body and blood seems to imply that the bread and wine are merely symbols of the Body and Blood, and are not changed into them. This, however, cannot be the way A took the words, as he is quoting them to show how 'at the consecration this bread becomes the body of Christ' (14: cf. 23). A therefore sees no incompatibility between the real and the symbolic presence; the Body and Blood are really present and are symbolised by the bread and wine. In this sense he has already spoken of the 'likeness of the precious blood' in sect. 20.
    This use of the term 'figure' or its equivalent is also found in the *Apostolic Tradition* (23.1), and in the Byzantine Liturgy of St Basil (Jasper and Cuming, *Prayers of the Eucharist*, p. 119), and is perhaps an instance of oriental influence in A's liturgical text. So according to Cyril we receive Christ's body 'in the form (*type*) of bread' (MC 4.3); the bread and wine are the sign (*antitype*) of Christ's body and blood (MC 5.20; cf. note 23). Nevertheless, this use of figure-terminology to express real presence in symbols was also known in the western writers like Tertullian and Pope Gelasius. Cf. Darwell Stone, *A History of the Doctrine of the Eucharist*, i. 29-37; 58-123.
    [46]The account is closer to 1 Cor. 11.23-24 than to the gospels. 'Which shall be broken' is not in the best NT texts, but is included in some eucharistic liturgies, such as the *Apostolic Tradition*, and Sarapion's *Euchologion*. For the connection between the breaking of bread and the breaking of Christ's body, cf. Introduction, pp. 51-52.
    [47]Cf. Mt. 26.27-28.

Christ: 'Take and drink of this, all of you, for this is my blood'.

23. Notice each detail. The day before he suffered, it says, he took bread in his holy hands. Before it is consecrated, it is bread; but when the words of Christ have been uttered over it, it is the body of Christ. Listen to what he says then: 'Take and eat of this, all of you, for this is my body'. And the chalice, before the words of Christ, is full of wine and water. But when the words of Christ have done their work, it becomes the blood of Christ which has redeemed the people. So you can see the ways in which the word of Christ is powerful enough to change all things. Besides, the Lord Jesus himself is our witness that we receive his body and blood. Should we doubt his authority and testimony?

24. Let us return to my argument.[48] That manna rained down from heaven for the Jews was a mighty and awe-inspiring work. But think; which is greater, manna from heaven or the body of Christ? Surely the body of Christ, who is the maker of heaven. Besides, those who ate the manna are dead. But those who eat this body have their sins forgiven and will never die.[49]

25. So the answer 'Amen'[50] you give is no idle word. For you are confessing in spirit that you receive the body of Christ. So, too, when you come up from communion, the bishop says to you: 'The body of Christ'. And you say 'Amen', that is, 'It is true'. What your lips confess let your heart hold fast. For you must realise that this is a sacrament that was preceded by its symbol.[51]

[48]Cf. S 4.13 with note 28. The Eucharist is greater than the manna, its Jewish equivalent, not only because it was founded by Christ, but also because the Eucharist gives eternal life.

[49]Cf. Jn. 6.49, 58; 11.26.

[50]Similarly in the Jerusalem liturgy of St James, the people exclaim 'Amen' after the words of institution over the bread, and again after the words over the cup (Jasper and Cuming, *Prayer of the Eucharist*, p. 92). In the 1969 Roman liturgy the people are allowed a choice of forms of acclamation after the consecration.

A's explanation is confused. He passes from the Amen after the consecration to the Amen which is the response to the words 'The body of Christ', which are spoken when communion is given.

[51]I.e., your Amen is an acknowledgement of the truth of what was said in the previous section about the manna and Christ's body. But perhaps the text is corrupt.

26. And you must understand how great a sacrament it is. Notice what he[52] says: 'As often as you did this, you will do it in commemoration of me, until I come again.'

Anamnesis

27. Then the priest says:[53] *Therefore we call to mind his most glorious passion, his resurrection from the dead and his ascension into heaven.*

Prayer of the Offering

And we offer you this spotless sacrifice, this spiritual sacrifice, this bloodless[54] sacrifice, this holy bread and chalice of eternal life, and we beseech and pray you to take up this offering by the hands of your angels[55] to your altar on high, just as you were graciously pleased to

---

[52]'He' must mean the bishop, as in sect. 25. Cf. 1 Cor. 11.24, 26: 'Do this in remembrance of me ... For as often as you eat this bread and drink the cup, you proclaim the Lord's death until he comes'.

[53]The Roman canon translated literally continues: 'Therefore, O Lord, we your servants and your holy people call to mind the blessed passion of your son, Jesus Christ our Lord, his resurrection from the dead, and his glorious ascension into heaven, and we offer to your illustrious majesty from your gifts and presents a clean offering, a holy offering, a spotless offering, the holy bread of eternal life and the chalice of perpetual salvation. May you be graciously pleased to look down on these things with favourable and serene countenance and to receive them as you were graciously pleased to receive the gifts of your just servant Abel and the sacrifice of our father Abraham and the offering the high priest Melchizedek made to you, a holy sacrifice, a spotless offering. Beseechingly, we ask you, almighty God, bid these things to be carried by the hands of your holy angel to your altar on high in the sight of your divine majesty so that all of us who share in this altar and receive the most holy body and blood of your Son, may be filled with every heavenly blessing and grace, through the same Christ our Lord. Amen.'

The last few lines form an Epiclesis over the People, which is absent from A's text.

[54]Cf. Cyril, MC 5.8 and Introduction, p. 47, note 240.

[55]This prayer that God will send his angel(s) to carry the offering up to the heavenly altar takes the place of the eastern Epiclesis over the Offerings *after* the consecration. Cf. H. W. Codrington, 'The Heavenly Altar in the Byzantine Liturgy and Elsewhere', *Eastern Churches Quarterly*, 3 (1938) 125-130. However, the fourth-century *Apostolic Constitutions* contain a rite which includes after the consecration not only an Epiclesis over the Offerings but also a prayer that God will receive the offering on his heavenly altar 'through the mediation of his Christ' (viii.12-13). Since the Roman Canon has 'angel' in the singular, it is possible that the sacrifice is thought to be carried up by Christ, as in the *Apostolic Constitutions*. 'Angel' was

receive the gifts of your just servant Abel, the sacrifice of our father Abraham, and the offering the high priest Melchizedek made to you.[56] 28. What is it the apostle says about every time you receive it? 'As often as we receive it, we proclaim the death of the Lord'[57] If we proclaim his death, we proclaim the remission of sins. If whenever his blood is shed, it is shed for the remission of sins,[58] I ought always to receive him so that he may always forgive sins.[59] Since I am always sinning, I always need the medicine. 29. We have gone as far as we could today at this stage of our explanation. Tomorrow (Saturday) and Sunday, we will speak as best we can of the order of prayer.[60] May our Lord God preserve in you the grace which he has given you, and may he deign to illuminate more fully the eyes he has opened through his only-begotten Son, our king and saviour, our Lord God by whom and with whom he has praise, honour, glory, magnificence and power, with the Holy Spirit now and for ever into endless ages. Amen.

a title attributed to Christ in some early Christian works (e.g. Hermas, *Shepherd*, Vis. v. 2. Cf. J. Daniélou, *The Theology of Jewish Christianity*, pp. 117ff.). In the Latin text of Is. 9.6 that A follows in S 2.4, the Prince of Peace is to be called 'the Angel of Great Counsel'. For the heavenly liturgy, cf. Theodore, BH 4.15 with note 26.

[56]Gen. 14.18 ('Melchizedek, king of Salem, brought out bread and wine') was habitually taken to be a prefiguration of the Eucharist. To 'bring out' (*ekpherein*) was taken to mean 'offer' (*prospherein*). For Melchizedek cf. S 4.12 with note 24, and 5.1-2 with notes 2 and 3. The liturgies have changed Melchizedek's title from 'priest of the Most High God' (Heb. 7.1), to 'high priest'. Cf. G. Jeanes, 'Early Latin Parallels to the Roman Canon?', *JTS* 37 (1986), pp. 427-431.

[57]Cf. 1 Cor. 11.26.

[58]Cf. Mt. 26.28.

[59]One of the effects of the Eucharist is to forgive sins. Cf. S 5.17 and Theodore BH 5.33-35 with note 59. In S 6.24 (not included in this collection), commenting on the petitions of the Lord's Prayer, 'Give us this day our daily bread and forgive us our trespasses ...', A concludes: 'Therefore receive every day in order to seek pardon for your debt every day'.

[60]The text is suspect, and should perhaps be slightly amended to read: 'tomorrow and Saturday we will speak as best we can about the Lord's Prayer and the order of prayer' (Cf. S 1.2 with note 4). The 'order of prayer' is a scheme for prayer according to which we should pass from point to point as if we were composing a speech (S 6.11, 23 not in this collection). A discusses the Lord's Prayer twice in S 5.18-29 and 6.24. For a discussion of the text of this passage, cf. Botte, *Des Sacraments etc.*, pp. 210-211. If the reading given in the text is retained, A's six sermons were given from Tuesday to Sunday; the emendation makes the days Monday to Saturday, which is perhaps more likely.

SERMONS ON THE SACRAMENTS
V
SYMBOLS OF THE EUCHARIST

1. Yesterday in our instruction we got as far as the sacraments of the sacred altar, and we learnt that a prefiguration of these sacraments was given in times past in the days of Abraham when blessed Melchizedek, who had 'neither beginning of days nor end',[1] offered sacrifice. Listen, O man, to what the apostle Paul says to the Hebrews. Are there any who say that the Son of God belongs to time? It says there that the days of Melchizedek have neither beginning nor end.[2] If the days of Melchizedek have no beginning, could the days of Christ? The figure is not greater than the reality.[3] You recognise that he is at once 'the first and the last':[4] the first, because he is the creator of all, the last, not because he will come to an end, but because he completes all things.

The Water mixed with the Wine

2. We have said that the bread and the chalice are placed on the altar. What is put into the chalice? Wine. What else? Water. You will say: 'What for? Melchizedek offered bread and wine. What is the meaning of the water that is added?' Here is the reason.[5]

---

[1]Heb. 7.3. Cf. S 4.10-12, 27. The solemn apostrophe, 'O man', is perhaps borrowed from Rom. 2.1, 3.

[2]A argues against those who say the Son had a beginning in time (i.e. the Arians, who regarded him as a creature) that, since according to Hebrews Melchizedek had no beginning, Christ, his superior, must also have had no beginning.

[3]Since the OT foreshadows Christ, he must be greater that the OT figures. For this Platonic theory of symbols and realities, cf. Theodore, BH 4.15 with note 26.

[4]Apoc. 1.17; 22.13.

[5]A gives three reasons why water is mixed with the wine — (1) It symbolises Christ, prefigured by the rock which gave water; (2) It stands for the 'living water' Jesus promised (Jn. 4.10); (3) It symbolises the water that flowed from Jesus' side. In fact in the ancient world it was normal to add water to the wine, and we need look no further for the origin of the practice. The Roman Mass takes the mixture to be a symbol of the union of the divinity with the humanity. Another tradition made the added drop of water stand for the Church's self-offering united to Christ's (cf. Cyprian, Ep. 63.13).

3. First of all, what was the meaning of the prefiguration given in the time of Moses? The Jewish people were thirsty and murmured because they could not find water; so God commanded Moses to touch the rock with his staff. He touched the rock, and the rock gave forth an abundance of water.[6] So the apostle says: 'They drank from the rock which followed them, and the rock was Christ'.[7] A very mobile rock, this rock which followed the people. You also must drink, so that Christ may follow you. Consider this mystery. Moses, that is, as a prophet, touched the rock with his staff, that is, with the word of God; as a priest he touched the rock with the word of God, and water flowed forth, and the people of God drank. The priest, therefore, touches the chalice, water flows into the chalice, and it 'wells up to the eternal life',[8] and the people of God who have received his grace drink from it.

4. This is one point you have learnt. Listen now to something else. During the Lord's passion, because the great sabbath was at hand and our Lord Jesus Christ or the thieves were still alive, people were sent to strike them. When they came they found the Lord Jesus Christ already dead. Then one of the soldiers touched his side with a spear, and from his side flowed blood and water.[9] Why water? Why blood? Water to cleanse, blood to redeem.[10] Why from his side? Because the source of guilt was to be the source of grace. Guilt came through the woman, grace through the Lord Jesus Christ.[11]

Holy Communion

5. You have to come to the altar,[12] the Lord Jesus calls you,

[6]Ex. 17.1-6.

[7]1 Cor. 10.4. A omits the adjective 'supernatural' (*pneumatikes*) which St Paul attributes to the rock. Jewish tradition elaborated legends concerning the travels of the following rock (cf. Strack-Billerbeck, iii. 406ff.; R. Murray, *Symbols of Church and Kingdom*, pp. 205-238).

[8]Jn. 4.14.

[9]Cf. Jn. 19.34.

[10]Probably for St John the blood and water stood for the Eucharist and baptism.

[11]Cf. Jn. 1.17. Eve, the source of sin, came from Adam's side; therefore it is fitting that the means of redemption should come from Christ's side.

[12]Elsewhere (e.g. S 3.15) A has spoken to the baptized coming to the altar to see for the first time what is there. Here he means that the people come up for holy communion.

or your soul, or the Church,[13] when he says: 'Let him kiss me with the kisses of his lips'.[14] Do you wish to attribute them to your soul? Nothing could be sweeter.

6. 'Let him kiss me'.[15] He sees that you are cleansed of all sin, because your faults are washed away. So he judges you worthy to receive the heavenly sacraments, and so he invites you to the heavenly feast: 'Let him kiss me with the kisses of his lips'.

7. Now because of what follows,[16] it is your soul or human nature or the Church that speaks; it sees that it is cleansed of all sin, and worthy to approach the altar of Christ: for what is the altar except an image of Christ's body?[17] It sees the marvellous sacraments, and says: 'Let him kiss me with the kisses of his lips': that is: 'Let Christ give *me* a kiss'.

8. Why? 'Because your breasts are better than wine':[18] that is, your thoughts, your sacraments are better than wine: which in spite of the sweetness, the happiness, the joy it gives, is still a worldly joy; but in you there is also a spiritual joy. So Solomon now refers to the nuptials of Christ and the Church, of the spirit and the flesh, of the spirit and the soul.

9. Solomon goes on to say: 'Your name is oil poured out; therefore the maidens love you'.[19] Who are these maidens, except those souls which have rid themselves of the old age of

---

[13]A gives three allegorical interpretations of the Song of Songs. His third interpretation, that the bride is the Church, is in keeping with OT symbolism. Many modern scholars, however, regard the book simply as a series of marriage-poems in origin; though even so the book was doubtless included in the Jewish scriptures as an illustration of the covenant under the traditional marriage-symbolism. If so, this later application, as well as the original composition, is to be considered as inspired.

[14]Cant 1.2 (LXX). A may be referring with typical allusiveness to the Kiss of Peace before communion Cf. Introduction, p. 44. A writes of the Kiss of Peace in *Epistle* 41.14-15.

[15]A first imagines Christ addressing the words to a soul he loves.

[16]I.e., because of the continuation in the Song of Songs, quoted in sect. 8ff., it is evident that the words, 'Let him kiss me', are spoken *to* Christ, not by him, as in sect. 5.

[17]Here the association with the Song of Songs makes A see the body as the body of a lover. In S 4.7 the context suggests the dead body of Christ.

[18]Cant 1.2 (LXX).

[19]Cant 1.3. The Song of Songs claims to be written by Solomon.

the body, and have been made young again through the Holy Spirit?[20]

10. 'Draw us, so that we follow the scent of your perfumes'.[21] See what he means: you cannot follow Christ unless he draws you himself. To teach you this, he says: 'When I am lifted up, I will draw all things to myself'.[22]

11. 'The King has brought me into his chamber'.[23] The Greek reads: 'into his store-room' or 'his cellar': the place where the best vintages, the best perfumes, the sweetest honey are stored, the choicest fruits and dainties, so that your meal may be garnished with dainties in abundance.

12. So you have come to the altar, you have received the body of Christ. Learn from another source the nature of the sacraments you have received. Listen to what blessed David says, who saw the mysteries beforehand in spirit: he rejoiced and said that nothing further was lacking.[24] Why? Because he who receives the body of Christ will never go hungry again.[25]

13. How often have you listened to the Twenty-second Psalm without understanding it? See how fittingly it is applied to the heavenly sacraments. 'The Lord feeds me. I want for nothing. He has led me to a place of refreshment. He has brought me to the waters which refresh me, he has revived my spirit. He has led me by the paths of justice, for his name's sake. Though I should walk in the midst of death's shadow, I shall fear no evil, because you are with me. Your rod and your staff have comforted

[20]In A's allegorical interpretation, the maidens stand for the newly-baptized soul in its newness of life.

[21]Cant 1.4 (adapted).

[22]Jn. 12.32 (adapted). This emphasis on the need of grace corrects the balance after such passages as S 1.1; 5.7, where it is said we must be worthy of the sacraments. A's disciple, St Augustine, was to elaborate this idea in his well-known 26th Treatise on St John's Gospel. Cf. Chrysostom, BH 2.2, p. 152.

[23]Cant 1.4. A's standards of scholarship differ from those of today. He meticulously compares texts, only to choose whichever has the richest allegorical meaning.

[24]Cf. Ps. 23.1: 'I shall not want'. The psalm (22 in LXX and Latin) is quoted in full below. In another work of A's (*De Elia*, 10.34; PL 14.708-709) this psalm seems perhaps to be sung as a communion chant. Cyril also quotes the psalm in the same context (MC 4.7).

[25]Cf. Jn. 6.35.

me'.[26] The rod is his sovereign right, the staff his suffering; Christ's everlasting godhead, but his bodily suffering as well.[27] With the one he created, with the other he redeemed. 'You have prepared a meal for me, in the sight of those who afflict me. You have anointed my head with perfume. And your cup which inebriates, how glorious it is!'[28]

14. You have come to the altar, you have received the grace of Christ, you have taken the heavenly sacraments. The Church rejoices in the redemption of so many, and is exultant with spiritual gladness when she sees at her side his family clothed in white.[29] You can find this in the Song of Songs.[30] With joy she invites Christ, because she has prepared a banquet which seems fit for a heavenly feast. So she says: 'Let my brother come down into his garden and pluck the fruit from his trees'.[31] What are these fruit trees? You are the tree which, in Adam, lost its sap; but now, through the grace of Christ, you have come to fruitfulness like orchard trees.

15. The Lord Jesus has willingly accepted the invitation, and in his heavenly graciousness has answered the Church: 'I have come down into my garden: I have gathered a vintage of myrrh with my perfumes. I have eaten honey with my bread, and I have drunk wine with my milk. Eat, brothers,' he says, 'and drink deep.'[32]

16. 'I have gathered a vintage of myrrh with my perfumes'. What is this vintage? You should know the vine, and recognise the vintage. 'Thou didst bring', he says, 'a vine out of Egypt':[33] that is, the people of God. You are the vine, you are the vintage

---

[26]Ps. 23.1-4 (with many verbal changes). The beginning of the psalm is usually quoted in the form, 'The Lord is my Shepherd'.

[27]The rod is the royal sceptre, the sign of Christ's divinity; the staff, less appropriately, stands for the cross. The implied proposition that Christ created by his divinity and redeemed by his humanity seems to make the Incarnation unnecessary; on the contrary, what Christ did for us he did as both God and man.

[28]Ps 23.5 (LXX).

[29]For the baptismal white garment, cf. S 4.5-6 and Introduction, p. 31ff.

[30]Cf. Cant 8.5 (LXX), quoted in S 4.5.

[31]Cant 4.16 (based on LXX).

[32]Cant 5.1 (based on LXX).

[33]Ps. 80.8.

planted like vines. You have given fruit like a vintage. 'I have gathered a vintage of myrrh with my perfumes': that is to say, for the sweet fragrance which you have received.[34]

17. 'I have eaten honey with my bread'. You see that in this bread there is no bitter taste: it is all sweetness. 'I have drunk wine with my milk'.[35] You see that your joy is one which is uncontaminated by any stain of sin. So often as you drink, you receive the remission of your sins: you are inebriated in spirit. 'Do not get drunk with wine', the apostle says, 'but be filled with the Spirit'.[36] He who is drunk with wine staggers and totters. He who is drunk with the Spirit is firmly rooted in Christ. This is a splendid drunkenness which brings sobriety of soul. So we bring to a close our brief reflections on the sacraments.[37]

[34]Cf. S 1.3. Myrrh perhaps recalls the myron.

[35]Perhaps an allusion to the milk and honey which were administered to the neophyte at his first communion in some churches. Cf. Introduction, p. 39f.

[36]Eph. 5.18.

[37]The rest of Book V consists of an explanation of the Lord's Prayer.

SERMONS ON THE SACRAMENTS
VI
CHRIST'S TRUE BODY AND BLOOD ARE RECEIVED

1. Our Lord Jesus Christ is God's true Son, not as men are God's sons by favour, but as God's Son from his Father's substance.[1] So too it is his true flesh which we receive, as he told us himself, and his true blood which is our drink.[2]

2. Perhaps, however, you will say what Christ's disciples once said when they heard him saying, 'Unless one eats my flesh and drinks my blood, he will not abide in me or have eternal life.'[3] Perhaps you will say: 'How can this be true? I see the likeness of blood, but I cannot see real blood.'[4]

3. First of all, I explained[5] to you how Christ's word is so effectual that it can change and transform the fixed natural species. Secondly, when Christ's disciples could not bear to hear him saying that he would give them his flesh to eat and his blood to drink, they left him. Peter was the only one to say, 'You have the words of eternal life. To whom can I go if I leave you?'[6] And so, to prevent more people from saying this because of a certain horror of blood,[7] and at the same time to preserve the grace of redemption, you receive the sacraments in symbolic form but you receive the grace and efficacy of Christ's real human nature.[8]

4. 'I am the bread which came down from heaven', he said.[9]

---

[1] Arius had held that the Son was not 'true God' but a mere creature, divine only 'by participation' or 'by grace' (Athanasius, *Or. Contra Arianos*, 1.9; PG 26.29). In denial of this heresy the Council of Nicaea declared that the Son was 'of one substance' (*homoousios*) with the Father.

[2] Cf. Jn. 6.55.

[3] Jn. 6.54, with phrases from 6.53, 56.

[4] Cf. S 4.20, where the same answer is given to this objection as at the end of 6.3.

[5] S 4.14-20. The objection is answered in two ways: (1) we know from other instances that Christ can change the nature of things; (2) we might be repelled if the eucharistic species looked like blood.

[6] Jn. 6.68 (adapted).

[7] A's squeamishness is apparent again here; cf. 1.2 and Introduction, p. 18 with note 80.

[8] For the contrast between the symbol and reality of the sacraments, cf. Cyril, MC 5.20 with note 23.

[9] Jn. 6.41. To the objection that, since Christ's flesh originated in this world, it is not true that the Bread came down from heaven, A replies that the divinity and

But his flesh did not come down from heaven; he took flesh on earth from the Virgin. How then can the bread have come down from heaven, and living bread, too? Because one and the same Jesus Christ our Lord possessed both divinity and a body,[10] you too, by receiving his flesh, share in his divine substance by means of his food.

The Trinity

5. And so you have learnt about the sacraments; now you know everything in full. You have been baptized in the name of the Trinity. In everything we have done the mystery of the Trinity has been preserved. The Father, the Son and the Holy Spirit are present everywhere; they exercise a joint causality, a single sanctifying action,[11] although some aspects do seem to be peculiar to the individual Persons.

humanity are so closely united that by receiving the Bread (i.e. the flesh) we receive also the divinity, which *did* come down from heaven; therefore the Bread can be said to have come down from heaven.

[10]This formula at first sight appears Apollinarian; i.e. it suggests that Christ had no human soul, but was simply body plus divinity. However, A's Christology was orthodox. He adopts the divinity/body terminology in preference to the divinity/humanity terminology in order to emphasize the identity of the humanity with the eucharistic body.

[11]As later theologians put it, all activity the Trinity exercises on created things is common to all three persons; their individuality lies only in their relationships with one another (*omnia ... sunt unum, ubi non obviat relationis oppositio*, Council of Florence, *Decree for Jacobites* DS 1330). However, Scripture and Tradition have assigned different roles, or at least emphases, to each Person: the Father is regarded as the Creator, the Son as the Redeemer and Revealer, the Spirit as the Sanctifier. Although A is arguing against the Arians (cf. 6.10) that the three Persons are equal because in the sacraments they exercise a single causality, he also maintains that each contributes to this single action in his own way. In A's words, 'some aspects do seem to be peculiar to the individual persons' (*quaedam veluti specialia esse videantur*). To reconcile this emphasis on the role of the individual Person with the unity of the divine action, some theologians have had recourse to the theory of 'appropriation': every divine action in creation is common to all three Persons, but it helps us to understand the individual Person if we for convenience attribute certain divine actions to one or other of the three persons. Others would say that, though the actions are performed jointly by the three Persons, each Person contributes to that action in his peculiar way: the Father as originator, the Son as Word (the Father's Revelation or Purpose), the Spirit as the mutual gift of Father and Son. A tries to define the 'peculiar aspects' by the latter procedure.

6. How? God anointed you, the Lord put his sign on you and placed the Holy Spirit in your heart.[12] So you received the Holy Spirit in your heart. But there is another point: just as the Holy Spirit is in your heart, so too Christ is in your heart. How can this be? You have it in the Song of Songs, where Christ says to the Church: 'Set me as a seal upon your heart, as a seal upon your arm.'[13]

7. God anointed you, then, Christ put his sign on you. In what sense? You were given a sign in the form of his cross and of his passion.[14] You received the seal in his likeness to enable you to rise again in his form and live after the model of the one who was crucified to sin and lives to God.[15] And your 'old self',[16] too, was drowned in the font and crucified to sin, but rose again to God.

8. Again, you have another example of the individual effects: God called you, in baptism you are crucified together with Christ — a kind of individual effect; and there is another individual effect, so to speak, when you receive the spiritual seal.[17] You can see here the distinction of Persons, but the whole mystery of the Trinity is interconnected.

---

[12]Cf. S 3.8 with notes, and Introduction, pp. 37-38. The text of this sentence is probably corrupt. It is clear from the corresponding passage in M 42 that A is speaking not about the 'messianic' Anointing with Chrism but the conferring of the Gift of the Spirit. A is indicating the distinct functions of each of the three Persons in this rite: God (the Father) anoints us (cf. 2 Cor. 1.21); the Son gives us the sign or seal which conforms us to his likeness; the Holy Spirit dwells in our hearts. The passage shows that there was an anointing associated with this rite, which involved a third anointing after the earlier use of oil and chrism — unless the word 'anointed' is simply metaphorical; cf. Theodore, BH 3.27 with note 65.

[13]Cant 8.6. Again A puts OT words on Christ's lips.

[14]These words suggest that the anointing was performed by means of a sign of the cross.

[15]Cf. Rom. 6.10.

[16]Rom. 6.6.

[17]In this section A seems to be seeking 'individual effects' or 'the distinction of persons' not, as in sect. 6-7, by showing how each person contributes differently to the joint effect of a particular sacrament, but by showing how at different stages of the process of Christian initiation different persons of the Trinity are predominant. The Father predominantly calls us to faith (cf. 1 Thess. 4.7; 2 Thess. 2.14); we are crucified with the Son in baptism; we receive the Holy Spirit at confirmation.

9. Besides, what did St Paul tell you the day before yesterday in the reading? 'There are varieties of gifts, but the same Spirit; and there are varieties of service, but the same Lord; and there are varieties of working, but it is the same God who works them all in every one.'[18] God, he says, works them all. But you have also read concerning the Spirit of God: 'These are worked by one and the same Spirit, who apportions to each one individually as he wills.'[19] Notice that the text says that the Spirit apportions according to his will, not out of obedience.[20] Therefore the Spirit has apportioned grace to you as he wills, not as he is ordered — necessarily so, because the Spirit of God is the Spirit of Christ. You must believe that he is the Holy Spirit of God, the Spirit of Christ, the Spirit the Paraclete.

10. The Arians believe they are diminishing the status of the Holy Spirit if they call him the Spirit the Paraclete. But if Paraclete means anything, it means 'Comforter'.[21] And have we not heard in the reading that the Father himself is the 'God of comfort'?[22] So, you see, they think they can diminish the Holy Spirit's status in the very point in which the eternal Father's power is proclaimed so devoutly.

11. Now let me tell you how we ought to pray.[23]

---

[18]1 Cor. 12.4-6.

[19]1 Cor. 12.11. A's argument is obscure; his thought may be as follows: (1) 'Gifts' are attributed to the Spirit, 'service' to the Son, 'working' to the Father. Therefore there is a 'distinction of persons'. (2) 'Working' is attributed to God (the Father) (1 Cor. 12.6) and the Spirit (1 Cor. 12.11). Therefore the Trinity is interconnected. (3) This thought leads him on to the equality of the Spirit: he acts 'as he wills', not 'under obedience to the Father'.

[20]If the Holy Spirit were not equal to the Father, he would act in obedience to the Father, not according to his own will.

[21]Scholars are generally agreed that A's understanding of the title 'Paraclete' is not correct. In general usage the word applied to one who was called in as a helper, especially as an advocate to plead on one's behalf.

[22]2 Cor 1.3. Eunomius, a follower of Arius, preferred to speak of the 'Paraclete' rather than the 'Holy Spirit' because he thought in this way to make him seem inferior to the Father. Cf. Gregory of Nyssa, *Ref. Conf. Eunom.* 185 (PG 45.459-52; Jaeger ii, pp. 389-391), a passage on which A seems to be drawing in this section. Gregory wrote about 383, some eight years before the date normally ascribed to this work of A's.

[23]The rest of the work is the treatise on the 'order of prayer' promised in S 4.29.

JOHN CHRYSOSTOM

Antioch, the capital of Syria, was the home of the next two authors, John Chrysostom and Theodore of Mopsuestia. They studied together under Diodore of Tarsus at this great centre of theological thought, but they acquired very dissimilar reputations. Whereas Chrysostom was recognized by the Church as a saint and a doctor, Theodore was condemned as a heretic more than a century after his death at the Second Council of Constantinople (553).

John Chrysostom's life was much more troubled than that of his fellow-student. Theodore's unimportant diocese of Mopsuestia afforded him leisure for study and a flow of theological writing which established him in a position of great influence in the Church; even Julian of Eclanum, Pelagius' disciple and St Augustine's adversary, found a welcome with Theodore, a fact which did no good to the latter's reputation for orthodoxy in the critical eyes of the following century. John, on the other hand, remained longer at Antioch, where he won deserved fame as a preacher (his nickname Chrysostom means 'golden-mouthed') before being chosen in 397 to rule the troublesome See of Constantinople, the capital of the Eastern Empire. Here his outspoken criticism of the rich, including the Emperor's wife, led to his exile in 403. He died in 407, while being conveyed to a still more remote place of banishment.

It is probable that both he and Theodore preached their baptismal sermons as priests at Antioch.[1] If so, the two men must have held the office of catechetical preacher there in close succession.[2] Chrysostom explains baptism in advance; he gives his reasons for this procedure in sections 12 and 28 of the sermon reproduced here. However, unlike the other three sets of baptismal sermons, Chrysostom's do not include a systematic explanation of the Eucharist. The two sets of the instructions, however, though explaining almost identical ceremonies, differ

---

[1] Cf. P. W. Harkins, *St John Chrysostom: Baptismal Instructions*, pp. 15-18 (*Ancient Christian Writers*, Vol. 31).

[2] But see p. 165, n. 1.

enormously in treatment: Theodore's genius is speculative, Chrysostom was more concerned with stirring the emotions and giving moral instruction.

Both preachers make much of the awe which the sacraments should inspire. In his treatise *On the Priesthood*, Chrysostom elsewhere elaborates upon the awesome aspect of the Eucharist in what seems to modern taste too vivid and literal detail:

Fearful and most awesome were the rites before the coming of grace ...
But if you examine the ceremonies of the age of grace, the old things that seemed so fearful and awesome you will find to be trifles ... When you see the Lord sacrificed and lying [on the altar], and the high priest standing by the victim and praying over it, and everyone stained red with that precious blood, do you feel you are standing on earth among men? Are you not transported at once to heaven?[3]

There are extant three sets of baptismal sermons preached by Chrysostom. The Greek texts have to be sought in three different editions.[4]

The following sermon comes from a collection of eight found in 1955 on Mount Athos. I am grateful to the help of my friend Michael Bossy, S.J., in making this translation.

[3]III.iv.176-177 (PG 48.642). For the application of the concept of awe to the Eucharist, cf. Cyril of Jerusalem, MC 5.9 and E. Bishop, 'Fear and Awe attaching to the Eucharistic Service', in R. H. Connolly, *The Liturgical Homilies of Narsai*, Cambridge Texts and Studies, 1909, pp. 92-97.

[4]*Sources Chrétiennes*, vol. 50, ed. A. Wenger and Vol. 366, ed. A. Piédagnel (the latter homilies sometimes go by the name of the earliest editor A. Papadopoulos-Kerameus); and a homily on baptism included in another series of Chrysostom's sermons, and edited by B. de Montfaucon in PG 49. The sermon translated in the following pages is No. 2 of the Wenger collection. P. W. Harkins, *op. cit.*, translates all three sets. For convenience references to the sermons are given to this omnibus edition, with the initial ACW.

BAPTISMAL HOMILY II

1. Today I am going to speak a few more words to those who have been enrolled[1] among the household of Christ, to teach them the power of the weapons which they are about to receive and the indescribable goodness of the love God shows to the human race. I hope that as a result they may approach him with great faith and confidence and enjoy his generosity more liberally.

God's Generosity even towards Sinners

Consider, my beloved, the abundance of God's goodness from the beginning. For if, without your having worked for it nor shown any qualification, he thinks you worthy of such a gift and pardons all the sins you have committed in your life, what return are you likely to merit from a loving God if after such great kindness you learn to be grateful and determine to make a contribution of your own?

2. In human affairs nothing similar has ever been seen. On the contrary, many men on many occasions, after undergoing many labours and troubles in hope of recompense, return home empty-handed. Those from whom they expected a return have proved ungrateful for all their exertions, or else they have themselves often been snatched away from this world before they could fulfil their own aim. But in the service of our Master we need never suspect anything of the sort. Even before we begin our efforts and offer anything of our own, he forestalls us and shows his own generosity, so that his many kindnesses may induce us to take thought for our own salvation.[2]

3. And so from the very beginning he has never ceased to bless the human race. For as soon as he created the first man, at once he put him to dwell in the garden of Paradise and gave him a life of ease, allowing him the freedom of all that was in the garden except for a single tree. But once the man had

---

[1] They have given in their names; cf. Introduction, pp. 7-9.
[2] We cannot show ourselves worthy of grace without grace. Cf. Ambrose, S 5.10 with note 22.

intemperately allowed himself to be deceived by the woman, he rode roughshod over the command that was given to him and abused the great honour that had been paid him.

4. Here too you see the extent of God's love for man. It would have been just if one who had been so ungrateful for the benefits prepared for him had been judged unworthy of any further pardon and set outside God's providence. Not only did God not do this, but he was like a loving Father with an undisciplined son. In his instinctive love for the boy, he does not measure punishment by the fault; nor does he completely let him go free, but chastises him with moderation so as not to drive him to greater evil and the shipwreck of his life. In the same way God in his goodness expelled man for his great disobedience from this comfortable way of life and condemned him to toil and hardship so as to check his pride for the future in case he should kick over the traces again.[3]

It is almost as if God had said to him:

5. 'This ample ease and freedom which you enjoyed has led you to this act of grave disobedience and has made you forget my commandments. You had nothing to do, and this has given you thoughts above your own nature[4] ("It is idleness that is the teacher of all vices"[5]). Consequently I am condemning you to toil and hardship, so that by working the land you may have a continual reminder of your own disobedience and of the worthlessness of human nature. For since you have had great dreams and refused to remain within your own limits, I order you to go back to the dust from which you have been taken. "You are dust and to dust you shall return".'[6]

6. To increase his sorrow and make him perceive his own fall, God made him dwell not far from Paradise[7] and walled off his

---

[3]The punishment is a blessing in disguise. Ambrose and others said this of the punishment of death, which put a happy limit to man's sinful life (S 2.17). JC's point, however, is that the sense of loss roused the first man to sorrow.

[4]An allusion perhaps to the Greek proverb: 'Being a man one should think human thoughts' (cf. Aristotle, *Nic. Eth.* 1177b32).

[5]Ecclus 33.27.

[6]Gen. 3.19.

[7]This midrashic detail occurs frequently in JC and in the Syriac fathers. Cf. R. Murray, *Symbols of Church and Kingdom*, pp. 221-222.

entry into it, so that the continual sight of what he had forfeited by his heedlessness might serve as a perpetual warning and make him in future more careful to keep the commands that were given to him. For when we do not remember as we should how fortunate we are in the enjoyment of some blessing, as soon as we are deprived of it the sense of loss makes us take great notice of it and increases our distress. And this is just what happened then in the case of the first man.

7. If you wish to learn of the evil demon's treachery and our Master's resourceful plan, consider what the devil has tried to effect in man by his deceit and what kindness our Master and Protector has shown towards man. That evil demon, in envy of man's home in Paradise, by promising him greater hopes, deprived him even of what he had already. In leading him to dream of an equality with God[8] he brought him to the punishment of death. Such are his incitements: he not only deprives us of the blessings we have, but attempts to face us with a fall from a greater height. But even so, God in his love did not abandon the human race. He showed the devil the futility of his attempts and showed man the extent of the care he has for him — through death he gave him immortality. Just think. The devil threw man out of Paradise; the Master brought him into heaven. The profit is greater than the loss.

8. But as I said at the start — and this is the reason for these remarks — God considered that one who was heedless of such blessings was worthy once more of his great kindness. So if you, who are the soldiers of Christ, try to be grateful for these indescribable gifts that are being granted to you and if you are vigilant to preserve them once they are granted, who can say what kindness you will win from him, if you succeed in preserving them? He it was who said: 'To everyone who has will more be given, and he will have abundance.'[9] One who makes himself worthy of what he has already received deserves to enjoy greater blessings still.

---

[8] Cf. Gen. 3.5: 'You will be like God.'
[9] Mt. 25.29.

The Need of Faith

9. I ask all of you who have been found worthy to be inscribed in this heavenly book[10] to bring a generous faith and a firm resolve. What is performed here requires faith and the eyes of the soul: we are not merely to notice what is seen but to go on from this to imagine what cannot be seen.[11] Such is the power of the eyes of faith. The eyes of the body can only see what falls under the sense of sight, but with the eyes of faith it is just the reverse. They see nothing that is visible, but they see what is invisible just as if it lay before their eyes. For faith is the capacity to attend to the invisible as if it were visible. 'Now faith is the assurance of things hoped for, the conviction of things not seen.'[12]

10. What is the meaning of these words? Why have I said that one must not attend to the visible but develop spiritual eyes? I will tell you. I said it so that when you see the font with its water and the hand of the priest touching your head, you will not think that this is mere water nor that it is simply the hand of the bishop[13] that is laid upon your head. It is not a man who performs the rites but the gracious presence of the Spirit who sanctifies the natural properties of the water and who touches your head along with the hand of the priest.[14] I was right, then — was I not? — to speak of the need we have of the eyes of faith if we are to believe in what is unseen instead of despising what our sense perceives.[15]

11. As you know, baptism is a burial and a resurrection: the old self is buried with Christ to sin and the new nature rises from the dead 'which is being renewed after the image of its

---

[10]See note 1.

[11]Cf. Ambrose, S 1.10; 3.12.

[12]Heb. 11.1.

[13]In this paragraph and throughout, the terms 'priest' and 'high priest' apparently both refer to the bishop.

[14]Ambrose (S 1.15) and Theodore (BH 3.9) explain that it is the bishop's blessing of the water which makes the Holy Spirit present in the baptismal water. Cf. sect. 25-26 of the present homily, with note 37.

[15]Ambrose (S 1.9ff.) uses Naaman's contempt of the Jordan to illustrate the sense of anti-climax the candidate may feel when he sees the font.

creator.'[16] We are stripped and we are clothed,[17] stripped of the old garment which has been soiled by the multitude of our sins, clothed with the new that is free from all stain. What does this mean? We are clothed in Christ himself. St Paul remarks: 'As many of you as were baptized into Christ have put on Christ.'[18]

Exorcisms

12. Since you are on the threshold of the time when you are to receive these great gifts, I must now teach you, as far as I can, the meaning of each of the rites, so that you may go from here with knowledge and a more assured faith. So you need to know why it is that after the daily instruction we send you off to hear the words of the exorcists.[19] This rite is neither a simple one nor a pointless. You are about to receive the heavenly King into your house. So those who are appointed for this task, just as if they were preparing a house for a royal visit, take you on one side after our sermon, and purify your minds by those fearful words, putting to flight all the tricks of the evil one, and so make the house fit for the presence of the King. For no demon, however fierce and harsh, after these fearful words and the invocation of the universal Lord of all things, can refrain from flight with all speed. And, in addition, the rite imprints great reverence in the soul and leads it to great sorrow for sin.

13. The wonderful, unbelievable thing is that every difference and distinction of rank is missing here. If anyone happens to be in a position of worldly importance or conspicuous wealth, if he boasts of his birth or the glory of this present life, he stands on just the same footing as the beggar in rags, the blind man or the lame. Nor does he complain at this since he knows that all such differences have been set aside in the life of the spirit; a grateful heart is the only requirement.

[16]Col. 3.10; cf. Rom. 6.4, 6.

[17]A reference to the stripping before baptism, which he mentions without comment in sect. 24. Cf. Introduction, p. 21.

[18]Gal. 3.27.

[19]Cf. Introduction, pp. 9-11.

14. Such is the effect of these marvellous, awesome words and invocations. But something else is made known to us by the outward attitude — the bare feet and the outstretched hands. Just as those who suffer bodily captivity show by the appearance they present their dejection at the disaster that has struck them, so do those men who have been captives of the devil. As they are about to be freed from his tyranny and go beneath the yoke that is easy,[20] first of all they remind themselves by their appearance of their previous situation[21] and try to understand what they are being saved from and what they are hastening to. This then becomes for them a reason for greater gratitude and thankfulness.

The Duties of Sponsors

15. Will you allow me now to address some words to your sponsors[22] so that they may know the rewards they are worthy of if they show great care for you and the punishment that will ensue if they become negligent? Consider this, my beloved. Those who act as guarantors for money accept a greater responsibility than the debtor who receives the money. If the borrower proves generous he lightens the load of the guarantor, but if not he prepares a greater crash for him. It is for this reason that the Wise Man offers his advice: 'If you offer yourself as surety, be concerned as one who must pay.'[23] If those who stand as surety for money are responsible for the full sum, those who guarantee that others will pay their account of virtue in matters of the spirit have an even greater duty to show vigilance, advising, counselling, correcting with a paternal affection.

16. They should not consider that what they are doing is a routine action. Rather they should be fully aware that they will share the credit if they guide their charges to the path of virtue by their advice, but that if they are negligent, then grave

---

[20]Cf. Mt. 11.30: 'My yoke is easy, and my burden is light.'

[21]In another sermon (ACW 10.14-15) JC explains in greater detail how this posture denotes captivity. He adds there the detail that the candidate, like the captive, is stripped. Cf. Introduction, p 10.

[22]On the sponsors, cf. Theodore, BH 2.19.

[23]Ecclus. 8.13.

condemnation will fall upon them. For this reason it is the custom to call them 'spiritual fathers', in order that they may learn from their office the affection they owe to their charges in giving them spiritual instruction. For if it is a noble thing to lead those who are in no way connected with us to a desire of virtue, we have a much greater duty to fulfil this obligation to one whom we have received to the position of our spiritual son. To sum up, negligence brings no small danger to those of you who are acting as sponsors.

Renunciation of Sin and Profession of Faith

17. I turn now to the sacraments and the covenant between yourself and the Lord into which you are about to enter. In business, when a man wishes to entrust his affairs to another, it is necessary for a contract[24] to be signed between the two parties. The same is true now, when the Lord of all things is about to entrust to you affairs that are not mortal and passing away and decaying, but spiritual and heavenly. The contract is also called a pledge of faith,[25] since we are doing nothing that can be seen but everything can be discerned by the eyes of the spirit. Meanwhile it is necessary for the contract to be signed, not with ink on paper but with the spirit in God. The words that you pronounce are inscribed in heaven, the agreement spoken by your lips remains indelibly before God.

18. Now consider once again the posture of captivity. The priests who introduce you first of all tell you to kneel down and pray with your hands raised to heaven, and by this attitude of body recall to your mind the one from whom you have been delivered and the other whom you are about to join. After that the priest approaches each in turn and demands your contracts and confessions[26] and instructs each one to pronounce those fearful and awesome words: *I renounce you, Satan.*

[24]Ambrose also regards the Renunciation as a contract (S 1.5). Cf. Introduction, p. 20.

[25]JC uses the word 'faith' in two senses: (1) a pledge; (2) belief. Ambrose has a similar play on words in S 1.8.

[26]In Cyril the 'contract' takes the form of a confession of faith (MC 1.9). Although JC gives an explicit 'contract' (sect. 21), perhaps a confession of faith follows; cf. Harkins, *op. cit.*, p. 222, note 39.

19. Tears and deep sighs now force themselves upon me. I have recalled the day on which I too was judged worthy to pronounce these words. As I reckon up the weight of the sins which I have gathered from that day to this, I am confused in mind and stung in conscience as I reflect upon the shame with which I have covered myself by my subsequent negligence. And so I beg all of you to show some generosity towards me, and since you are about to approach our king — he will receive you with great alacrity, he will dress you in the royal robe[27] and will grant every kind of gift that you desire, at least if you seek spiritual gifts[28] — beg a favour for me too. Pray that God may not ask an account of my sins but grant me pardon, and for the future count me worthy of his support. I have no doubt that you will do this in your affection for your teachers.

20. But I must not allow myself to lose the thread of my argument any more. The priest then instructs you to say, *I renounce you, Satan, your pomp, your worship and your works.* There is great power in these few words. For the angels who are present and the invisible powers rejoice at your conversion and, receiving the words from your lips, carry them to the common master of all things, where they are inscribed in the books of heaven.

21. Have you seen the terms of the contract? After the renunciation of the Evil One and all the works he delights in, the priest instructs you to speak again as follows: *And I pledge myself,*[29] *Christ, to you.* Do you see the overwhelming goodness of God? From you he receives only words, yet he entrusts to you realities, a great treasure. He forgets your past ingratitude; he remembers nothing of your past; he is content with these few words.

---

[27]Probably an allusion to the Baptismal Garment. JC only hints at it in this sermon here and when he describes the rite of baptism (sect. 25 and 27). There is however an unmistakable reference to the Garment in a later sermon of this series: 'They [the newly-baptized] have put on the royal robe; they almost outshine the sky and appear brighter than the stars' (ACW 4.3; cf. Introduction, pp. 31-33).

[28]'Earnestly desire the spiritual gifts' (1 Cor. 14.1).

[29]Cf. Introduction, pp. 20-21. The Greek word *suntassomai* can mean simply 'I pledge myself; I make a contract', but sect. 22 shows that JC also took it to mean 'I enlist'.

Anointing with Chrism

22. Then once you have made this covenant, this renunciation and contract, since you have confessed his sovereignty over you and pronounced the words by which you pledge yourself to Christ, you are now a soldier and have signed on for a spiritual contest. Accordingly the bishop[30] anoints you on the forehead with spiritual myron,[31] placing a seal on your head and saying: *N. is anointed in the name of the Father, the Son and the Holy Spirit.*

23. Now the bishop knows that the Enemy is enraged and is sharpening his teeth going around like a roaring lion,[32] seeing that the former victims of his tyranny have suddenly defected. Renouncing him, they have changed their allegiance and publicly enlisted with Christ. It is for this reason that the bishop anoints you on your forehead and marks you with the seal, to make the devil turn away his eyes. He does not dare to look at you directly because he sees the light blazing from your head and blinding his eyes. From that day onwards you will confront him in battle, and this is why the bishop anoints you as athletes of Christ before leading you into the spiritual arena.[33]

Stripping and Anointing with Oil [34]

24. Then after this at the appointed hour of the night, he strips you of all your clothes, and as if he were about to lead you

---

[30]The words 'the bishop' do not appear in the Greek in sections 22-23.

[31]In JC the anointing with chrism precedes the anointing with olive-oil. See Introduction, pp. 28-29. JC does not connect the 'seal' with the gift of the Holy Spirit. For the 'seal', cf. Introduction, pp. 36-38.

[32]Cf. 1 Pet. 5.8.

[33]In these sections JC confuses the metaphors of the soldier and the athlete. The effect of this anointing is to imprint a mark which shows that the new Christian belongs to Christ and also keeps the devil at a distance. JC overlooks here the 'messianic' significance of the anointing; cf. Introduction, p. 28.

[34]When he describes this rite in another series of homilies (ACW 11.27; Whitaker, p. 37), the more obvious interpretation of the Greek suggests that chrism is used; however it is possible that *touto to aleimma* means 'the latter unguent' (i.e. olive oil), rather than 'this same unguent' (i.e. chrism). In BH 2.24 the material is described as 'spiritual (olive) oil'. Evidently there is a considerable interval after the anointing with chrism; the candidates leave the church and return later for the rest of the ceremonies. In another sermon of a different series

into heaven itself by means of these rites,[35] he prepares to anoint your whole body with this spiritual oil so that his unction may armour all your limbs and make them invulnerable to any weapons the Enemy may hurl.

Baptism

25. After this anointing he takes you down into the sacred waters, at the same time burying the old nature and raising 'the new creature, which is being renewed after the image of the creator'.[36] Then by the words of the priest and by his hand the presence of the Holy Spirit flies down upon you[37] and another man comes up out of the font, one washed from all the stain of his sins, who has put off the old garment of sin and is clothed in the royal robe.[38]

26. To give you a further lesson that the substance of the Father, the Son and the Spirit is one,[39] baptism is conferred in

JC states explicitly that the renunciation etc. takes place on the Friday (ACW 11.19. Cf. Harkins, *op. cit.*, pp. 221-222; Wenger, *op. cit.*, pp. 79-80). In our sermon, however, although there is no explicit day allotted to the renunciation, the lack of any indication of a change of day leaves a strong impression that the renunciation is made on Saturday. Hippolytus also gives an interval in the ceremonies, which is spent in prayer, presumably in the church (*Ap. Trad.* 20.9). Hippolytus, however, divides the ceremonies at a different point.

The Greek does not specify who performs the stripping and the anointing. The bishop probably delegated this menial and messy office to a deacon or a priest, as in Ambrose's rite (S 1.4), or perhaps in the case of women to a deaconess (cf. Harkins, *op. cit.*, p. 225).

[35]This language is reminiscent of that of the Mystery Religions. Cf. Introduction, pp. 63-66.

[36]Col. 3.10. Cf. Rom. 6.4; Col. 2.12.

[37]JC's rite contains no specific sacrament for the giving of the Holy Spirit: cf. Theodore, BH 3.27 with note 65. This seems to have been the original pattern for initiation in the Syrian churches; cf. Introduction, pp. 37-38. The terms in which JC describes the Holy Spirit descending or flying down on (*epiphoitesis, ephiptatai*) the candidate resemble the terms which other authors apply to the descent of the Holy Spirit (or the whole Trinity) on the *water* (Ambrose, S 1.15; Theodore, BH 3.9) or the *bread and wine* (Cyril, MC 5.19) in response to the epiclesis. The conclusion is inescapable that for Chrysostom it is baptism which is the moment when the Holy Spirit is received. So too in section 10, the Spirit both sanctifies the water and touches the candidate's head at the same time as the bishop does so.

[38]See note 27.

[39]A piece of polemic against heretics who deny the full divinity of the Son and the Holy Spirit. Theodore (BH 3.20ff.) and, less explicitly, Ambrose (S 1.19; cf. 6.5-

this form. As the priest pronounced the words, *N. is baptized in the name of the Father and of the Son and of the Holy Spirit,* he plunges your head into the water and lifts it up again three times, by this sacred rite preparing you to receive the descent of the Holy Spirit. For the priest is not the only one who touches your head; Christ also touches it with his right hand. This is shown by the actual words of the one who baptizes you. He does not say, 'I baptize N.', but rather, 'N. is baptized'. This shows that he is only the minister of the grace and merely lends his hand since he has been ordained for this by the Spirit. It is the Father, Son and Holy Spirit, the indivisible Trinity, who bring the whole rite to completion. It is faith in the Trinity that bestows the grace of remission of sin, and the confession of the Trinity that grants us the adoption of sons.[40]

The Greeting

27. The ceremonies that follow are well able to teach us the afflictions from which those who have been counted worthy to receive this sacred rite have been set free and the blessings which they have been granted. As soon as they come up from those sacred waters all present embrace them, greet them, kiss them, congratulate and rejoice with them, because those who

9) also take the opportunity that this part of the ceremony affords to develop a similar argument. The Council of Nicaea (A.D. 325) had only defined the Father and Son to be of one substance (*homoousioi*); JC says the same of the Holy Spirit.

JC's argument is not worked out as thoroughly as Theodore's. His thought seems to be that the fact that the three Persons share one substance is shown by: (1) the three immersions coupled with one trinitarian formula; (2) the part played by the Son (whose minister the bishop is) and the Holy Spirit (who ordained the bishop).

[40]The mention of a 'confession of the Trinity' suggests that the candidate makes a profession of faith at the moment of immersion, as in Cyril (MC 2.4), Ambrose (S 2.20) and the *Ap. Trad.* (21.12-18). However in no contemporary source is there evidence for the use of *both* the minister's declaration ('I baptize you' or 'N. is baptized') *and* the profession of faith by the candidate during immersion. JC's words should therefore be taken to mean what Theodore says more explicitly: the bishop professes faith in the Trinity when he says 'N. is baptized in the name' (BH 3.15-16); the candidate subscribes to this profession by bowing down under the water (3.18-19).

before were slaves and prisoners have all at once become free men and sons who are invited to the royal table. For as soon as they come up from the font, they are led to the awesome[41] table which is laden with all good things. They taste the body and blood of the Lord and become the dwelling place of the Spirit;[42] since they have put on Christ, they go about appearing everywhere like angels on earth and shining as brightly as the rays of the sun.[43]

Conclusion

28. It is not without good reason and careful thought that I have explained all these things to you in advance, my loving people. Even before you actually enjoy them, I wanted you to feel great pleasure as you fly on the wings of hope.[44] I wanted you to take up a disposition of soul worthy of the rite and, as the blessed Paul advised you, to 'set your mind on things that are above',[45] raising your thoughts from earth to heaven, from the visible to the invisible. We see such things more clearly with the eyes of the spirit than the perceptions of the senses.

29. But since you have come near the royal entrance-hall and are about to approach the very throne where the king sits distributing his gifts, show complete unselfishness in your requests. Ask for nothing worldly or natural, but make a request that is worthy of the giver. As you step out of the sacred waters and express your resurrection by the act of coming up from them, ask for alliance with him so that you may show great vigilance in guarding what has been given to you, and so be immune from the tricks of the Enemy. Pray for the peace of the Churches. Intercede for those who are still wandering. Fall on your knees for those who are in sin so that we may deserve some

---

[41]JC applies the language of awe more fully in his sermon *On the Priesthood* (quoted on p. 151).

[42]Again JC associates the gift of the Holy Spirit not with a specific rite of confirmation, but with another part of the initiation.

[43]Cf. Mt. 13.43. Another oblique reference to the White Garment; see note 27.

[44]Contrast this passage with the reasons given by Cyril (MC 1.1) and Ambrose (S 1.1) for not explaining baptism until after it has been received.

[45]Col. 3.2.

pardon. You were once diffident; God has given you great assurance. You were once slaves; he has enrolled you among the chief of his friends. You were once captives; he has raised you up and adopted you as sons. He will not refuse your demands; he will grant them all, true again in this to his own goodness.

30. In this way too you will draw God to still greater kindness. When he sees you showing such concern for those who are your own members[46] and anxious about the salvation of others, because of this he will count you worthy to receive great assurance. Nothing so warms his heart as our compassion for our members and the affection that we show for our brothers, the great forethought we show for the salvation of our neighbour.

31. And so, dearly beloved, in this knowledge, prepare yourselves with joy and spiritual delight to receive this grace so that you may enjoy the gift in its abundance. And so may we all together, living lives that are in keeping with the grace we have received, be counted worthy to win the eternal and indescribable blessings through the grace and loving kindness of our Lord Jesus Christ with whom to the Father and the Holy Spirit be glory, power, honour now and always, for ever and ever. Amen.

[46]'We are members one of another' (Eph. 4.25).

THEODORE OF MOPSUESTIA

Theodore was ordained at Antioch about 383, and served there as a priest until in 392 he became Bishop of Mopsuestia, a town some 100 miles away, where he remained until his death in 428. It was probably during his time at Antioch that he preached the 16 catechetical sermons.[1] He was a perceptive and imaginative theological thinker, and was the source from which Nestorius derived much of his terminology and ideas.

By the last decades of the fourth century a marked cleavage had developed between the theology current at Alexandria and Antioch. The two schools followed different methods in explaining scripture, the Antiochenes favouring the more literal sense against the allegorical interpretations of the Alexandrians; but it was in the field of Christology that the divergence was most pronounced. The Alexandrian tendency (exemplified by both the Doctor of the Church Athanasius, as well as the heretic Apollinarius, whose thought was subject to Alexandrian influences though his home was in Asia Minor) was to assume that the eternal Word replaced or made irrelevant some of the faculties of Jesus' human soul; this viewpoint had the advantage of emphasising the unity of the divine and human natures, but at the cost of the completeness of the humanity. The Antiochenes, on the other hand, stressed the completeness of Jesus' human nature, with the result, however, that they had difficulty in explaining the union of the divine and human natures except in terms which could apply to any saint. Theodore, for example, preferred to speak of the Word 'assuming a *man*' (cf. BH 3.21, 24; 5.2, 10) rather than 'becoming *flesh*', thus preparing the way for the Nestorian heresy[2] that

---

[1]For the indications, which are far from conclusive, that these sermons were preached at Antioch, not Mopsuestia, see R. Tonneau and R. Devreesse, *Homilies Catéchetiques*, Studi e Testi 145 (1949) p. xvi. If this theory is correct, it is surprising that, although the two sets of rites described by Theodore and his friend Chrysostom are on most points identical, there are some significant differences, viz. with regard to the Renunciation and Profession of Faith, and the Gift of the Spirit. On this last point, see Theodore, BH 3.27, note 65, last paragraph.

[2]Though whether Nestorius himself was 'Nestorian' in this sense is a much discussed question.

Christ consisted of two persons, a human and a divine, united in moral union and functional collaboration. The Christological orthodoxy of Theodore is much debated, and is hard to establish because of the systematic destruction to which his writings were submitted after his condemnation. A set of commentaries on St Paul's Epistles, and fragments from a very influential work on the Incarnation,[3] did however escape destruction. R. A. Greer and J. N. D. Kelly both defend him;[4] on the evidence of the BH they seem to be right.

But whatever the verdict should be, there remain elements in his thought which the present age finds congenial and stimulating. His emphasis on the resurrection in connection with the Mass and the redemption, and his perception of the eschatological role of sacraments, which are only the first instalment of our heavenly destiny, have inspired some of the modern thinking in the liturgical and catechetical movements. However, it is generally agreed that his allegorization of the ceremonies of the Mass, so that, e.g., the Offertory Procession is made to represent the leading of Jesus to Calvary, distracts from the true understanding of the eucharistic action.

Among Theodore's works which perished after the condemnation in the sixth century was the Greek original of these catechetical sermons. They survive only in Syriac translation. The English version printed in this collection is based on the French translation of R. Tonneau,[5] and owes much to the assistance of my friend Robert Murray, S.J., who checked my version against the Syriac.

Theodore has many merits, but conciseness is not one of them. His work occupies a disproportionate amount of space in this book, and the imbalance would have been even more pronounced if I had not allowed myself a certain liberty in

---

[3] A long extract from the *de Incarnatione* is readily available in English in M. Wiles and M. Santer, *Documents in Early Christian Thought*, Cambridge, 1975, pp. 57-61.

[4] R. A. Greer, *Theodore of Mopsuestia, Exegete and Theologian*, London 1961. J. N. D. Kelly, *Early Christian Doctrines*, London, 4th ed. 1968, pp. 303-309.

[5] See note 1. It was not until 1932-1933 that the Syriac text was first published by A. Mingana; it is accompanied by an English translation (Woodbrooke Studies 5 and 6, Cambridge 1932-3).

removing some of his repetitions. Many otiose adjectives and similar insignificant flourishes have been dropped without indication. But I have used two signs to mark larger omissions. Dots indicate that some words have been omitted between sentences as they appear in the English. An asterisk means that I have compressed the expression within a sentence. I trust this license does no violence to Theodore's thought. The saving in space and, more important, the avoidance of some turgidity should provide ample compensation.

The first eleven of the catechetical sermons are the Lenten instructions given to the candidates for baptism. The last five (called here *Baptismal Homilies*) teach the candidate the meaning of the sacraments of initiation. The first, which deals with preliminaries, is not included in this collection. The second and third explain the ceremonies connected with baptism; the fourth and fifth explain the Eucharist.[6] Unlike Cyril and Ambrose, who required the candidate to be baptized before hearing an explanation of the sacrament, Theodore and John Chrysostom explain baptism in advance; but in all four sets of sermons the instruction on the Eucharist is held back until after the neophyte's baptism and first communion.

[6]There is unfortunately a confusing variety of systems for numbering these few sermons. Numbered 2-5 here, they bear the numbers 13-16 in Tonneau's edition, and 3-6 in Mingana's and in Whitaker.

BAPTISMAL HOMILY II

Synopsis[1] — You stand again on sackcloth, bare-footed, with your outer garment removed and your hands stretched out to God in the attitude of prayer. First you fall on your knees, holding the rest of your body upright. Then you say, 'I renounce Satan, all his angels, all his works, all his service, all his vanity and all his worldly enticements. I pledge myself by vow, I believe and I am baptized in the name of the Father, of the Son and of the Holy Spirit.' Kneeling on the ground, but with the rest of your body upright, you look up to heaven and stretch out your hands in the attitude of prayer. The bishop, wearing light, shining vestments of linen, signs your forehead with the oil of anointing, saying: 'N. is signed in the name of the Father and of the Son and of the Holy Spirit.' Your sponsor, standing behind you, spreads a linen stole over your head and raises you to your feet.

Preliminary Rites

1. I have already instructed you sufficiently about the rites which according to ancient tradition the candidates for baptism must celebrate. When you present yourselves to give in your names, in the hope of finding a dwelling-place in heaven, the exorcisms are, so to say, a law-suit with the devil; you are freed from slavery to him by God's judgment. So you recite the words of the Creed and the Lord's Prayer;[2] and there and then through the mediation of the bishops you make an undertaking to persevere in love towards God's being. This undertaking will be the source of wonderful blessings for you if you think about his being in the right way — that is to say if you believe that it is Father, Son and Holy Spirit[3] — and if you live in this world

---

[1]The 'synopsis' with which each homily begins seems to be a summary of what follows, rather than a quotation from some kind of Ritual.

[2]The names are given in in the course of a rite of Election or Enrolment; see Introduction, p. 7ff. For the Recitation of the Creed and of the Lord's Prayer, see Introduction, pp. 12-14.

[3]Theodore has in mind the heresies which denied the divinity of the Son (Arianism) and of the Holy Spirit (Pneumatomachianism). The condemnation of the latter at the Council of Constantinople was as recent as 381.

as far as you are able in a way which befits people who have a dwelling-place in heaven. But now you need to learn what takes place in the mystery itself ...

Renunciation of Sin

2. *You stand again on sackcloth, bare-footed, with your outer garment removed and your hands stretched out to God in the attitude of prayer.* In all this you adopt the posture of the exorcism[4] by which you symbolized your former captivity and slavery to the Tyrant, which was your severe punishment. For it is appropriate that you should abandon this posture and these memories before you approach the mystery which promises a share in the good things to come ...

3. *First you fall on your knees, but keep the rest of your body upright.* You stretch out your hands to God in the attitude of one at prayer. For we have fallen into sin and the sentence of death has thrown us to the ground; but, as St Paul said, 'at the name of Jesus Christ the knee should bow, and confess in praise of God his Father that Jesus Christ is Lord'.[5] By this confession we show what the divine nature bestows on us through the administration[6] of Christ our Lord, whom it raised up to heaven as Lord of the Universe and 'pioneer of our salvation'.[7] It remains then for all of us, who in St Paul's words have 'fallen to the ground',[8] to attain this. So you are called by faith in Christ our Lord to share through the mystery in these indescribable benefits; you must kneel as a sign of your ancient fall and adore God, the source of good.

4. *The rest of your body should remain upright,* looking up to heaven. By this attitude you present, so to speak, a request to God, asking him like a petitioner for liberation from your ancient fall and a share in the joys of heaven. While you are

---

[4]For T's rites of exorcism, see Introduction, p. 9f.

[5]Phil. 2.10-11 (adapted).

[6]The underlying Greek word (*oikonomia*) means 'management' (literally 'housekeeping'), and comes to refer to the Incarnation, by which God the Son 'arranges' his influence on human history.

[7]Heb. 2.10.

[8]Acts 26.14.

kneeling like this the appointed ministers come and address to you in effect the very words which the angel who appeared to St Cornelius spoke to him:[9] 'Your prayers have been heard.' God has had regard for the tribulations that have gripped you from the beginning and pitied you for your long, cruel service as a slave to the Tyrant. He has deigned to deliver you from this slavery and to give you a share in the indescribable gifts of heaven, so that once you have received them you will be completely free from evil* ...[10] What is the undertaking that you make at this moment which releases you from your long-standing ills and gives you a share in the gifts you hope for?

5. *'I renounce Satan and all his angels, all his service, all his vanity and all his worldly enticements. I pledge myself by vow, I believe, I am baptized in the name of the Father, of the Son and of the Holy Spirit.'* Now the deacons come to you and tell you to recite these words. The time has come for me to explain to you their efficacy, so that you may know the force of the undertaking which opens the way to the enjoyment of such a gift. Once, beginning with the first members of your race, you obeyed the devil, and he inflicted on you many great tribulations.[11] So you must promise to turn away from him now that you have experienced suffering at his hands. That is why you say, 'I renounce Satan'. Up till now, even if you had wished, you would not have dared to speak these words, frightened and enslaved as you were. But now that the divine judgment has granted you your liberty through the exorcisms, you recover your voice and boldly proclaim that you

---

[9]Cf. Acts 10.4.

[10]The preacher wishes to prepare the minds of his congregation so that baptism will cause a profound conversion in their lives, and so allows himself to leave the impression that evil will now have no influence or attraction for them.

[11]Because of the unity of the human race Theodore, like many other Fathers, says that 'you' or 'we' fell. The language is deliberately ambiguous: he means not only that all mankind was affected by Adam's sin, but also that each individual is personally associated in the guilt of his sin. It was rare for the Fathers to attempt to answer the question that seems to later theologians to expose the weakness of this theory of original sin: how can later generations incur the guilt of Adam's disobedience? The next section, however, suggests that Theodore also accepts another explanation of original sin: we do not simply inherit the effects of Adam's sin, but 'freely submit to the devil' subscribing to Adam's sin by our own personal sins. Cf. BH 3.11.

renounce him ... At the same time you show that you have so far been associated with him, but that you are parting with him now; for no one claims to renounce a thing if he has never had anything to do with it ...

6. Hardly for a moment have you realized the harm you suffered from your familiarity with him, hardly have you received the power to recover from it, when you have to say, 'I renounce Satan'. By this you mean: Now we have nothing in common with him. I have hardly realized the evils in which he tried to involve us every day; hardly understood the extent of the harm suffered by Adam, the father of us all, when he listened to the devil, the extent of the ills he incurred, together with those who freely submitted themselves to the devil and down the years chose to become his slaves. But now that a great and marvellous grace has appeared[12] through Christ himself, a grace that has freed us from the Tyrant's oppression, liberated us from this slavery, won for us good things in wonderful abundance — now I know my benefactor, I recognise my Saviour. For truly my benefactor is my Saviour, who created me when I was not, who grants me favours every day, who does not turn away from me even when I rebel ... Once for all I renounce Satan, I avoid his company and pledge myself by vow never to seek it again. I shall have nothing to do with him, I shall avoid him like a dangerous enemy, for he was the cause of evils without number ... This is the meaning of 'I renounce'.

7. If Satan made war on us single-handed, if he were the only one to harm us, this expression 'I renounce' would be sufficient, for it would prevent you from accepting his friendship.* But, invisible though he is, he can attack us with visible weapons, by means of men whom he has conquered and made instruments of his malice to harm others. That is why you add, 'And all his angels'.

8. 'His angels' are men who have contracted from him some ill-will which leads them to harm others. Originally, since no one had yet fallen so as to become a ready tool for injuring others, the serpent was the instrument he used to beguile and

---

[12]Cf. 2 Tim. 1.9-10.

ruin men. But once he has men in his trap, he always uses those whom he finds suitable for his purpose of harming others. This is what St Paul meant when he said: 'I am afraid that as the serpent deceived Eve by his cunning, your minds will be led astray from a sincere devotion to Christ'[13] ... This is why, after saying, 'I renounce Satan', you add, 'and all his angels'. By Satan's angels you mean all those who carry out his purpose of ruining and deceiving the human race. We must take 'angels of Satan' to refer to all those who devote themselves to profane wisdom and spread the error of paganism. 'Angels of Satan' are poets whose stories promote idolatry and whose 'wisdom' supports the error of paganism ... 'Angels of Satan' are leaders of heresies who, since the coming of Christ our Lord, have in Christ's name taught ungodly dreams and presented them to the world. Mani, Marcion, Valentinus[14] were 'angels of Satan', who dissociated visible things from the creative power of God; visible things, they said, owe their existence to another principle apart from God. Paul of Samosata[15] was an 'angel of Satan'; he taught that Christ our Lord was a mere man, and denied the individuality of the divinity of the Only-Begotten Son that existed before time began. Arius and Eunomius[16] were 'angels

---

[13]2 Cor. 11.3 (adapted).

[14]Mani (c. 216-c. 277) was the Persian prophet whose followers, the Manichees, St Augustine joined for a while in his youth. The central doctrine of the sect was its dualistic belief in two Creators, one good, one evil. Matter was the creation of the evil principle: man is a spiritual spark imprisoned in evil matter. Marcion (fl. 140) separated the vindictive Creator, who was the God of the Old Testament, from the God of Love who revealed himself in Christ. Valentinus, a contemporary of Marcion's, in order to insulate God from contact with matter, postulated a descending hierarchy of spirits emanating from God; only the inferior spirits have any contact with material creation. Mani, Marcion and Valentinus agree in teaching that matter is too sordid to be the concern of the Almighty; therefore other deities or spirits must be responsible for it.

[15]Paul of Samosata's teaching is not available to us in any impartial source, but he seems to have held erroneous views about the Trinity and the Person of Christ. With regard to the Trinity he is said to have taught that only the Father had a substantial existence; the Word was simply the Father's will, and the Spirit his grace dwelling in men. Christ was a mere man inspired by the Word (cf. J. N. D. Kelly, *Doctrines*, pp. 117-118; 158). Paul was condemned at the Synod of Antioch in 268.

[16]Arius' (d. 336) heresy arose from an attempt to reconcile the unity of God with the distinction between the Father and the Son. Since God is one, he taught, the

of Satan'. They dared to say that the nature of the divinity of the Only-Begotten Son is created and did not exist from the beginning, but according to the law of nature passed from nothingness to a state of becoming. They copy the pagan myths and assert that the Son's substance is created, and yet, like the pagans, say they believe him to be God by nature. They imitate the childishness of the Jews, who do not recognize that the Son came from the Father and exists without beginning by his Father's substance, true Son that he is; instead they say he is Son in the sense in which the Jews call men sons of God, who hold the rank of sons by grace and not by their substance.

9. Apollinarius[17] was another 'angel of Satan'. He gave a false interpretation to belief in the Father, the Son and the Holy Spirit; in the guise of orthodoxy he declared our salvation to be imperfect, maintaining that Christ did not assume a human intelligence, so that, unlike our body, our intelligence does not receive a share of grace. 'Angels of Satan' are the leaders and teachers of error in any heresy, honoured though they may be with the name of bishop or priest; they all serve Satan's purposes, and in the name of their position in the Church fall headlong into error.* Other 'angels of Satan' again are those who give men any wicked, shameful advice against the divine laws, so as to lead them into the service of evil. All these you have promised to renounce; so you ought to have nothing to do with them in future. You have presented yourself to Christ; you have been enrolled in God's Church; being born in baptism you look forward to becoming the body and member

Son must be a creature, created in time, though he can be called divine 'by grace'. The Council of Nicaea (325) had declared in its Creed, against Arius, that the Son was 'one in substance' with the Father, but almost immediately a reaction set in against this unscriptural term. One heretical school of thought, led by Eunomius (d. c. 394), held that the Son was 'unlike' the Father, and inferior to him, though the Father was able to confer true divinity upon him.

[17]Apollinarius (d. c. 390) tried to explain the union of the human and divine elements in Christ by maintaining that the divinity took the place of the rational soul. This view was quickly rejected by the Church, among other reasons because it made the redemption impossible. The Son redeemed us by assuming our nature; but sin lies precisely in the rational soul that Apollinarius maintained the Son did not assume. Gregory of Nazianzus' slogan, 'What is not assumed is not restored', pin-points the weakness of Apollinarius' theory.

of Christ our Lord; you will share with him and be attached to him, your Head, and keep apart from all those who dare to abandon the Church's creed.

10. When you have said, 'I renounce Satan and all his angels', you continue, 'and all his service'. It is not only men who are in the Evil One's service; you must also recoil in horror from the open blasphemies done in the name of religion. All pagan practices are works of Satan: not only sacrifices and idolatry and all the old cult, but everything that derives from it and corrupts the soul. The pursuit of astrology is clearly the service of Satan — the scrutiny of the movements of the sun, the moon and the stars before beginning a journey or undertaking any business, and the belief that their course can help or harm us; in short, the study of the movement of the stars in the hope of learning the future from them is clearly the service of Satan ... Ritual washings and purifications, amulets, the practice of hanging up fermenting dough, the inspection of the bodies of animals or the movement and cries of birds[18] — all such things are the service of Satan. To put your trust in any Jewish observances is service of Satan. The worship found among heretics in the name of religion is service of Satan. It may bear a superficial resemblance to the worship of the Church, but it lacks the gift of the grace of the Holy Spirit, and it is wicked to perform it.[19] It follows that it is service of the devil and illustrates our Lord's saying: 'Not everyone who says to me, "Lord, Lord," shall enter the kingdom of heaven, but he who does the will of my Father who is in heaven.'[20] For surely it is useless to invoke our Lord with an ungodly mind and in the company of the ungodly ... Just as in the theatre the actors who play the part of kings are not taken for real kings despite their

[18]In Roman society there were officials appointed to predict the future from their study of natural phenomena: the *auspex* derived omens from the behaviour of birds, the *haruspex* from the formation of a slaughtered animal's entrails. The use of fermenting dough as a charm or means of divination is not elsewhere attested, so far as I know.

[19]It is only comparatively recently that most Christians have become convinced that there can be heretics in good faith, whose worship is a channel of grace, and who are not without the grace of the Holy Spirit.

[20]Mt. 7.21.

royal appearance — we know this is only play-acting; appearances do not blind our eyes to the reality — so too the rites that the heretics perform in the name of religion, whether they be baptism, the Eucharist or anything else, are play-acting and the service of Satan. We should recoil from it, for its purpose is evil.*

11. Then you say: 'And all his vanity'. Satan's vanity is a plain description of everything pagans do in the name of religion; all those actions they flaunted in the eyes of the world they performed out of vanity to dazzle the spectators and lead them astray. Today the grace of God has abolished all this, but we must be no less chary of the rites of the heretics. When Satan saw that the name of Christ had put an end to the error of paganism, he at once took other steps to lead men astray. He devised heresies and raised up their leaders to imitate the Church's invocations and outward forms, and so deceive the simple and lead them to damnation.

12. Next you say: 'And all his worldly enticements'. What do you mean by 'worldly enticements'? The theatre, the circus, the stadium, athletics, songs, organ-playing, dances — seeds which the devil sows in the world in the guise of amusement to lead men's souls to ruin. It is easy to see the dangers such pursuits hold for men's souls. You must avoid such things if you share in the Mystery of the New Covenant, if you have enrolled as a citizen of heaven, a fellow-heir of the blessings to come,[21] if you hope that, being born again in baptism, you will henceforth become a member of Christ our Lord, our common Head, in Heaven. We, his members, must live lives that are worthy of him. That is why at this moment, in the attitude I have described, you pronounce these vows ...

Profession of Faith

13. When you say, 'I renounce', you reject Satan without reserve and show that you will never turn back or take pleasure again in his company; so too, when you say, 'I pledge myself by vow', you show that you will stand firm and unshakable at God's

[21]Cf. Phil 3.20; Rom. 8.17.

side, that you will never on any account abandon him, and that for the rest of your life you will value more than anything else the privilege of living in company with him and in accordance with his laws.*

14. But you must also add, 'I believe', for, as St Paul said, 'whoever would draw near to God must believe that he exists'.[22] Since God is invisible by nature, to face him and promise to persevere as members of his household you need faith. The blessings that God is preparing for us in heaven by the administration[23] of Christ our Lord, the blessings that we hope for when we present ourselves for baptism — these are invisible and indescribable too. For this reason too we must have faith in the invisible blessings in store for us ... That is why the words, 'I believe', are followed by the words, 'I am baptized'. For it is with faith in what is to take place that you came forward to receive the holy gift of baptism; you mean to be reborn, to die with Christ and rise again with him, in order that this second birth may replace your first and obtain for you a share in heaven. As long as you are by nature mortal, you cannot reach your home in heaven; but when you discard this mortality in baptism and rise again with Christ and receive the sign of this new birth you hope for, you are revealed as a citizen of heaven and become a fellow-heir to the heavenly kingdom.

15. To the foregoing words you add: 'In the name of the Father and of the Son and of the Holy Spirit.' For such is God's nature. It is the Substance[24] which exists from all eternity, the cause of all, which created us in the beginning and now is renewing us; it is Father, Son and Holy Spirit. We approach this nature now and offer it our vows, as is just, because it has been and remains the cause of the countless great blessings we have received. We make to it our vows and promise in future to believe in it; we invoke it when we are baptized; we hope to receive from it the blessings which are given to us now in

---

[22]Heb. 11.6. Unlike Chrysostom, T describes a rite which involves a profession of faith in the Trinity, as well as an explicit Act of Adhesion to Christ. See Introduction, p. 20.

[23]Cf. note 6.

[24]The underlying Greek word is *ousia*.

symbol and in anticipation, and to enjoy them for ever when we rise in reality[25] from the dead and share in the inheritance of our home in heaven.

16. You pronounce these vows and this covenant in the attitude I have described, *kneeling on the ground*, as a sign that you are paying God a debt of adoration and that you are recalling your ancient fall to earth. But *the rest of your body is upright*, and you *look up to heaven and stretch out your hands in the attitude of prayer*.[26] In this way you express your adoration of God in heaven and your hope of receiving from there the power to rise from your ancient fall. The time has already come for you to receive the first instalment of the mystery, the promise of the indescribable blessings of heaven.

Anointing with Chrism[27]

17. When you have pronounced these vows and this covenant, the bishop comes over to you. Instead of his usual clothes, he is wearing a delicate, shining linen vestment. He is wearing new garments which denote the new world you are entering; their dazzling appearance signifies that you will shine in the next life; its light texture symbolizes the delicacy and grace of that world. This is the symbolic meaning of his dress: he inspires you with fear but at the same time fills you with love; because it is

[25]This contrast is central to T's sacramental theology. He contrasts the immediate effects of baptism, which we receive 'in symbol and in anticipation' ('symbolically' alone would not convey the full meaning of the underlying Greek word *tupoi*, as the effects begin in this life), with the 'reality', i.e. the full realisation of the effects which will take place only in heaven. To quote other terms T uses, the sacraments bestow the 'guarantee (advance payment) of our inheritance' (BH 3.6-7), 'first-fruits of the mystery' (3.7), the 'promise of the blessings of heaven' (2.16), the 'share in the heavenly blessings' (2.20), the 'potentialities' of man's 'immortal and incorruptible nature' (3.10). After baptism we are *already* risen (3.5; cf. 3.7, note 15). Baptism confers the 'seed' of the future risen life (3.28).

[26]There are many representations in early Christian art which show people standing at prayer with hands stretched out, a posture which is still adopted at Mass by the priest in the Roman rite.

[27]The Syriac makes no distinction between the use of oil and of myron in the two prebaptismal anointings. It is to be presumed, however, that T's practice was the same as Chrysostom's in the use of myron for this 'messianic' anointing. Both T and JC put the Anointing with Chrism before the Anointing with Oil.

new it communicates the dignity of the sacrament. *Then he signs your forehead with the oil of anointing saying: 'N. is signed in the name of the Father and of the Son and of the Holy Spirit.'* This is the first instalment of the sacrament he is administering to you. He does so 'in the name of the Father and of the Son and of the Holy Spirit', because he must begin the sacrament with the name from which you hope to receive all these favours. Already he is prompting you to invoke the Trinity; you must look to it and live your life according to its will in preference to everything else. The seal[28] that you receive at this point marks you out for ever as the sheep of Christ, the soldier of the King of Heaven. As soon as a sheep is bought, it is given a mark to identify its owner; it feeds in the same pasture and lives in the same fold as the other sheep that bear the same owner's mark. And when a soldier is chosen for his height and build to serve the empire, he is at once given a tattoo on his hand to show the name of the emperor in whose service he has enlisted. You have been chosen for the kingdom of heaven; you too can be identified as a soldier of the King of heaven.[29]

18. First you receive a sign on your forehead. This is the highest and noblest part of the body; when we are talking to somebody, it is to this part that we direct our eyes.* So you receive this mark on the forehead to show what a great privilege you are receiving. 'For now we see in a mirror dimly, but then face to face.'[30] 'We all, with unveiled face, beholding the glory of the Lord, are being changed into his likeness from one degree of glory to another; for this comes from the Lord who is the Spirit', says St Paul.[31] This is why we have to receive the seal on the upper part of the face. In this way the demons can see it a long way off and are deterred from coming close to

---

[28]S. Brock, *The Holy Spirit in the Syrian Baptismal Tradition*, p. 107, distinguishes between *rushma* (sign) and *hatma* (seal). However, comparison with other homilies, such as Chrysostom, BH 2.23, indicates that the Greek original here must have *sphragis* (seal). For the seal, see Introduction, p. 29f. Chrysostom also compares this anointing to the branding of a sheep (ACW 10.16). The seal which Theodore associates with the Holy Spirit is discussed in the next Homily, sect. 27.

[29]See Introduction, p. 28.

[30]1 Cor. 13.12.

[31]2 Cor. 3.18.

harm us in future; and we proclaim that God has granted us the privilege of beholding him henceforth with face unveiled, if only we display before him the sign that we are members of his household and soldiers of Christ our Lord.[32]

19. When the bishop has completed this ceremony of sealing your forehead, he pronounces the words I have mentioned to show that he has set you apart for the future and appointed you a soldier of the true king and a citizen of heaven. The seal shows that all this belongs to you. Immediately *your sponsor stands behind you, spreads a linen stole over your head and raises you to your feet.* You get up off your knees to show that you have abandoned your ancient fall, and have nothing to do with the earth and earthly affairs. God has accepted your adoration and entreaty. You have received the seal to show that you have been chosen for heavenly service. You have been called to heaven. Henceforth this is the home and the life you must make for; you must keep aloof from all earthly things ... To begin with, you stand naked, like prisoners and slaves; but when you receive the sign, you spread the linen cloth over your head to symbolize the freedom to which you are called,[33] for this is the decoration that free men wear both indoors and out.

20. Now that you carry the identification-mark of a soldier of Christ our Lord, you may receive the rest of the sacraments and so acquire the full armour of the Spirit[34] and your share in the heavenly blessings. How this happens I shall explain in detail later. What I have said is sufficient for today. So let us end our instruction in the usual way, offering praise to God the Father, to his Only-Begotten Son and to the Holy Spirit, now and for ever. Amen.

[32] In this paragraph T states the following reasons why the sign is received on the forehead, but the development of his thought is confused: (1) the forehead is a sign of dignity; (2) it reminds us that we will meet the Lord 'face to face' (i.e. in familiar intercourse as opposed to the obscurity of sacramental signs); (3) to proclaim our allegiance openly; (4) to scare away the devil.

[33] For the significance of the linen stole, see Introduction, p. 33; BH 4.23 with note 52.

[34] Cf. Eph 6.11, 13, 17.

BAPTISMAL HOMILY III

Synopsis — Then you come forward to be baptized. First you strip completely; then you are anointed all over the with the oil of anointing in the prescribed manner. The bishop begins the ceremony with the words: 'N. is anointed in the name of the Father and of the Son and of the Holy Spirit.' Then you go down into the water that has been blessed by the bishop. The bishop stands and lays his hand on your head saying: 'N. is baptized in the name of the Father and of the Son and the of the Holy Spirit.' He wears the same vestments as before. He lays his hand on your head with the words, 'In the name of the Father', and while pronouncing them pushes you down into the water. If you were free to speak at this moment, you would say, 'Amen'. You bow down under the water, then lift up your head again. Meanwhile the bishop says, 'and of the Son', and guides you with his hand as you bend into the water as before. When you raise your head, the bishop says, 'and of the Holy Spirit', pressing you down into the water again with his hand. Then you come up out of the font and put on a dazzling garment of pure white. The bishop comes to you and puts a seal on your forehead saying: 'N. is sealed in the name of the Father and of the Son and of the Holy Spirit.'

Recapitulation

1. I concluded yesterday's instruction at the point where you had been sealed with the oil of baptism to mark you out for service in the heavenly army as one chosen and approved. Now the kingdom of heaven was revealed in the person of Christ our Lord in his economy,[1] when after his passion and resurrection he ascended into heaven and established his kingdom there. And we, who have been called to this service, ought to have an affinity with heaven, for we are all now bound for the place where our king is, since he said himself: 'I desire that they also may be with me where I am.'*[2] We hope to 'reign with him', as

---

[1] *Oikonomia.* Cf. BH 2.3, note 6.
[2] Jn. 17.24.

St Paul said, if we show our love for him by endurance,[3] because when we are in heaven with him we shall share in his great glory ... So as soon as you stand up after receiving the seal, you have a linen cloth spread over your head to signify your state of freedom. Since you have been chosen to serve in the heavenly army you have been set free from all contact with earthly things and assumed the liberty of heaven. If an earthly ruler will not countenance the presence of a slave in his army,[4] all the more should one who serves in the army of heaven be free from slavery. Our share in heavenly things has set us all free; in St Paul's words, 'the Jerusalem above is free, and she is our mother'.[5]

New Birth

2. These then are the effects of the sealing, and you know all you need to know about the ceremony, for I described it yesterday. Today I must explain the next ceremonies, for at this stage you have to come forward for baptism itself. Baptism contains the signs of the new birth which will be manifested in reality when you rise from the dead and recover all that death has stolen from you ... You will gain this new birth by rising from the dead to a second existence, just as when you were born of a woman you entered upon the existence that death takes away from you. You will gain this in reality when the time comes for you to rise again to your new birth; but now you have faith in Christ our Lord, and while you are waiting for the resurrection you must be content with receiving symbols and signs of it in this awesome sacrament which affords you certainty of sharing in the blessings to come.

3. You come forward then for baptism, the symbol of this birth you hope for. This is why Christ our Lord calls it a second birth in his words to Nicodemus: 'Unless one is born anew, he cannot see the kingdom of God'[6] ... Nicodemus, taking Jesus

[3]2 Tim. 2.12.

[4]On the almost inflexible principle that only free men could serve in the Roman army, see J. B. Bury, *History of the Later Roman Empire*, vol. 1, p. 39.

[5]Gal. 4.26.

[6]Jn. 3.3ff.

to mean that this birth was like birth from a woman, asks: 'How can a man be born when he is old? Can he enter a second time into his mother's womb and be born?' ... So Christ our Lord says no more about the second birth that we shall receive in reality at the resurrection, for he knows that this is a truth too sublime for Nicodemus to grasp. Instead he tells him about the symbolical birth that takes place at baptism, and which believers must undergo in order to pass by means of the signs to the enjoyment of the reality. 'Unless', he says, 'one is born of water and the Spirit, he cannot enter the Kingdom of God.' He explains the means, water, and he reveals the cause, the Spirit. That is why he adds the words: 'That which is born of the flesh is flesh, and that which is born of the Spirit is spirit.' He says no more about the water, because it merely serves as a sacramental sign; he speaks of the Spirit because this birth is due to the Spirit's operation. This is clearly his meaning: just as one who is born in the flesh and of the flesh is by nature subject to death, pain, corruption and all kinds of change,[7] so we are to expect that when we are born, so to speak, of the Spirit, we shall become by nature free from all these afflictions.*

4. But Nicodemus repeated the question: 'How can this be?' Jesus answered: 'The wind blows where it wills and you hear the sound of it, but you do not know whence it comes or whither it goes; so it is with everyone who is born of the Spirit.'[8] He does not say a word about water; he refers to the reliability and credibility of the Spirit to establish his teaching against all doubt. For the expression 'blows where it wills' indicates the Spirit's power to accomplish his will in anything ... Therefore Christ's words are conclusive: 'so it is with everyone who is born of the Spirit' ...

5. For the same reason St Paul says: 'All of us who have been baptized into Christ Jesus were baptized into his death. We

---

[7]Liability to change is commonly regarded in Greek philosophy as an imperfection, because it indicates an incomplete realisation of the ideal as well as the possibility of corruption. T, however, probably is thinking of liability to moral change, i.e. sin.

[8]In fact Nicodemus' question, 'How can this be?' comes after these words of Jesus'. 'Wind' and 'spirit' are used to translate different meanings of the same word in the gospel text.

were buried therefore with him by baptism into death, so that as Christ was raised from the dead by the glory of the Father, we too might walk in newness of life.'[9] Before Christ's coming, God's sentence enabled death to exercise sovereign power over us, and it was quite beyond our strength to break our bonds, so firm was death's hold on us. But by his death and resurrection Christ our Lord altered the sentence and undid death's hold on us, so that now the death of those who believe in Christ is like a prolonged sleep. This is implied in St Paul's words: 'Christ has been raised from the dead, the first-fruits of those who have fallen asleep.'[10] By 'those who have fallen asleep', he means those who have died since the resurrection of Christ, for they will rise again and cast off their death.* So it is because Christ our Lord has abolished the power of death by his own resurrection that St Paul says: 'All of us who have been baptized in Christ Jesus were baptized into his death'; we know, he means, that Christ our Lord has already abolished death. Believing this we come to him for baptism, because we wish now to share in his death so as to share like him in the resurrection from the dead. So when I am baptized and put my head under the water, I wish to receive the death and burial of Christ our Lord, and I solemnly profess my faith in his resurrection; when I come up out of the water, this is a sign that I believe I am already risen.

6. These things only happen to us in symbols, but St Paul wishes to make it clear that we are not concerned with empty symbols but with realities, in which we profess our faith with longing and without hesitation. So he continues: 'If we have been united with him in a death like his, we shall certainly be united with him in a resurrection like his.'[11] He proves the present by the future, taking the splendour of what is to come as evidence of the value of these symbols, the symbols contained

---

[9]Rom. 6.3-4.

[10]1 Cor. 15.20. Several of the Fathers held that between death and the resurrection of the body the separated soul did not yet enter heaven or hell (cf. Tertullian, *de Anima*, 58; PL 2.795-798). For the Syriac tradition that the souls of the dead sleep (though not without consciousness) until the general resurrection, see P. Kruger, 'Le sommeil des âmes dans l'oeuvre de Narsai', *L'Orient Syrien*, 4 (1959) 196-210.

[11]Rom. 6.5.

in baptism, the work of the Holy Spirit. You receive baptism only because you hope for the blessings to come: by dying and rising with Christ and being born to a new life, you come to share in the reality of the signs that attracted you* ... This second birth is the work of the Holy Spirit, whom you receive in the sacrament as a kind of guarantee. So you can see what a great sacrament this is, how awesome and deserving belief its symbolism ... That is why St Paul says: 'In him we have believed and were sealed with the Holy Spirit of promise, who is the guarantee of our inheritance to the praise of his glory.'[12] He calls this grace that the Holy Spirit gives us here on earth 'the Spirit of promise' because we receive it as a promise of future gifts. He calls it also 'the guarantee of our inheritance', because it enables us already to share in the gifts to come.

7. Similarly he says in another place: 'It is God who establishes us with you in Christ, and has anointed us; he has put his seal upon us and given us his Spirit in our hearts as a guarantee.'[13] In yet another place he says: 'And not only the creation, but we ourselves, who have the first-fruits of the Spirit, groan inwardly as we wait for adoption as sons, the redemption of our bodies.'[14] We have the first-fruits of the Spirit, he says, on this earth, because we receive the fullness of grace only when we enjoy the reality. 'We wait for adoption as sons, the redemption of our bodies', he says, meaning that in this life we receive adoption in anticipation;[15] we shall receive the reality when we are born again and rise from the dead, becoming at once immortal, incorruptible and free from all physical evil ...

Stripping and Anointing with Oil

8. *Then you come forward to be baptized. First you strip completely.* Originally Adam was 'naked and not ashamed'[16] but once he had disobeyed the commandment and become mortal, he

---

[12]Eph. 1.13-14 (adapted).

[13]2 Cor. 1.21-22 (RSV modified).

[14]Rom. 8.23.

[15]Literally 'in sign' (*tupoi*). T refers not so much to the sacramental *sign*, but the sacramental effect, which is an anticipation of the full reality found only in heaven.

[16]Gen. 2.25.

needed a covering; you, on the other hand, are to present yourself for baptism in order to be born again and become immortal in anticipation, and so you must first take off your clothes.[17] For they are proof of mortality, convincing evidence of the humiliating sentence which made man need clothes. When you have done this, *you are anointed all over with the oil of anointing in the prescribed manner, this is a sign of the garment of immortality you will receive through baptism ... You are anointed all over:* unlike clothes, which only come in contact with part of the body, and even if they touched the whole surface of the body would still not come in contact with the internal organs, our whole nature will 'put on the imperishable'[18] at the moment of the resurrection, by virtue of the working of the Holy Spirit within us.* When this anointing is conferred upon you, *the bishop begins the ceremony with the words: 'N. is anointed in the name of the Father and of the Son and of the Holy Spirit',* and the appointed ministers anoint your body all over.

Prayer over the Water

9. Next, at the time I have already explained to you, *you go down into the water that has been blessed by the bishop.* You are not baptized in ordinary water, but in the water of second birth. Now ordinary water cannot become this other thing except by the coming of the Holy Spirit.[19] Consequently the bishop beforehand pronounces a prescribed form of words, asking God to let the grace of the Holy Spirit come upon the water and make it capable of begetting this awesome birth, making it a womb for sacramental birth.[20] For when Nicodemus asked:

[17]Cf. Introduction, p. 21.

[18]1 Cor. 15.53. The consequence of the reversal of the Anointings with Oil and Chrism is that the effect of strengthening the candidate against the devil is attributed to the chrism rather than the oil. The only effect of the Anointing with oil which T mentions is its action as a symbol of the resurrection of our bodies as well as of our souls. Chrysostom, on the other hand, does take this anointing to give strength against the Enemy, even though he has already attributed this effect to the Anointing with Chrism. Cf. Introduction, p. 28.

[19]Note the implication that the water is changed (transubstantiated?). Cf. Introduction, p. 23f.

[20]Cf. Introduction, p. 24.

'Can a man enter a second time into his mother's womb and be reborn?', our Lord replied: 'Unless one is born of water and the Spirit, he cannot enter the Kingdom of God.' He means that just as in natural birth the mother's womb receives a seed, but it is God's hand that forms it according to his original decree, so too in baptism the water becomes a womb to receive the person who is being born, but it is the grace of the Spirit which forms him there for a second birth and makes him a completely new man. A seed settling in the mother's womb has neither life nor soul nor sense; but God's hand forms it so that it emerges a living man, endowed with soul and senses and a nature capable of any human action. So too here: the one baptized settles in the water as in a kind of womb, like a seed showing no sign of an immortal nature; but once baptized and endowed with the divine grace of the Spirit, his nature is reshaped completely. Once mortal, it becomes immortal; once corruptible, it becomes incorruptible;[21] once changing, it becomes unchanging; by the almighty power of him who forms it.

10. A baby born of a woman has the potentiality of talking, hearing, walking and working with his hands, but is too utterly weak for any action of the kind; yet, in due time, by God's decree he becomes capable of these actions. So too one who is born by baptism possesses in himself all the potentialities of his immortal and incorruptible nature, but cannot use or exhibit them until the moment God has ordained for us to be born from the dead and attain full enjoyment of our freedom from corruption, death, pain and change. We are endowed with the potentiality for these things at baptism but gain the effective use of them only when we are no longer merely natural but spiritual,[22] and the working of the Spirit has made the body incorruptible and the soul immutable, holding them both in his own power and preserving them. As St Paul says, 'What is

---

[21]Cf. 1 Cor. 15.53-54.

[22]T is using the terms 'natural' and 'spiritual' in the sense in which St Paul uses them in the quotation which follows: 'natural' applies to our condition in this life, 'spiritual' to our condition in the next.

sown is perishable, what is raised is imperishable. It is sown in weakness, it is raised in power. It is sown in dishonour, it is raised in glory. It is sown a merely natural body, it is raised a spiritual body'.[23] He means that it is the power of the Holy Spirit that will make us imperishable, glorious and powerful, working upon our bodies and souls, making the former immortal and the latter immutable. The body that will rise from the dead and that man will assume will not be merely natural now but spiritual. Now it is not in the nature of water to work these effects; they are the result of the working of the Spirit at baptism by water. So first of all the bishop pronounces the prescribed words of consecration, praying that the grace of the Holy Spirit may come upon the water and by his holy and awesome coming endow the water with power to produce all these effects. In this way the water becomes an awesome womb of the second birth; in this way all who go down into the water are formed again by the grace of the Holy Spirit and born again in another, higher nature ...

Baptism

11. So the water you enter is like a crucible in which you are reshaped to a higher nature: you lay aside your old mortality and assume a nature that is completely immortal and incorruptible. You are born in water because you were formed originally from earth and water,[24] and when you fell into sin the sentence of death made you totally corruptible. This is what a potter[25] does when a vase he is shaping from clay becomes

---

[23] 1 Cor. 15.42-44 (adapted).

[24] T presumably has in mind Gen. 2.6-7: 'A mist went up from the earth and watered the whole face of the ground — then the Lord God formed man of dust from the ground'. Ambrose (S 2.19) makes a clearer connection between earth and water: since water comes from the earth, by ritual 'burial' beneath the baptismal water we fulfil the sentence: '... return to the earth, for out of it you were taken' (Gen. 3.19).

For this ambiguous use of the pronoun '*you*' (*you* fell), to refer to the first man, the whole human race and the individual members of the congregation, cf. BH 2.5, note 11.

[25] This simile of the potter is used to explain original sin by many of the Greek Fathers: Adam's sin produced a hereditary flaw in our nature, which can only be

spoilt: he shapes it again in water and so it recovers its true form. This is why God told Jeremiah to go to the potter; and when he had seen the potter doing this God said to him: 'O house of Israel, can I not do with you as this potter has done?'*[26] For we too were formed from earth and clay — 'You too were formed from a piece of clay, like me.'[27] Pardon 'those who dwell in houses of clay, for we too are of the same clay'.[28] We too fell and were corrupted by sin. Then sentence of death involved us in complete decay, but our Creator and Master subsequently shaped us afresh by his immeasurable power: he abolished death by the resurrection and gave all of us hope of salvation from death and of a better world than this, in which we shall not only survive, but become immortal and incorruptible …

13. When the potter has made a vase, he can reshape it in water, as long as it retains the plastic quality of clay and has not yet come into contact with the fire; but once it has been baked there is no longer any way of reshaping it. So it is with us now: since we are by nature mortal, we need to undergo this renewal by baptism; but once we have been formed afresh by baptism and received the grace of the Holy Spirit, who will harden us more than any fire, we cannot undergo a second renewal or look to a second baptism,[29] just as we can only hope for a single resurrection, since Christ our Lord also, as St Paul said, 'being

---

cured when our bodies are broken up at death and reshaped at the resurrection. Cf. Theophilus of Antioch (flor. 188), *Ad Autolycum*, 2.26 (PG 6.1093); Methodius of Olympus (d. 311), *Symposium*, iii.5 (PG 18.68), *de Resurrect.*, 6-7 (PG 18.269-273); Gregory of Nyssa (d. 394), *Or Cat.* 8 (PG 45.36); Chrysostom, ACW 9.21-26. Thus death is a blessing as well as a punishment. Cf. Ambrose, S 2.17.

[26]Jer. 18.6.

[27]Job 33.6 (LXX).

[28]Job 4.19 (LXX).

[29]T gives this common simile of the potter an original twist to illustrate the fact that baptism cannot be repeated. The Church only gradually gained a clear grasp of the possibility of the forgiveness of sins committed after baptism. Although some local churches were slower in coming to this conclusion than others, by T's time it seems to have won general acceptance (cf. J. N. D. Kelly, *Doctrines*, pp. 436ff.). The reason why T says nothing here of the forgiveness of sins after baptism is perhaps that he wishes to stress the conversion of life that baptism should bring about; he takes it for granted that there will not be any deliberate sins after baptism. But he does allow later for this possibility (BH 5.33-34).

raised from the dead will never die again; death no longer has dominion over him'.*[30]

14. This then is the effect of the gift of baptism. But to teach you once for all who it is who is the cause of all these blessings, who is now recasting you, who is raising you to a higher nature, who is making you immortal instead of mortal, imperishable instead of perishable, *the bishop stands and lays his hand on your head saying: 'N. is baptized in the name of the Father and of the Son and of the Holy Spirit.' He wears the same vestments as before,* when he sealed your forehead while you knelt, and when he blessed the water. He wears it now while performing the ceremony of baptism, because it is appropriate that he should perform all the rites of the sacrament in the same vestments which symbolize this new world to which the sacrament transports you. He says, *'N. is baptized in the name of the Father and of the Son and of the Holy Spirit',* to teach you by these words who it is who is the cause of this grace ... This formula corresponds to our Lord's commission: 'Go therefore and make disciples of all nations, baptizing them in the name of the Father and of the Son and of the Holy Spirit'.[31] These words show that the effects are produced entirely by the Father, the Son and the Holy Spirit, who exist from all eternity, and are the cause of all things. To them we owe our original existence, and by them we now hope to be renewed ... It is evident that the one who originally saw fit to make us mortal and corruptible is none other than the one who is now making us immortal and incorruptible ... He made us originally according to his good pleasure and in the end brought us to a state of excellence, to teach us that the first state too was his doing; the thought that we owe our attainment of excellence to him should make us realise that we would never have existed in the first place if he had not brought us into existence.[32]

---

[30]Rom. 6.9.

[31]Mt. 28.19.

[32]The baptismal formula shows that our new life comes from God; therefore our natural creation must also have been due to him. The contrast between the 'first state' and the 'state of excellence' does not quite coincide with the distinction between the natural and the supernatural, for in T's thought the state of excellence does not begin until the next life.

15. This is why, when the bishop places his hand on your head, he does not say, 'I baptize', but 'N. is baptized'; for no man, only divine grace, is capable of making such a gift.* He goes on at once to say who it is who signs and baptizes: the words 'In the name of the Father and of the Son and of the Holy Spirit' show who is responsible for the effect, and proclaim that he himself is simply the obedient minister ... For just as Peter's words, 'In the name of Jesus Christ of Nazareth, stand up and walk',[33] show that Christ is the cause of the man's recovery of his powers, so too the bishop's words show that the Father, the Son and the Holy Spirit are the cause of the gifts we receive at baptism.* This is the cause of our renewal, of our second birth, of our reshaping as new men, free from death, decay, suffering and change, of our exchange of our former slavery for a state of liberty, in which we are free from all our ills and enjoy for ever these indescribable blessings.

16. *In the name of the Father, etc.* means 'at the invocation of the Father, etc.'. Similarly Isaiah said: 'Lord, apart from you we know no other; we call on you by name'.[34] He meant this: We acknowledge no other Lord apart from you, the Creator of all things; you have put an end to all our ills; from you we expect to receive the enjoyment of all our blessings; it is you, the Creator of all things, whom we have learnt to invoke in all our needs; you alone can produce and give every gift at will. So at this stage the bishop says, 'In the name, etc.', meaning that we are baptized invoking the Father, the Son and the Holy Spirit, the cause of all things, that can accomplish whatever it wills. But he does not say: 'In the name of the Father and in the name of the Son and in the name of the Holy Spirit.' Each of them has his own name which he does not share with the others ... But the name that the bishop pronounces is not that by which the Father, the Son and the Holy Spirit are invoked individually: the name which he invokes and by which we call upon the cause of these blessings, is the divine nature existing from all eternity, the nature shared by the Father, the Son and the Holy Spirit; we call upon them in a single invocation.* We do not call upon

---

[33]Acts 3.6 (alternative reading).
[34]Is. 26.13 (LXX).

the Father as one cause and the Son as another and the Holy Spirit as a third. The invocation is addressed to One, and towards this One we look for the enjoyment of the graces of baptism ...[35]

17. Consider then that these names act as a prayer.[36] When the bishop says, 'In the name of the Father', take him to mean, 'Grant, Father, these everlasting, inestimable blessings for which this man is now baptized.' So too with the Son and the Holy Spirit.* When Peter said, 'In the name of Jesus Christ of Nazareth, stand up and walk,'[37] he meant, 'Grant, O Jesus Christ, to this man that he may stand up and walk.' So too when the bishop says 'In the name, etc.', all he means is: 'O Father, Son and Holy Spirit, grant to this person who is baptized the grace to be born again.' Peter's words, 'In the name of Jesus Christ, stand up and walk,' have the same meaning as his later words, 'Aeneas, Jesus Christ heals you';[38] in both cases he showed who was really responsible for the cure ...*

18. Then the bishop lays his hand on your head with the words, '*In the name of the Father', and while pronouncing them pushes you down into the water.* You obediently follow the signal he gives by word and gesture, and bow down under the water. You incline your head to show your consent and to acknowledge the truth of the bishop's words that you receive the blessings of baptism from the Father. *If you were free to speak at this moment you would say 'Amen'* — a word which we use as a sign of our

---

[35]T is arguing from the baptismal formula that, although all three Persons of the Trinity cause the sacramental effect, they do so, not as three co-operating individuals, but by virtue of the single divine essence. Indeed in whatever way God exerts influence on his creation, he does so by virtue of this essence that all three persons share; otherwise there would be three individual Gods, instead of one God in three Persons. The argument is developed in sections 20 and 21. Ambrose hints at a similar argument in his treatment of Mt. 28.19 (S 2.22; cf. 6.5-8).

[36]Sacraments are not only signs that cause the grace God gives the Christian. They are also prayers in which the Church asks God to grant the grace. This is another way of saying that an essential element in the rite is the epiclesis, in which God is asked to send the Holy Spirit upon the sacramental materials and/or upon the person receiving the sacrament.

[37]Acts 3.6.
[38]Acts 9.34.

agreement with what the bishop says. This is implied in St Paul's question: 'How can anyone in the position of an outsider say the "Amen" to your thanksgiving?'[39] St Paul's words show that 'Amen' is the people's response to the bishop's thanksgiving, by which they express agreement. But since at the moment of baptism you cannot speak, but have to receive the sacrament of renewal in silence and awe,[40] you bow your head when you immerse yourself to show your sincere agreement with the bishop's words.

19. *You bow down under the water, then lift your head again. Meanwhile the bishop says, 'And of the Son', and guides you with his hand as you bend down into the water as before.* You make the sign of consent as before, signifying that you accept the bishop's declaration that it is from the Son that you hope to receive the blessings of baptism. *You raise your head, and again the bishop says, 'And of the Holy Spirit', pressing you down into the water again with his hand.* You bend beneath the water again, humbly acknowledging by the same sign that you hope for the blessings of baptism from the Holy Spirit ... Then you come up out of the font to receive the completion of the mystery.[41]

20. Three times you immerse yourself, each time performing the same action, once in the name of the Father, once in the name of the Son and once in the name of the Holy Spirit. Since each Person is named, you understand that each enjoys equal perfection, and each is able to dispense the graces of baptism. You go down into the font once, but you bend beneath the water three times in accordance with the bishop's words, and you come up out of the font once. This teaches you that there is only one baptism, and that the grace dispensed by the Father, the Son and the Holy Spirit is one and the same. They are inseparable one from the other, for they have one nature. So although each Person can confer the grace, as is shown by your

---

[39] 1 Cor. 14.16.

[40] This passage shows that the phrase 'the awesome rite of initiation' was no *cliché*, but an expression of the religious awe that the baptismal ceremonies were intended to inculcate.

[41] An allusion to Confirmation (cf. Introduction, p. 36).

immersion at each of the names, we do not consider baptism to be complete until the Father, the Son and the Holy Spirit have all been invoked. Since their substance is one and their divinity is one, it follows that it is by a single will and a single operation that the Father, Son and Holy Spirit regularly act upon their creatures.[42] So we too can hope for new birth, second creation and in short all the graces of baptism only upon the invocation of the Father, the Son and the Holy Spirit — an invocation which we believe to be the cause of all our blessings.

21. It is in this sense that St Paul says: 'One Lord, one faith, one baptism, one body and one Spirit, one God and Father of us all, who is through all and in all.'[43] He does not mean that the Lord is not God or Spirit, and God is not Lord or Spirit, and the Spirit is not Lord or God. For necessarily the Lord is also God and Spirit, and God is also Lord and Spirit, and the true Spirit — the Holy Spirit — is also God and Lord. No, what he is teaching us is this: the one Lordship is the one Godhead. For the Substance of the Father, the Son and the Holy Spirit is one, without body or limit. It is the Substance which at baptism grants us adoption, this Substance in which we believe, are baptized and become a single body by the power of the Holy Spirit at baptism. This power makes us sons of God and the one body of Christ our Lord, whom we call our Head, since he shares our nature and he was the first to rise from the dead so that we might share in these blessings through him. By naming the Father, the Son and the Holy Spirit we received the cause of all blessings. St Paul indeed would not have said that there was one faith in the Father, the Son and the Holy Spirit if he had believed that their nature was distinct; he would not have said that there was one baptism in the name of the Father, the Son and the Holy Spirit if he had believed that their will, their power and their activity were distinct.[44] It is clear that there is

[42]See note 35.

[43]Eph. 4.4-6 (adapted). In the following lines the word 'Substance' stands for the Greek *ousia*.

[44]T misunderstands the text from Ephesians. St Paul does not in fact say in this passage that we have faith in the Father, Son and Holy Spirit; nor that we are baptized in their name. Paul instances the one faith and one baptism, not as

one faith, because there is one Being in which we believe. There is one baptism, because those whom we invoke have one will, one operation and one power, which enables us all to be born again and to become the one body of Christ whom we call our Head. In his human existence he was assumed[45] from among us and became the first to rise from the dead, in this way assuring for us a share in his resurrection, which allows us to hope that our bodies too will be like his: 'But our commonwealth is in heaven, and from it we await a Saviour, the Lord Jesus Christ, who will change our lowly body to be like his glorious body.'[46]

22. This prediction will be fulfilled in reality at the resurrection; at baptism we merely perform the signs and symbols.[47] For the same reason[48] we are called, according to St

evidence of the unity of the Father, Son and Holy Spirit, but to show the unity that should exist among Christians. T's anti-Arian concern makes him so insistent on the unity of the Substance of the Trinity that he regrettably uses language suggesting that the Substance is a fourth entity logically prior to the Father, the Son and the Holy Spirit. This unfortunate mode of expression is more typical of Western than Eastern writers.

[45]T's Christology bears the peculiar features of the Antiochene school of thought. Instead of St John's formula, 'The Word became flesh' (Jn. 1.14), he speaks of the Word 'assuming' a 'man'. This terminology was capable of an unorthodox interpretation, for it could be taken to imply that the Incarnation was simply a union of wills between the Second Person of the Trinity and an independently existing human being. This indeed was the interpretation that the disciples of Nestorius read into the words, and later generations posthumously condemned T as a result. Most probably, however, T used the terms in an orthodox sense to express two truths; first, that Jesus' humanity was complete; secondly, that we are saved, not by direct union with his *divine* life, but by a share in his *human* life and his resurrection from the dead (cf. Theodore, *de Incarnatione*, vii; Wiles and Santer, *Documents in Early Christian Thought*, pp. 60-61). To make this second point more clearly T emphasises the share that our *bodies* will receive in the glory of Christ's risen body.

[46]Phil. 3.20-21. The Syriac translation read 'service' instead of 'commonwealth'.

[47]In this and the following two sections the word corresponding with the Greek *tupos* occurs several times, and is translated here four times 'sign' and twice 'anticipation'. Cf. BH 3.7, note 15. Our baptism is the '*tupos*' of heaven; Christ's baptism is the '*tupos*' of ours. Although this sentence may suggest that for T baptism is only a symbol of the after-life, it is clear from other passages (e.g. 3.23) that he believes the sacrament has an immediate effect, which is, however, only a first instalment of the glory of our risen lives in heaven. Cf. BH 2.15, note 25.

[48]I.e., because we share even bodily in Christ's resurrection.

Paul's saying, the body of Christ our Lord, who is our head: Christ is the head 'from whom the whole body, nourished and knit together, grows with a growth that is from God.'[49]

Our Baptism and Christ's Baptism

Our Lord himself, before his resurrection from the dead, was seen to receive baptism at the hands of John the Baptist in the River Jordan in order to present in anticipation a sign of the baptism that we were to receive by his grace. For us he was 'the first-born from the dead', in St Paul's words, 'that in everything he might be pre-eminent';[50] therefore he chose for your sake to be the first not only in the reality of the resurrection but also in sign … St John the Baptist said to him: 'I need to be baptized by you, and do you come to me?', showing in this way the difference there was between himself and Jesus. But Jesus replied: 'Let it be so now; for thus it is fitting for us to fulfil all righteousness.'[51] Righteousness, he meant, is established by the grace of baptism,[52] and it is fitting that your hands should introduce it among those who are subject to the Law. So the Law too is publicly honoured, since through it righteousness entered the world.

23. Our Lord, then, was baptized by John, but not with John's baptism. For John's baptism was a baptism of repentance for the remission of sins, and our Lord had no need of it as he was free from all sin. He was baptized with our baptism, and presented an anticipation of it. Consequently he also received the Holy Spirit, who appeared descending in the form of a dove and 'remained on him',[53] as the evangelist says. For John did not have the power to confer the Spirit; he said himself: 'I baptize you with water; but among you stands one whom you do not know; he will baptize you with the Holy Spirit and with fire' …[54] The power to confer the Spirit belonged to our Lord.

---

[49]Col. 2.19.
[50]Col. 1.18.
[51]Mt. 3.14-15.
[52]There is a similar argument in Ambrose, S 1.15.
[53]Jn. 1.32.
[54]Jn. 1.26; Mt. 3.11

He gives us 'the first-fruits of the Spirit'[55] now, and promises to give us the full measure at the resurrection, when our nature will be fully capable of being transformed in reality to a state of excellence.*

24. You were baptized then, with the same baptism that Christ our Lord received in his humanity. This is one reason why you are baptized 'in the name of the Father and of the Son and of the Holy Spirit', because the very events at Christ's baptism foreshadowed your baptism in sign. When the Father said aloud from far off, 'This is my beloved son, with whom I am well pleased', he was referring in fact to the grace of our adoption, which is the purpose of baptism ...[56] This adoption is far superior to Jewish adoption, which was subject to change. God is saying in effect: 'I say, "You are gods, sons of the Most High, all of you; nevertheless, you shall die like men".'[57] This adoption remains firm and unshakeable, because anyone who is adopted in this way will remain immortal. For these signs enable him to pass to the adoption which will take place at the resurrection, transforming him into an immortal and incorruptible nature. The Son also was present in the one who was baptized, and united with the one who was assumed,[58] confirming our adoption as sons. So the Holy Spirit too was there: he descended in the form of a dove and 'remained on him'. And so Christ too was baptized in the name of the Father and of the Son and of the Holy Spirit.

25. When the bishop says, 'In the name of the Father', he recalls the Father's words: 'This is my beloved Son, with whom I am well pleased.' When he says, 'Of the Son', take these words

---

[55]Rom. 8.23.

[56]Mt. 3.17. T should not be regarded as a supporter of the Adoptionist heresy that before the baptism Jesus was no more than a man. He says elsewhere (*de Incarnatione*, vii, Wiles and Santer, p. 60) that the union of the divine Word with the humanity began with the beginning of life within Mary's womb. The Nicene Creed, in fact, contains an implicit denial of Adoptionism: '... incarnate by the Holy Spirit out of the Virgin Mary.'

[57]Ps. 82.6-7.

[58]T is not attempting to distinguish between 'the one who was baptized' and 'the one who was assumed'. The two phrases refer to the same human being, who was united to God the Son.

to refer to him who was present in the man who was baptized, and acknowledge that he has obtained adoption for you. When he says, 'Of the Holy Spirit', remember the one who descended in the form of a dove and remained on him, and in short expect that your adoption too will be confirmed by the same Spirit. For, as St Paul said, 'those who are led by the Spirit of God are sons of God'.[59] The only genuine adoption is that granted by the Holy Spirit; but it is not genuine if the Spirit is not present to produce the effect and encourage us to receive the gift in which we have faith. And so, by the invocation of the Father, the Son and the Holy Spirit, you have received the grace of adoption.

Then you come up out of the font. You have received baptism, second birth. By your immersion you fulfilled the sentence of burial; by coming up you received a sign of the resurrection. You have been born again and have become a completely different person.[60] You no longer belong to Adam, who was subject to change, because he was afflicted and overwhelmed by sin; you belong to Christ, who was entirely free from sin through his resurrection, and in fact had committed no sin from the beginning of his life. For it was fitting that he should have from the beginning a claim to the immutable nature that he received in full at the resurrection.[61] So it is that he confirms for us the resurrection from the dead and a share in his freedom from corruption.

The Baptismal Garment

26. As soon as *you come up out of the font, you put on a dazzling garment of pure white.* This is a sign of the world of shining splendour[62] and the way of life to which you have already

---

[59]Rom. 8.14.

[60]T refers very obliquely to Rom. 6.3ff. This obviously relevant text, with its juxtaposition of baptism with death and resurrection, is quoted much more explicitly by Ambrose at this point in his exposition (S 2.20; 3.2).

[61]T implies that the resurrection changed Jesus' spiritual state, as well as his physical condition.

[62]Cf. Mt. 13.43: 'The righteous will shine like the sun in the kingdom of their father.'

passed in symbol. When you experience the resurrection in reality and put on immortality and incorruptibility, you will not need such garments any longer; but you need them now, because you have not yet received these gifts in reality, but only in symbols and signs ...

The Final Anointing: The Gift of the Spirit?

27. When you have received grace by means of baptism, then, and put on this shining white garment, *the bishop comes to you and puts a seal on your forehead, saying: 'N. is sealed in the name of the Father and of the Son and of the Holy Spirit.'* When Jesus came up out of the water, he received the grace of the Holy Spirit, which came and remained on him in the form of a dove. This is why he too is said to have been anointed by the Holy Spirit: 'The Spirit of the Lord is upon me,' he said, 'and therefore the Lord has anointed me.'[63] 'Jesus of Nazareth, whom God anointed with the Holy Spirit and with power.'[64] This shows that the Holy Spirit never leaves him, just as the anointing attaches to those who are anointed by men with oil[65] and never leaves them. You too, then, must be sealed on the forehead. *While the bishop is putting the seal on you, he says: 'N. is sealed in the name of the Father, etc.'* This sign shows you that, when the Father, the Son and the Holy Spirit were named, the Holy Spirit came upon you. You were anointed by him and received him by God's grace. He is yours and remains within you. You

---

[63]Lk. 4.18 (adapted) quoted Is. 61.1. In BH 5.12 however T seems to link Jesus' anointing with his resurrection.

[64]Acts 10.38 (adapted).

[65]The mention of oil seems to imply that an anointing forms part of this 'sealing', which confers the Holy Spirit. The inclusion of such a rite would constitute a departure from the prevalent practice in Syria, including that of Chrysostom. See Introduction, p. 37, with note 202. The *Apostolic Constitutions,* which is generally held to have been put together in Syria, or even Antioch, in the second half of the fourth century, gives three main versions of the baptismal ceremonies, all of which include a post-baptismal anointing, which is not however associated with the gift of the Spirit: iii.16 (post-baptismal anointing with myron as a seal); vii.22 (ditto); vii.44 (post-baptismal anointing with myron, for steadfastness in the good odour of Christ) (Whitaker, pp. 31-32, 34). In all three of these versions the gift of the Spirit is connected with the anointing *before* baptism.

enjoy the first-fruits of him in this life, for you receive now in symbol the possession of the blessings to come. Then you will receive the grace in its fullness, and it will free you from death, corruption, pain and change; your body too will last for ever and will be free from decay, and your soul will not be liable to any further movement towards evil.

28. Such, then, is the second birth which we receive at baptism, and which you are now about to approach. We hope

Why then is T at variance with the Syrian tradition in giving after baptism a rite conferring the Spirit? Why in particular does his version differ from that of his fellow-townsman and contemporary, Chrysostom?

One way of attempting to solve these difficulties is to take the simple, radical solution of declaring T's section 27 to be a later addition made to bring this homily into line with subsequent liturgical practice. (Thus L. L. Mitchell, *Baptismal Anointing*, p. 41). However, if this paragraph is a later addition made for this purpose it is a surprisingly fumbling one. The text does not say that the rite itself is for conferring the Spirit after baptism. If some editor wished to insert a reference to a post-baptismal rite for the giving of the Spirit, why did he describe a rite whose purpose is to show that the Spirit *has already been given?*

This obscurity in the reference to anointing has led some scholars (e.g. G. W. H. Lampe, *The Seal of the Spirit*, p. 202, n.4) to maintain that in this section there is no evidence for an anointing after baptism. For T does not say explicitly that the 'seal' is given in the form of an anointing. The words 'anoint' may, with the exception of one clause, be used throughout this section (as in Lk. 4.18, just quoted) simply as a metaphor to describe the gift of the Holy Spirit. The exception is the reference to anointing 'by men with oil' (as opposed to anointing 'by the Holy Spirit'). It could at first sight be taken to be a simile illustrating the permanence of the presence of the Spirit in Christ, not a description of a ceremony performed at this stage in the service. However, if this is so, the simile is peculiarly inept, as the possibility of recourse to a bath makes nonsense of the statement that anointing 'never leaves them'. It seems better, therefore, to take this mention of anointing with oil as a description of the sealing that is given after baptism.

Consequently it seems that T is agreeing with Chrysostom in connecting the gift of the Spirit with the imposition of the bishop's hand at the moment of baptism. Indeed T places much of his teaching about the Spirit in the context of baptism, viz. 3.10, 13, 24-25. Where T's rite differs from JC's is in containing a post-baptismal sealing to signify the Spirit already given in baptism. Nevertheless the resulting discrepancy between the ceremonies which T and JC describe does seem surprising, as they were performed in the same region, perhaps even the same city of Antioch with not many years between them (cf. Introduction, p. 165). However, with our present experience of rapid liturgical change, we should not reject the possibility that in a space of a few years there should be two or more versions of the same ceremonies at Antioch. It seems likely that T's form, which includes the post-baptismal ceremony, represents a later stage in evolution than Chrysostom's.

that this baptism will enable us to pass in reality to this dread birth of resurrection. Baptism assures us of the resurrection, a resurrection which in signs and symbols we already enjoy sacramentally by faith.* The fact that we receive a double birth, and pass from the first to the second, need not surprise us, because even in our physical existence we receive a double birth, first from a man and then from a woman. First we are born from a man in the form of sperm.[66] Everyone knows that the seed bears no resemblance to a human being until it has been conceived, shaped and brought to birth by a woman according to the laws of nature decreed by God.* So too at baptism we are born in seed, but not yet in the immortal nature which we hope to attain at the resurrection: we do not yet bear the least resemblance to it. But if in faith and hope of the future blessings we shape ourselves by a Christian life, when the time of the resurrection comes, according to God's decree we shall receive a second birth from the dust and assume this immortal and incorruptible nature. 'Christ our Saviour', says St Paul, 'will change our lowly body to be like his glorious body.'[67]

29. When you have undergone the sacramental birth of baptism in this way, you will come forward to receive the food of immortality, the food that will be in keeping with your birth. On a later occasion you will be able to learn about this food and the way in which it is offered to you. But now after this instruction you are going to receive the birth of baptism;[68] you have come forward now to share in the indescribable light by means of this second birth. So for the moment our words have, so to speak, wound you tightly in swaddling bands to keep you in mind of this birth which is about to take place. Here, then, we shall let you rest in silence; at a suitable time we shall bring you to this divine food and explain it to you. But now let us end our address in the usual way, praising God the Father, his only-begotten Son and the Holy Spirit, now and for ever. Amen.

---

[66]The ancients did not know that the mother provided the *ova* to be fertilized by the sperm.

[67]Phil. 3.21 (adapted).

[68]T (like Chrysostom) does not explain the Eucharist until the next homily, delivered after the neophyte has received his first communion.

BAPTISMAL HOMILY IV

Synopsis—The important point to grasp is that the food we take is a kind of sacrifice we perform. The duty of the High Priest of the New Covenant is to offer this sacrifice which revealed the nature of the New Covenant. We ought to believe that the bishop who is now at the altar is playing the part of this High Priest, and that the deacons are so to speak presenting an image of the liturgy of the invisible powers. They wear vestments which are in keeping with their true role, for their outer garments have a greater splendour than their personal appearance. On their left shoulders they drape a stole which hangs down equally on either side. We must see Christ now as he is led away to his passion, and again later when he is stretched out on the altar to be immolated for us. This is why some of the deacons spread cloths on the altar which remind us of winding sheets, while others stand on either side and fan the air above the sacred body. All this takes place amid general silence. Then comes the time for prayer aloud. The deacon announces it, and everyone stands in silence while the bishop begins the Prayer over the Offerings. At the conclusion of the prayer he gives thanks on his own behalf, and all present reply 'Amen'. Then the bishop prays: 'Peace be with you', to which the congregation replies, 'And with your spirit'. The bishop then begins to give the Kiss of Peace, and the church herald in a loud voice orders all the people to exchange the Kiss of Peace among themselves. Next the bishop washes his hands, and after him all the priests present, however many there may be, do the same. The names of the living and the dead are read from the church records. Then the bishop comes forward to perform the liturgy, while the church herald proclaims: 'Turn your eyes to the offering'.

Eucharistic Food

1. It is usual to wrap babies in swaddling-bands when they are born; for their bodies are newly-shaped and still soft, and we wish to keep them from suffering any injury, and so hold them still so that they retain their new shape. First you make them lie motionless in their swaddling-bands and only later offer them

their natural food. In the same way you have just been born by baptism. We have, so to speak, wrapped you up tightly in the swaddling-bands of instruction to let the memory of the grace you have received harden within you. We broke off the instruction to let you rest, for we had said enough. But today by the grace of God I shall try to give you the food you need, for you need to know what it is and precisely where its greatness lies.

2. When you have undergone the real birth of the resurrection, you will eat another kind of food which is wonderful beyond description; you will feed upon the grace of the Spirit, which will make your bodies immortal and your souls unchanging ... It enables those who have been born by the resurrection to remain firm, so that their bodies do not decay, and their souls experience no change inclining them to evil.

3. But for the present we are born in anticipation[1] at baptism in the hope of this expected birth. For at this moment we receive the first-fruits of the grace of the Holy Spirit, which we shall possess then; today we are given an advance payment of what we shall receive in full through the resurrection in the world to come, and which will make us immortal and unchanging. So we need a food which is suitable for our life in this world to feed us symbolically with the grace of the Holy Spirit. In St Paul's words, 'As often as you eat this bread and drink the cup, you proclaim the Lord's death until he comes.'[2] These words show that, when our Lord comes from heaven, he will reveal the future life and bring the resurrection for all of us ...

4. In this world we owe our existence to two things, birth and nourishment; we derive our existence from our birth, but in order to continue in existence we need nourishment, and without it birth is inevitably followed by decay. In the world to come we likewise derive our existence from our birth and

---

[1]Here and in sections 5 and 6, the Greek word behind this phrase is probably *tupoi*; it also underlies the words 'symbol' and 'symbolical' throughout this homily. Cf. BH 2.15, note 25; 3.7, note 15.
[2]1 Cor. 11.26.

resurrection; but since we are immortal our existence will be permanent. St Paul says: 'We know that if the earthly tent we live in is destroyed, we have a building from God, a house not made by hands, eternal in the heavens.'[3] St Paul describes the future life in such terms for this reason: in this world we win by the labour of our hands the nourishment that enables us to remain alive, but at the resurrection, when we become immortal and take up our abode in heaven, we shall no longer need food produced by the labour of our hands; the gift of immortality, which we shall enjoy then, will take the place of food and keep us alive by the power of grace.*[4]

5. This, then, is the future that awaits us through the resurrection. But since we are born now at baptism symbolically and by signs, we need also to receive under the same symbols nourishment which is in keeping with the new life we receive at baptism, and which will enable us to preserve this life. Every animal that is born by nature from another receives the kind of nourishment it needs from the body of the mother that gave it birth.* And we too have received divine grace in anticipation, and so need nourishment from the other world which is the origin of our birth. The abolition of our Lord's death by his resurrection reveals to us the birth that will be ours in the world to come through our resurrection. St Paul was thinking of the food for our symbolical birth in this world at baptism when he said: 'All of us who have been baptized into Christ Jesus were baptized into his death. We were buried therefore with him by baptism into death, so that as Christ was raised from the dead by the glory of the Father, we too might walk in newness of life. For if we have been united with him in a death like his, we shall certainly be united with him in a resurrection like his.'[5]

---

[3]2 Cor. 5.1.

[4]According to T, St Paul is emphasising the permanence of life in heaven. It is permanent by virtue of the gift of immortality, and so will not need the transient support of the eucharistic food. The argument, continued in section 6, is that, since the Eucharist proclaims the death of Christ, and the death of Christ is the source of our new birth and resurrection, the Eucharist is the food for Christians in their new birth.

[5]Rom. 6.3-5. Since there is no obvious connection between this passage and the Eucharist, Tonneau thinks something has dropped out of the text; but see note 4.

6. St Paul teaches us that Christ's death pointed to the resurrection. We were buried with him in anticipation by baptism, in order to share his death in this world by faith and so share also in his resurrection. The death of Christ our Lord procures for us not only the birth of baptism but also symbolic food. We have St Paul's word for this: 'As often as you eat this bread and drink the cup,' he says, 'you proclaim the Lord's death until he comes.'[6] He means that when we receive the offering and take part in the mysteries, we proclaim our Lord's death, which obtains for us the resurrection and the enjoyment of immortality. Since we have received sacramental birth through the death of Christ our Lord, it is fitting that we should also receive from his death the food of immortality. We have to obtain food from the source from which we derived our birth, in conformity with the law of nature that all living creatures are nourished by the parents that gave them life.

7. Our Lord also bears witness to this fact. When he gave us this sacrament he said: 'Take, eat; this is my body which is broken for you for the forgiveness of sins'; and: 'Take, drink; this is my blood which is poured out for you for the forgiveness of sins.'[7] He means that by death he will give us the world to come where our sins will be forgiven. It is our duty to take part in the sacrament and symbolically proclaim his passion, which will procure for us the possession of the future blessings together with forgiveness of our sins ...

8. The nature of signs and symbols should be appropriate to our present condition.* Just as we received new birth in water, which is so useful, or rather, indispensable for life in the world that one cannot even make bread without it; so too we receive as nourishment bread and wine mixed with water, because these things are especially conducive to life and help us to maintain it. In this world we do enough to maintain our life if we use the appropriate symbols, pondering on this spiritual food which we confidently expect will make us immortal and secure for us the everlasting enjoyment of the blessings we hope for when we receive this holy sacramental food.*

[6] 1 Cor. 11.26.
[7] Mt. 26.26-28; 1 Cor. 11.24-25 (adapted).

9. This, then, is the reason why he gave us the bread and the chalice: these are the food and the drink which keep us alive in this world. But he called the bread his body and the chalice his blood because the passion affected his body and wounded it and made his blood flow. He used food and drink as symbols of the two means of his passion, his body and blood, in order to make known to us our enduring, immortal life,[8] in expectation of which we receive this sacrament which gives us, so we believe, a firm hope of the blessings to come.

10. When he gave his apostles the bread he did not say, 'This is the symbol of my body', but, 'This is my body.' So too with the chalice, he did not say, 'This is the symbol of my blood', but, 'This is my blood' — and with good reason. For he wanted us to turn our attention from the nature of the bread and the chalice once they received the grace and the presence of the Holy Spirit,[9] and to receive them as the body and blood of our Lord. For even our Lord's body did not enjoy immortality and the power to confer immortality by its own nature, but by the gift of the Holy Spirit.[10] It was by resurrection from the dead that this body was united with the divine nature,[11] and so became immortal and the source of immortality for others.

11. This is why, when our Lord said, 'He who eats my flesh and drinks my blood has eternal life',[12] and when he saw the Jews murmuring and doubting his words, thinking that mortal

---

[8]I.e. Christ gave us his body and blood in the form of food to show that they are the source of life.

[9]The bread and wine are not only symbols, but are transformed into Christ's body and blood by the action of the Holy Spirit who is called down upon them (BH 4.11). See Introduction, p. 48, *Epiclesis.* T says more about the Real Presence later (e.g. BH 5.12, 24, 28, 36).

[10]The Father raised Jesus from the dead by the power of the Holy Spirit (cf. Rom. 8.11).

[11]These words seem to imply that Jesus was not united to the Second Person of the Trinity until the resurrection. In BH 3.24, he seems to hold that the union begins at Jesus' baptism. In fact, though he speaks imprecisely, he seems to date the union, as is orthodox teaching, to the beginning of the Incarnation, though here he seems to be saying that the body, as opposed to the human soul, is not fully united until the resurrection. Cf. note 56 to Homily 3.

[12]Jn. 6.54.

flesh cannot confer immortality, he sought to remove their doubts at once by adding: 'What if you were to see the Son of Man ascending where he was before?'[13] He said in effect: 'These words do not carry conviction with you now, because they refer to my body. But when you see me risen from the dead and ascending into heaven, you should certainly not find them harsh and shocking, because the facts themselves will convince you that I have passed to an immortal nature. How else could I ascend into heaven? And in order to show the source of this change, he at once added: 'It is the spirit that gives life, the flesh is of no avail.'[14] He would undergo this change, he meant, by the nature of the life-giving Spirit, which would transfer him to this state in which he would become immortal himself and confer immortality on others. This could not come from his own nature, because it is beyond the powers of the nature of flesh.* But if the life-giving Spirit gave our Lord's body a nature it did not possess before, we too, who have received the grace of the Holy Spirit by sacramental symbols should not regard the offering as bread and chalice any longer, but as the body and blood of Christ.[15] It is the descent of the grace of the Holy Spirit that transforms them, obtaining for those who receive them the gift which we believe the faithful obtain by means of our Lord's body and blood. This is what our Lord meant when he said: 'I am the bread which came down from heaven'; and: 'I am the bread of life.'[16] He showed what he meant by bread when he said: 'The bread which I shall give for the life of the world is my flesh.'[17] Since we need bread and other food to keep us alive, he calls himself the bread of life which came down from heaven, meaning: 'I am the true bread of life which

---

[13]Jn. 6.62. Christ's resurrection proves that he received the Spirit, which transforms his human nature, enabling him to give his flesh and blood as a source of life.

[14]Jn. 6.63.

[15]If the parallel were exact, it would imply that Jesus is no longer human after the resurrection. But, although T says the 'nature' of Christ's body was changed, he still refers to it as a body. It is, however, immortal now, and free from the need to eat, and the other physical limitations (cf. section 13).

[16]Jn. 6.41, 48.

[17]Jn. 6.51.

gives immortality to all who believe in me, by means of this visible body for the sake of which I came down. I have conferred immortality on my body, and by means of it I confer immortality on all who believe in me.' He could have said: 'I am the one who gives life'; but he said instead: 'I am the bread of life.' The immortality that is promised here we shall receive in sacramental symbols by means of the bread and the chalice. Therefore it was right that he should call himself and his body bread to teach us to honour him in the symbol.* He called himself bread because he wanted to explain these gifts and to use familiar things to remove our hesitation in receiving things that are exalted beyond description.

12. To keep alive we take nourishment in the form of bread — not that bread has this power of its own nature; it is only able to keep us alive because God decreed that it should have this power. This fact should convince us that we shall receive immortality when we eat the sacramental bread. For although it is not the nature of bread to produce this effect, once it has received the Holy Spirit and his grace, it can bring those who eat it to the enjoyment of immortality ... So too it is with our Lord's body, which the bread signifies: it received immortality and conferred it on others through the power of the Holy Spirit, even though it was quite devoid of immortality by its own nature.[18]

13. Our Lord's choice of bread for food and the chalice of wine mixed with water for drink was very appropriate. In the Old Testament it was already possible to call wine blood: 'He gave him wine, the blood of grapes, to drink,'[19] it says in one passage; and in another: 'He washes his garments in wine and his vesture in the blood of grapes.'[20] But Christ revealed clearly that it was wine that he gave: 'I shall not drink again the fruit of the vine until I drink it new with you in the kingdom of God.'[21] The kingdom of God he speaks of is the resurrection,

---

[18]T regards immortality as a gift of the Holy Spirit, not a natural property of the soul.

[19]Deut. 32.14 (adapted).

[20]Gen. 49.11.

[21]Mt. 26.29 (adapted).

because he establishes the kingdom of God in the world to come among those who rise again from the dead. Since he was to eat and drink with them after the resurrection before ascending into heaven — 'eating with them', St Luke says[22] — he shows that the passion is close at hand, and that he will not eat with them before the passion; but when he rises from the dead he will condescend to eat and drink with them to confirm the resurrection. This is the meaning of his words: 'I shall not drink again of the fruit of the vine until I drink it new with you in the kingdom of God.' I shall not take any food or drink with you, he meant, before the passion, because it is facing me immediately; but when I rise from the dead, I shall agree to eat and drink again with you, and in so doing I shall be doing something new. The new element consists in the fact that he who is risen from the dead and become immortal by nature eats and drinks. I will do violence to the nature of things in order that you may have unhesitating faith in me, believing that I have risen from the dead and that I, the risen one, whom you knew before, have eaten and drunk with you. Since you have many doubts about the resurrection, to convince you I must do violence to the nature of things and do something that has never been done before — eat and drink after taking an immortal nature. You above all need to understand my resurrection without hesitation, for you will have to explain it to others.

14. It is clear, then, that what Christ our Lord gave you in the chalice as a symbol of his blood is wine. It was diluted with water, either because this was the normal way of drinking wine, or else because it was appropriate that water should be added to the chalice, since it had also gone into the making of the bread — one cannot make bread without adding water to the mixture. We used this symbol for the birth of baptism, and use it again for the sacrament of food and drink. We commemorated our Lord's death in baptism, and recall it in holy communion, as St Paul said ...

---

[22]Cf. Lk. 24.43; Acts 1.4 (variant).

The Eucharistic Sacrifice: Christ the High Priest

15. *The most important point to grasp is that the food we take is a kind of sacrifice we perform.* It is true that we commemorate our Lord's death in food and drink, believing that these are the memorials of his passion, since he said himself: 'This is my body which is broken for you.'[23] But it is evident also that what we perform in the liturgy is a kind of sacrifice. *The duty of the High Priest[24] of the New Covenant is to offer this sacrifice which revealed the nature of the New Covenant.* It is clearly a sacrifice, although it is not something that is new or accomplished by the efforts of the bishop: it is a recalling of this true offering.[25] Since the bishop performs in symbol signs of the heavenly realities,[26] the sacrifice must manifest them, so that he presents, as it were, an image of the heavenly liturgy. For we who perform our priestly office outside the Old Law could not be priests unless we bore the image of the heavenly realities. St Paul says this of Christ our

[23]Adapted from 1 Cor. 11.24 and Mt. 26.28.

[24]I.e. Christ; the bishop is simply acting the part of the High Priest (BH 4.21).

[25]This admirably clear statement of eucharistic theology would probably have satisfied all parties in the Reformation controversies. It anticipates the theories of O. Casel and M. de la Taille that have had such an influence on Roman Catholic theology, as well as the agreements reached in such ecumenical dialogues as that of Faith and Order (*Baptism, Eucharist and Ministry*) and the Anglican-Roman Catholic International Commission: the Eucharist *makes effectually present* the once-for-all sacrifice of Christ. The word 'recalling', of course, implies not a mere commemoration, but actual participation in the eternal sacrifice. See the following note, and section 20.

[26]Realities: 'this word is always a very ordinary, un-metaphysical one roughly = *pragma*' (R. Murray). Nevertheless, the passage quoted from Hebrews envisages the heavenly liturgy in Platonic terms as an archetypal form of which the liturgies of the Old Law are a mere copy. Hebrews, however, does not consider the status of the earthly liturgy of the New Covenant, as T does here. T will not call it a mere shadow or copy; he prefers to call it a 'symbol' (or anticipation, *tupos*) (section 18), a 'recalling' (section 15), and 'image' (section 20). The bishop is the 'representation' (*eikon*) of the High Priest (19), and plays his part (21). The categories are basically Platonic.

T does not explain, however, the relationship between the heavenly liturgy and the sacrifice of Christ on the Cross. In Hebrews, the connection is clear; Christ, having made his definitive sacrifice on Calvary, enters into the heavenly sanctuary carrying his own blood offered in sacrifice; his perpetual presence at the Father's right hand to make intercession for us through this blood constitutes the heavenly liturgy.

Lord: 'If he were on earth, he would not be a priest at all, since there are priests who offer gifts and sacrifices according to the Law. They serve a copy and shadow of the heavenly sanctuary.'[27] He means that all the priests of the Old Law performed their duties on earth, where the commands of the Law were appropriate for mortals and sacrifices of slaughtered animals were in keeping with man's mortal stay on the face of the earth. For it is evident that this prescription and all the ceremonial of the Law, such as circumcision, the sabbath, holy days, the observance of feasts and the choice of food, was designed for mortal nature and is entirely out of keeping with one that is immortal ... but, as St Paul says, if Christ our Lord had had to perform a liturgy on earth, he would necessarily have had to exercise his priesthood according to the divine law and to perform the liturgy according to the regulations; otherwise he would not have been a High Priest at all.* But, as it is, he exercises his priesthood not on earth, but in heaven, since he died, rose again and ascended into heaven to raise all of us up too and make us ascend into heaven, for such is the covenant he made for those who were to believe in him ...

16. Christ exercises the true High Priesthood. He offered himself in sacrifice when he gave himself up to die for us all. But he became the first to rise from the dead, ascend into heaven and sit at God's right hand, in order to destroy all our enemies. In St Paul's words: 'When Christ had offered for all time a single sacrifice for sins, he sat down at the right hand of God, then to wait until his enemies should be made a stool for his feet. For by a single offering he has perfected for all time those who are sanctified.'[28] By 'his enemies' St Paul means those who make war on us, for our perfection clearly implies their destruction. He is right to call our Lord the High Priest, since he revealed himself as one who performed the High Priest's functions of first approaching God himself and then leading the rest to God after him ...[29] In St Paul's words, Christ our

[27]Heb. 8.4-5 (adapted).

[28]Heb. 10.12-14.

[29]This sentiment is in keeping with the theology of Christ's Priesthood expressed in Hebrews. Christ is the 'pioneer' (i.e. pathfinder, 2.10), who is able to bring others to the Father because he has run the same course himself (12.1-2).

Lord, who is the High Priest of us all, does not 'serve a copy and shadow of the heavenly sanctuary',[30] like the liturgy according to the Law; he is 'a minister in the sanctuary and the true tent which is set up not by man but by the Lord'[31], to teach us the heavenly mysteries. The author regards them as holy because they contain no contrary element of evil; when he speaks of 'the true tent which is set up not by man but by the Lord', he refers to heaven, because the tent prescribed by the Law was made by men, whereas heaven is not made by men but by God. This is the tent, he means, of which Christ is the minister, since he has ascended into heaven, where he performs the liturgy on our behalf, using every means to draw us there as he promised.[32]

For the same reason St Paul says in another passage: 'Who is at the right hand of God, who indeed intercedes for us.'[33] This intercession is not a kind of prayer offered for us in words; it consists of deeds. For having ascended into heaven, he performs service for us to God, and has undertaken to make us all ascend to his side in heaven.

17. According to St Paul, Christ our Lord would not have been a priest at all if he had been obliged to exercise his priesthood on earth,[34] unless he had followed the rites of the Law; for as the priesthood and liturgy of the Law were revealed by God on earth, it would not be right if what came from God were rejected and another liturgy were established on earth in its place. Christ is called High Priest — and rightly so — for this reason: he performs his priestly duties in heaven, where there is no communion with the things on earth. Accordingly no slight is paid to the priests of the Law; for according to another text[35] they are commissioned to deal with mortals and earthly beings, while Christ exercises his priesthood among other, much greater and more excellent things, among the immortal and heavenly realities. Indeed, is it not evident that it would not be possible, for us either, to be priests with a commission to

[30]Heb. 8.5.
[31]Heb. 8.2.
[32]Cf. Jn. 12.32.
[33]Rom. 8.34.
[34]Cf. Heb. 8.4.
[35]T is alluding perhaps to Heb. 5.1; 9.11.

exercise a priesthood on earth?[36] Certainly the priesthood of the Law was valid for mortal men of this world, whereas Christ is High Priest of the heavenly things, and will bring us all up there when the right time comes.

18. Since we are called by him to a New Covenant, in St Paul's words,[37] we have received this salvation and this life in hope. Since we do not see them, but wait to 'be away from the body and at home with the Lord', 'we walk by faith, not by sight';[38] for we have not yet attained to the realities, we have not yet reached the heavenly blessings. We continue in faith until we ascend into heaven and go to our Lord, when we shall no longer see him in a mirror dimly,[39] but face to face. We look forward to attaining to this state in reality at the resurrection, at the time God has ordained; in the meantime we approach the first-fruits of these blessings, Christ our Lord, the High Priest of our inheritance. Accordingly we are taught to perform in this world the symbols and signs of the blessings to come, and so, as people who enter into the enjoyment of the good things of heaven by means of the liturgy, we may possess in assured hope what we look for. So just as the true new birth is the birth to which we look forward at the resurrection, while what we undergo at baptism is a new symbolic birth, so too the true food of immortality is the food we hope to receive and will truly receive later by the gift of the Holy Spirit, while for the present we receive the food of immortality only in symbols or by means of symbols, through the grace of the Holy Spirit.*

The Bishop represents the High Priest

19. It follows that, since there needs to be a representation of the High Priest, certain individuals are appointed to preside over the liturgy of these signs. For we believe that what Christ our Lord performed in reality, and will continue to perform, is performed through the sacraments by those whom divine

---

[36]Presumably because only descendants of Levi enjoy the privilege.
[37]Cf. Heb. 9.15.
[38]2 Cor. 5.8, 7.
[39]Cf. 1 Cor. 13.12.

grace has called to be priests of the New Covenant when the Holy Spirit comes down on them to strengthen them and ordain them.[40] This is why they do not offer new sacrifices, like the repeated immolations prescribed by the Law. The priests of the Old Law were told to offer God many different victims — bulls, goats and sheep. They offered a succession of new victims; when one lot had been offered, killed and completely destroyed, others were offered in their place.* But with priests of the New Covenant it is just the reverse: they continue to offer the same sacrifice in every place and at every time. For there is only one sacrifice which was offered for us all, the sacrifice of Christ our Lord, who underwent death for our sake and by this sacrifice brought our perfection, as St Paul said: 'By a single offering he has perfected for all time those who are sanctified.'[41]

20. In every place and at every time we continue to perform the commemoration of this same sacrifice; for as often as we eat this bread and drink this chalice, we proclaim our Lord's death until he comes.[42] Every time, then, there is performed the liturgy of this awesome sacrifice, which is the clear image of the heavenly realities, we should imagine that we are in heaven.* Faith enables us to picture in our minds the heavenly realities, as we remind ourselves that the same Christ who is in heaven, who died for us, rose again and ascended to heaven, is now being immolated under these symbols. So when faith enables our eyes to contemplate the commemoration that takes place now, we are brought again to see his death, resurrection and ascension, which have already taken place for our sake.

21. Since Christ our Lord offered himself for us in sacrifice and so became in reality our High Priest, *we ought to believe that the bishop who is now at the altar is playing the part of this High Priest.* He is not offering his own sacrifice, for he is not the real High Priest here: he only performs a kind of representation of the liturgy of this sacrifice that is too great for words. By this means he performs for you a visible representation of these

---

[40]Literally, 'strengthen and establish them as sons of the sacrament'.
[41]Heb. 10.14.
[42]Cf. 1 Cor. 11.26. See note 25.

indescribable heavenly realities and of the spiritual, immaterial powers.[43]

The Deacons represent the Angels

Because Christ our Lord brought about for our sake this Incarnation[44] which is beyond explanation, all the invisible powers pay him service. In St Paul's words, they were indeed 'all ministering spirits sent forth to serve, for the sake of those who are to obtain salvation'.[45] We can discover the same truth in St Matthew's gospel: 'Angels came and ministered to him.'[46] Our Lord's own words show that this is so: 'Soon you will see heaven opened and the angels of God ascending and descending upon the Son of Man.'[47] The gospels record examples: the actions of the beings who sang at our Lord's birth, 'Glory to God in the highest, and on earth peace, and good hope to men',[48] and of those who at the resurrection told the women what had happened and at the ascension explained to the apostles the things they did not understand. So now, when this awesome liturgy is performed, *we ought to believe that the deacons are so to speak presenting an image of the liturgy of the invisible powers.*[49] For by the grace of the Holy Spirit the deacons have been put in charge of the celebration of this awesome liturgy.

22. For this reason, all of us who have been called to a form of ministry are called ministers of Christ. St Paul says: 'Inasmuch then as I am an apostle to the gentiles, I magnify my ministry.'[50] But all agree that the name 'deacon' (minister) belongs properly to those who are in charge of this liturgical ministry, and so resemble the 'ministering spirits sent forth to serve.'[51]*

23. *They wear vestments which are in keeping with their true role, for their garments give them a more impressive appearance than they*

---

[43]I.e. the spirits or angels.
[44]*Oikonomia.* See BH 2.3, note 6.
[45]Heb. 1.14.
[46]Mt. 4.11.
[47]Jn. 1.51 (alternative reading).
[48]Lk. 2.14 (alternative reading).
[49]For the comparison of deacons to angels, cf. Ambrose S 1.6 with note 13.
[50]Rom. 11.13.
[51]Heb. 1.14.

possess on their own account ... On their left shoulders they drape a stole,[52] *which hangs down equally on either side,* that is to say, in front and behind. It signifies that the ministry they perform is not one of slavery but of liberty, for the realities which they serve guide all who are worthy of God's great household the Church to freedom. They do not drape the stole round their neck so that both ends hang down behind, because no domestic servant dresses like that, but only free men who are their own masters.* The deacons wear the stole on their shoulder because they have a servant's position; but the stole is itself a sign of the freedom to which all of us who believe in Christ have been called and towards which we are hastening in our journey to what St Paul calls 'the household of God which is the church of the living God, the pillar and bulwark of truth'.[53] For it is precisely in the service of all that the deacons have undertaken their duties.

24. Christ our Lord established these awesome mysteries for us. We look forward to their perfect fulfilment in the world to come, but we have already laid hold of them by faith, so that even in this world we can struggle not to abandon any part of our faith in them.[54] Accordingly we need this sacramental liturgy to strengthen our faith in the revelation we have received; the liturgy leads us on to what is to come, for we know that it contains, as it were, an image of the mysterious administration[55] of Christ our Lord, and affords us a shadowy vision of what took place. Accordingly at the sight of the bishop we form in our hearts a kind of image of Christ our Lord sacrificing himself to save us and give us life.[56] At the sight of the

---

[52]Literally 'orarium', a linen cloth originally carried to wipe the sweat from the face, which gradually became elongated and was then wrapped round the neck like a student's scarf. In this form it became recognized as a liturgical vestment. I can find no other evidence that, when worn in a particular way, it was a sign of slavery. Cf. BH 2.19.

[53]1 Tim. 3.15.

[54]T's emphasis on our efforts to preserve faith is a faint pre-echo of Pelagius' belief that salvation lay in our own power. Later generations, indeed, unjustly regarded T as the father of Pelagianism as well as of Nestorianism.

[55]*Oikonomia.* See BH 2.3, note 6.

[56]Mediaeval piety elaborated in greater detail the correspondence between the ceremonies of the Mass and the incidents of the passion. Such interpretations do not accord well with liturgical scholarship and are not popular today.

deacons who serve at the ceremony we think of the invisible ministering powers who officiate at this mysterious liturgy; for the deacons bring this sacrifice — or rather the symbols of the sacrifice — and lay it out on the awesome altar ...

The Preparation of the Gifts

25. By means of the signs *we must see Christ now being led away to his passion and again later when he is stretched out on the altar to be immolated for us.* When the offering which is about to be presented is brought out in the sacred vessels, on the patens and in the chalice, you must imagine that Christ our Lord is being led out to his passion.[57] He is not led out by the Jews; it would be intolerable that there should be any evil symbolism in the signs of our life and salvation.[58] These signs point to the invisible ministering powers which were present at the time of the saving passion and performed their ministry, as they did throughout our Lord's incarnate life ...[59]* When our Lord was praying in fear of the approaching passion, St Luke tells us 'there appeared to him an angel from heaven, strengthening him'.[60] Like spectators who shout to encourage athletes, the angel anointed him to help him to bear his sufferings, encouraging him to endure, and reminding him that the passion was short in comparison with the benefits it would

---

[57]For T the status of the offerings as they are presented at this point is radically different from their status after the Epiclesis. The offerings which are presented at this stage in the celebration (paragraph 25) are signs of the dead Christ; the Holy Spirit has not yet descended on them to make Christ present in his risen state (BH 4.11; 5.11). The presentation of the bread and wine described here is distinguished from the 'offering' itself, which takes place during the Eucharistic Prayer (BH 4.44-45); see Introduction, pp. 41-43.

[58]The carrying up of the offerings by the deacons symbolises the leading of Christ to his passion. The deacons represent the angels present at the passion, not the Jews that led Jesus to his death. This exclusion of the Jews from the symbolism is not necessarily due to anti-Semitism; as T says in the last two lines of this section, he does not want the deacons to be made to represent the executioners. In the modern Byzantine rite at the Great Entrance, the bread and wine are brought to the altar to the accompaniment of the words: '... that we may welcome the King of the Universe, invisibly escorted by the ranks of the Angels'.

[59]*Oikonomia.*

[60]Lk. 22.43.

produce; for he would gain great glory immediately after his passion and death and would be the source of many benefits, not only for mankind, but also for the whole of creation.* So you must regard deacons as representations of the invisible ministering powers when they carry up the bread for the offering — with this difference, that their ministrations and these commemorations do not send Christ our Lord to his life-giving passion.

26. They bring up the bread and place it on the holy altar to complete the representation of the passion. So from now on we should consider that Christ has already undergone the passion and is now placed on the altar as if in a tomb. *That is why some of the deacons spread cloths on the altar which remind us of winding-sheets, while others* after the body is laid on the altar *stand on either side and fan the air above the sacred body* and prevent anything from settling on it. This shows us the importance of the body on the altar; for it is the custom among the great ones of this world that at their funerals, as a mark of honour, attendants fan the body as it is carried on its bier.[61] The same practice must be observed now that the sacred, dread and incorruptible body submits to being laid out on the altar, soon to rise again with an immortal nature ...

27. Holy Scripture teaches us that there were angels beside the tomb sitting on the stone; they announced the resurrection to the women, and as long as Christ remained dead, stayed there to do him honour until they had seen the resurrection. They proclaimed that he is the common good of all mankind and the renewal of all creation, as St Paul said: 'If any one is in Christ, he is a new creature; the old has passed away, behold, the new has come.'[62] So now we re-enact this angelic service in

---

[61]The use of fans on handles to drive away the flies (the mention of birds in section 27 is unusual) and stir the air was known to the Greeks and Romans of classical times. Fan-bearers became a mark of dignity, as only the wealthy would be able to afford them. Fans then entered into liturgical use, where they served both the practical and the honorific function. Often they were made of peacocks' feathers, and in this form featured in papal ceremonial until very recently. See H. Leclercq, 'Flabellum', in DACL, vol. v, coll. 1610-1625. T concentrates on their use in funerals because he is looking for symbols of mourning.

[62]2 Cor. 5.17.

commemoration of those who during the Lord's passion and death at every moment came and stood by. This is why the deacons stand round waving their fans, offering a kind of honour and veneration to the body that is laid out on the altar; in keeping it free from the filth of bird-droppings, they remind all present to regard the body as awesome and truly holy, for by virtue of its union with the divine nature it is truly the Lord.*[63] So it is right that they should lay it out and stand watch by it with great reverence.

28. *All this takes place amid general silence;* for since the liturgy has not yet begun, it is appropriate that everyone should look on in fearful recollection and silent prayer while this great and august body is brought and laid out. For when our Lord died, the disciples also withdrew and remained for a while in a house in great recollection and fear. An indescribable silence reigned all round, while even the invisible powers remained in recollection, with their thoughts fixed on the coming resurrection. When the moment came for Christ our Lord to rise again, it was a source of indescribable joy and happiness to them. When the women came to honour the body, the angels announced to them the news of the resurrection. The women told the disciples, and they ran together eagerly to the tomb.

29. So now the same circumstances remind us of our Lord's passion. When we see the offering on the altar like a body laid in a tomb, recollection takes hold of all present because of the dread rites that are performed. So they are obliged with recollection and fear to watch what is being done, because at this moment, through the awesome liturgy as it is performed according to the priestly rules, Christ our Lord is to rise from the dead, proclaiming to all a share in his sublime blessings. This is why in the offering we recall our Lord's death: it is the

---

[63]As the Holy Spirit has not yet descended on the bread and wine to make Christ present in his risen state (BH 4.25 with note 57; 5.11), T's words here must refer not to the eucharistic body of Christ, but to the dead body that lay in the tomb. By paying honour to what is still only bread, T believes, one is honouring the 'awesome and truly holy' body in the tomb, which the bread and wine symbolise. This view that even the dead body of Jesus was still united with the divinity has been commonly held by Catholic theologians, among others by St Thomas (*Summa*, iii. 50.2).

proclamation of the resurrection and the sublime blessings.

Prayer over the Offerings

30. *Then comes the time for prayer aloud. The deacon announces it.* He must be able to give the sign for the various ceremonies and explain their purpose ...

31. When he has performed his duty of arousing all the congregation and suggesting suitable prayers, *everyone stands in silence while the bishop begins the Prayer over the Offerings.* We should address a prayer to God before any action that is connected with his service, especially this awesome liturgy which we can perform only with God's help.* *In the course of the prayer he gives thanks* to our Lord for the great favours he procured for the salvation and life of mankind, and for giving us knowledge of this wonderful sacrament which is the memorial of the sublime gift which he bestowed upon us through his passion — his promise that we should rise from the dead and ascend to heaven.

32. *He gives thanks on his own behalf* for the fact that Christ has made him a minister of so dread a sacrament. Then he makes this request, that God will grant him now the grace of the Holy Spirit by which he has been called to the priesthood, so that he may be worthy of his great ministry, and by the grace of God may be free from all evil intentions and fear of punishment, as he approaches these things that are infinitely beyond him.

33. When the bishop has concluded these prayers and others like them, *all present reply: 'Amen'*. This word is an exclamation of agreement with the bishop's prayer. St Paul mentions it: 'How can any one in the position of an outsider say the "Amen" to your thanksgiving when he does not know what you are saying?' ...[64]

34. When the congregation has said 'Amen', *the bishop prays: 'Peace be with you'.* It is a good practice to begin every ceremony in church with this phrase, especially the dread liturgy which is about to be celebrated. St Paul begins all his epistles with the words: 'Grace to you and peace', praying that we may receive

[64]1 Cor. 14.16.

these gifts which the incarnate life[65] of Christ our Lord has won for us.[66] By coming into this world he destroyed all wars and uprooted all hate and conflict directed against us — death, corruption, sin, passion, the assaults of demons, all causes of distress. He liberated us from all this by his resurrection and set us altogether free from death and change; he raises us up to heaven where he grants us great confidence in his presence, and he prepares us for loving friendship with the invisible powers who are God's faithful servants. But St Paul in all his epistles puts the word 'grace' before 'peace'; for it is not by our own initiative or power but by God's grace that we have received such a precious gift.

35. It has always been laid down that those who are privileged to perform the duties of a priest must begin every ceremony in church with this prayer, especially the celebration of the dread sacrament. The bishop's prayer that all may enjoy peace proclaims the wonderful blessings of which this liturgy of the memorial of our Lord's death is the sign and the means.* *The congregation replies: 'And with your spirit'.*

36. In return they make the same prayer for him, showing the bishop and all present that, while the others need the bishop's blessing and prayer, he in turn needs their prayer. For this reason it has always been the custom that the prayers of the Church should include the needs of bishops as well as those of the rest; for we are one body of Christ our Lord[67] and all 'members one of another'.[68] The bishop plays the part of a more important limb than the others. I will explain what I mean. He is the eye or the tongue. As the eye he sees what everyone is doing, and with a priest's concern gives correction when it is called for; as the tongue he offers the prayers of all. But the eye and the tongue, if they are to do their work properly, need the healthy functioning of the other parts of the body; so too the bishop belongs to the body of the Church and

---

[65] *Oikonomia.* All of this takes place before the Eucharistic Prayer, which is described in the next homily.

[66] In the next two sentences T explains what he understands by 'peace', and then explains the need of 'grace'.

[67] Cf. 1 Cor. 12.27; Rom. 12.5

[68] Eph. 4.25.

needs to function healthily in order to exhibit the sound morals that befit a priest and to prove that he is worthy of his office and that he does his duty to the community.* That is why at the word 'peace' he blesses the congregation, and receives their blessing in turn when they say: 'And with your spirit'.

37. These words do not refer to the bishop's soul, but to the grace of the Holy Spirit by which his people believe he is called to the priesthood. St Paul speaks of God, 'whom I serve with my spirit in the gospel of his Son',[69] as if to say: by the gift of the grace of the Holy Spirit which has been given me to enable me to carry out the service of the gospel and you to be all united with my spirit. In other words, he says, now that God has given me power to do this and other similar things, I have no rest for my spirit; I have not been able to accomplish all that one who does service with the Holy Spirit for the good of others should accomplish, because he who should have helped me was absent.

38. This is the reason for the ancient custom of the Church that the congregation should reply to the bishop: 'And with your spirit'. When all is well with the bishop, the whole body of the Church feels the benefit, but when he is ailing, the whole community suffers. So all pray that this 'peace' will bring him the grace of the Holy Spirit to enable him to fulfil his duties and perform the liturgy worthily on behalf of the community. Conversely, the abundance of the grace of the Holy Spirit will give the bishop peace, making it easier for him to perform the prescribed ceremonies when in all his affairs and especially in the liturgy he shows that he has a clear conscience.

Kiss of Peace

39. When the bishop and the congregation have exchanged blessings, *the bishop begins to give the Kiss of Peace, and the church herald,* that is to say, the deacon, *in a loud voice orders all the people to exchange the Kiss of Peace,* following the bishop's example. This kiss which all present exchange constitutes a kind of profession

---

[69]Rom. 1.9. T's theory that 'with thy spirit' refers to the bishop's grace of ordination rather than his soul is hardly justifiable on linguistic grounds.

of the unity and charity that exists among them. Each of us
gives the Kiss of Peace to the person next to him, and so in
effect gives it to the whole assembly, because this act is an
acknowledgement that we have all become the single body of
Christ our Lord, and so must preserve with one another that
harmony that exists among the limbs of a body, loving one
another equally, supporting and helping one another,
regarding the individual's needs as concerns of the community,
sympathising with one another's sorrows and sharing in one
another's joys.

40. The new birth that we underwent at baptism is unique for
this reason, that it joins us into a natural unity; and so we all
share the same food when we partake of the same body and the
same blood, for we have been linked in the unity of baptism. St
Paul says: 'Because there is one loaf, we who are many are one
body, for we all partake of the same loaf.'[70] This is why before
we approach the sacrament of the liturgy we are required to
observe the custom of giving the Kiss of Peace, as a profession
of unity and mutual charity. It would certainly not be right for
those who form a single body, the body of the Church, to
entertain hatred towards a brother in the faith, who has shared
the same birth so as to become a member of the same body, and
whom we believe to be a member of Christ our Lord, just as we
are, and to share the same food at the spiritual table. Our Lord
said: 'Every one who is angry with his brother without cause
shall be liable to judgment.'[71] This ceremony, then, is not only
a profession of charity, but a reminder to us to lay aside all
unholy enmity, if we feel that our cause of complaint against
one of our brothers in the faith is not just. After our Lord had
forbidden any unjust anger, he offered the following remedy
to sinners of every kind: 'If you are offering your gift at the altar,
and there remember that your brother has something against
you, leave your gift there before the altar and go; first be
reconciled to your brother, and then come and offer your
gift.'[72] He tells the sinner to seek immediately every means of

[70] 1 Cor. 10.17.
[71] Mt. 5.22 (alternative reading).
[72] Mt. 5.23-24.

reconciliation with the man he has offended, and not to presume to make his offering until he has made amends to the one he has wronged and done all in his power to placate him; for we all make the offering by the agency of the bishop.

41. For although it is the bishop who stands up to make the offering, he is only acting as the tongue on behalf of the whole body.[73] We all make the offering in common, and all derive from it a common benefit and to all is extended an equal share of what has been offered. When St Paul says of the high priest that 'he is bound to offer sacrifice for his own sins as well as for those of the people',[74] he implies that the high priest is appointed to make a common offering for himself and for everyone else.

If anyone has wronged another, then, he must do all he can to make amends to the one he has wronged and to effect a reconciliation with him. If the injured party is present, the reconciliation should be made on the spot; if not, the offender must resolve to seek a reconciliation by all the means in his power when occasion offers. Only then may he come forward to take part in the offering. The injured party, on the other hand, must accept the other's offer of redress as readily as the offender made it.* He must put out of his mind all memories of the wrongs done to him and recall our Lord's words: 'If you do not forgive men their trespasses neither will your Father forgive your trespasses.'[75] We must regard the Kiss of Peace as a profession and a reminder of all this. Like St Paul, we should give one another peace 'with a holy kiss';[76] we must not be like Judas and kiss with the mouth only, while remaining set on showing hatred and malice to our brothers in the faith.

---

[73]T emphasizes the congregation's share in the bishop's priestly powers (cf. BH 5.5; 5.25 with note 48); 4.45 shows that the word 'offering' refers to the Eucharistic Prayer. Against this egalitarian expression of the bishop's powers should be set what T says in sections 37-38 about the peculiar powers and gifts of the bishop.

[74]Heb. 5.3. Since all share in offering, all must apply to themselves our Lord's command that one must not offer until one is reconciled.

[75]Mt. 6.15.

[76]Rom. 16.16.

Lavabo

42. *Next the bishop*[77] *washes his hands, and after him all the priests present, however many there may be, do the same.* They do not perform this ceremony to get their hands clean: decency requires that everyone should wash,[78] priests on account of their ministry, others on account of the offering they are about to receive. But the priests are appointed to offer the sacrifice for the whole community, and so they perform this ceremony to remind us all that when the sacrifice is offered we must all offer ourselves with clean consciences. Accordingly immediately after the Kiss of Peace by which we profess that we have laid aside all hatred and bitterness against our brothers in the faith and washed away the memory of grudges, we need to cleanse ourselves from every stain.

Reading of the Names of the Living and the Dead

43. All stand at a sign from the deacon and fix their eyes on the actions that are performed. *The names of the living and the dead* who have died believing in Christ *are read from the Church records.* These short lists of names, of course, include implicitly all the living and the dead. We learn from this the effect of the incarnate life[79] of Christ our Lord. For this liturgy, which is his memorial, benefits all, living and dead alike; the living contemplate their hopes for the future, while the dead are no longer dead but deep in sleep,[80] waiting in the hope for which Christ our Lord accepted the death that we commemorate in this sacrament.

Preparation for the Eucharistic Prayer

44. After the reading of these lists, *the bishop comes forward to perform the liturgy, while the Church herald* (i.e. the deacon who

---

[77]In this section 'bishop' and 'priest' translate the same Syriac word.

[78]Cf. Cyril of Jerusalem, MC 5.2: if the clergy had been dirty they would have washed before coming to church.

[79]*Oikonomia.*

[80]On death seen as sleep, see BH 3.5 with note 10.

announces to the congregation how to follow the actions of the bishop) *proclaims: 'Turn your eyes to the offering'.* *For the ceremony which is about to take place is a community affair. The community sacrifice is immolated and the community offering is presented on behalf of all, for those absent[81] as well as those present, in as much as they have shared the faith and been numbered as members of God's Church and lived out their lives in it. It is evident that 'to present the offering' and 'to immolate the offering' are synonymous terms, for what is immolated and offered to God is, as it were, a dread victim. Thus, St Paul says, Christ 'did this once for all when he offered up himself', 'it is necessary for this priest also to have something to offer'. [82] So, since our sacrifice is a representation of Christ's sacrifice, we call it the 'offering' or the 'delivering'[83] of the offering'. This is why it is appropriate for the deacon to prepare the ceremony with the words: *'Turn your eyes to the offering.'*

45. All have been warned to turn their eyes to the objects that have been placed in readiness ... Now the bishop begins the offering itself. How? You must be taught this too. But I have spoken for long enough: I shall keep this subject for another day, if God permits. And may God the Father, the Son and the Holy Spirit be praised for all things, now and for ever. Amen.

[81]The 'absent' include the dead.
[82]Heb. 7.27; 8.3. 'This priest', of course, refers to Christ.
[83]Literally 'sending up'. See BH 4.25 with note 57, and Introduction, pp. 41-43.

BAPTISMAL HOMILY V

Synopsis — The bishop begins the Eucharistic Prayer. First he blesses the people with the words: 'The grace of the Lord Jesus Christ and the love of God and the fellowship of the Holy Spirit be with you all.' The people reply: 'And with your spirit.' The bishop then says to the people: 'Lift up your hearts.' The people reply: 'To you, O Lord,' Then the bishop says: 'Let us give thanks to the Lord.' The people reply: 'It is right and fitting.' Then the bishop proceeds to offer up the offering and immolate the sacrifice on behalf of the community. The bishop[1] raises his voice and pronounces these words of praise: 'Holy, holy, holy is the almighty Lord. His praises fill all heaven and earth.' All fall silent again, with eyes cast down, while the Church herald proclaims: 'Let us all stand in great fear and trembling.' By virtue of the sacramental actions, this is the moment appointed for Christ our Lord to rise from the dead and pour out his grace upon us all. The bishop also prays that the grace of the Holy Spirit may come upon all the assembly. He offers a prayer for all whom it is customary to name in church, and then passes on to the commemoration of the dead. After these prayers the bishop pauses, then takes the sacred bread in his hands and looks up to heaven. He breaks the bread while praying for the people that the grace of Jesus Christ our Lord may come upon them. The people reply in the usual way. He traces the sign of the cross over the blood with the bread and over the bread with the blood. For this reason it is laid down that he should drop the life-giving bread piece by piece into the chalice. We must pray to our Lord first for those who brought this holy offering. The bishop blesses the people and wishes them peace; all present make the usual response with heads bowed in due reverence. The Church herald proclaims: 'Let us attend.' The bishop announces: 'What is holy for the holy.' All reply: 'One holy Father, one holy Son, one holy Spirit', and add: 'Glory be to the Father and to the Son

---

[1] R. Tonneau (*Studi e Testi* 145 (1939) p. 531, n. 7) thinks some words have dropped out here; they would have outlined the prayers described in sections 5 and 6. See note 11.

and to the Holy Spirit.' Then we all eagerly receive the offering. Accordingly the bishop, who is performing the offering, is the first to come forward and receive; then we each come forward, with eyes cast down and both hands extended; the right hand is stretched out to receive the offering, and the left hand held underneath. As he gives it the bishop says, 'The body of Christ.' You receive the chalice in the same way. So you say 'Amen' to his words, then receive the offering and swallow it so as to share in the mysteries. After you have received, you offer up thanksgiving and blessing to God, remaining with all the congregation for thanksgiving and blessing in accordance with the Church's custom.

1. This is the time that God has given me to complete what is lacking in your instruction. I began by speaking of the spiritual food which you eat when you receive the sacred sacrament. Then I taught you other things you needed to know concerning it. I was explaining the liturgy in which this food is perfected, and had reached the point at which, according to the Church's custom, the deacon proclaims: *'Turn your eyes to the offering'*. Then the bishop is required to begin the offering. But this was a suitable point for me to break off my instruction, as I had already spoken for some time, and to keep the priestly liturgy for today's homily, which will, please God, conclude what remains to be said.

The Eucharistic Prayer: Introductory
Responses

2. As soon as the deacon says: 'Turn your eyes to the offering', and all have obediently turned their eyes on the action taking place, *the bishop begins the Eucharistic Prayer. First he blesses the people with the words: 'The grace of the Lord Jesus Christ and the love of God the Father and the fellowship of the Holy Spirit be with you all'.*[2] He knows that now, before the liturgy, more than at any other time, the people need to receive this apostolic blessing. It is so rich in meaning and so solemn in character

[2] 2 Cor. 13.14 (adapted). This version of the text is regular in the Byzantine Liturgy.

that the bishop uses it as a beginning. Besides, it accords with scripture: 'God so loved the world', the evangelist wrote, 'that he gave his only Son, that whoever believes in him should not perish but have eternal life.'[3] He did not show this great love for men because he had received from us anything that deserved his good will; he did it of his generosity and mercy. But because of this love God's only Son, God the Word, simply and solely for our salvation, consented to assume[4] one of our race in order to raise him from the dead, and took him up into heaven, united him with himself, and made him sit at God's right hand. He enabled us to share in this process and gave us the Holy Spirit. For the present we receive the first-fruits of the Spirit as a guarantee; later we shall receive him in full, and then we shall have real communion with him and 'our lowly body' will be changed 'to be like his glorious body'.[5] That is why St Paul prayed in his epistles that the faithful might prove themselves worthy of the love which God in his generosity showed to all our race and which the grace of the Holy Spirit bestowed on us all. Again, that is why, when the bishop is on the point of celebrating this solemn liturgy which leads us to such great hopes, it is so appropriate that he should use these words to bless the people. However, some priests only say, 'The grace of our Lord Jesus Christ be with you all', thus abbreviating the apostle's words. *The people reply: 'And with your spirit'.* As always when the bishop blesses the people, wishing them 'grace' or 'peace', custom requires all present to make the response that I have already explained.

3. After the blessing the bishop prepares the people for what is to come with the words: *'Lift up your hearts.'* By these words he shows that, although it is our duty to perform this dread and sublime liturgy on earth, we must look to heaven and turn our thoughts to God, since we are making a commemoration of the sacrifice and death of Christ our Lord, who suffered for us and rose again, was united with the divine nature, and sits at God's right hand in heaven. So we too must fix our minds there and turn our hearts from this memorial to heaven.

[3]Jn. 3.16. T proceeds to show how this text mentions by implication the grace of Jesus, the love of the Father and the fellowship of the Spirit.

[4]On this Christological terminology cf. p. 165, and BH 3.21 and 24 with notes.

[5]Phil. 3.21. Cf. Rom. 8.23; Eph. 1.14.

4. *The people reply: 'To you, O Lord'*, thus professing their willingness to comply. When the bishop has duly prepared the congregation's minds and hearts in this way, he says: *'Let us give thanks to the Lord.'* We owe our thanks to God, the source of all these favours, especially for these things which were done for us and which we are about to commemorate in the liturgy. Accordingly *the people reply: 'It is right and fitting'*, acknowledging that it is right for us to give thanks, either because God, who gave us those gifts, is so great, or because it is right that people who have received favours should not be ungrateful to their benefactor.

The Preface

5. Then, when we are all standing in silence and profound awe, *the bishop proceeds to offer up the offering and immolate the sacrifice on behalf of the community.* He is filled with awe both for himself and for us because our Lord suffered death for us all, a death which will be commemorated in this sacrifice. At this moment the bishop is the tongue of all the Church, and in the liturgy he speaks the appropriate words, words of praise of God, acknowledging that all praise and glory is due to God, and that it is right[6] for us all to pay him adoration and worship, especially by his memorial of the grace which has been given to us and which is beyond the comprehension of mere creatures.

6. We were instructed and baptized in the name of the Father and of the Son and of the Holy Spirit, and to them we must turn for the fulfilment of what is performed in the liturgy. So now the bishop says: 'The majesty of the Father',[7] but adds the words: 'And of the Son', because the Son stands to the Father as one who is truly a Son, is like the Father, has the same Substance as he has,[8] and is in no respect inferior to him.* The bishop must also add the name of the Holy Spirit, thus

---

[6] A paraphrase of the opening words of the Preface, in which the bishop returns to his earlier invitation, 'Let us give thanks', and comments that it is right and fitting to do so.

[7] Presumably T's Preface contained a reference to the majesty of the Trinity.

[8] Cf. BH 2.8, with note 16.

acknowledging that he too is the divine Substance.[9] All creation, the bishop says, and especially the invisible powers, ever praise and glorify this divine, eternally existing nature. He makes special mention of the Seraphim[10] who raise this hymn of praise to God — this hymn, revealed by God to blessed Isaiah, which he recorded in his sacred book, and which all of us here assembled, with the invisible beings, sing in a loud voice: *'Holy, holy, holy is the Lord of hosts. His praises fill all heaven and earth'.*[11] Isaiah foresaw by the power of the Spirit the benefits that were to be conferred on the human race, when he heard in his vision the Seraphim speaking these words. It was by a revelation in a vision that the prophet came to know a kind of majestic liturgy, because it is too sublime for human nature and even the spiritual powers look on with great fear and reverence. This is why they lower their gaze and cover their feet and their face with their wing.[12] Besides this revelation of the liturgy, there was also revealed to the prophet at this moment the doctrine of the Trinity. For one godhead was proclaimed in threefold form when the Seraphim said 'Holy' three times, but 'Lord' only once. The threefold repetition of the word 'Holy' referred to the three persons of the Father, the Son and the Holy Spirit. We must believe that each of them is the Eternal One and truly holy; for divinity is truly holy and unchangeable, while creatures can be called holy or become so only by the gift of the divinity. But the next words, 'Lord of hosts', show that he is Lord and God of the Powers and Almighty God, for this is proper to the nature of the Trinity, which alone exists from all eternity and is God.*

7. So in this liturgy too, when the bishop has spoken of the Father, the Son and the Holy Spirit, he is bound to add: 'Praise

---

[9]This doctrine had been only recently defined at Constantinople in 381.

[10]For the mention in the Preface of creation and the Seraphim, cf. Cyril of Jerusalem, MC 5.6.

[11]Cf. Is. 6.3. In the Synopsis it is the bishop, not the congregation, who says the Sanctus. Hence Tonneau's conjecture that some words have dropped out (see note 1).

[12]Cf. Is. 6.2. Cyril of Jerusalem has a reference to the six wings in his liturgy, though he seems to follow the tradition according to which it is God's face which the Seraphim cover (MC 5.6 with note 10). T reads into the triple repetition of the word 'Holy' an invocation of the three Persons, who together form one 'Lord God'.

and adoration be offered to the divine nature by all creation'. He recalls the Seraphim, because scripture describes them singing the hymn of praise that all of us present recite in a loud voice, paying our worship to God, in company with the invisible powers.* We imitate their attitude and their tribute; for the Incarnation[13] of Christ our Lord has made it possible for us to become like them immortal and incorruptible and to pay our worship with them, when, as St Paul says, we 'shall be caught up to meet the Lord in the air; and so we shall always be with the Lord'.[14] For our Lord himself was not deceiving us when he said: 'They are equal to angels and are sons of God, being sons of the resurrection.'[15]

8. When Isaiah heard these words in his vision, he fell on his face and said: 'Woe is me! For I am lost; for I am a man of unclean lips, and I dwell in the midst of a people of unclean lips; for my eyes have seen the King, the Lord of hosts.'[16] It is as if he were grieving in his heart for the human race, considering what we are and the gifts we receive. That is what he meant when he said: 'I am a man'; in speaking of our common nature, he implied that the propensity to evil is common to it. In God's own words: 'The imagination of man's heart is evil from his youth.'[17] So, while lamenting for all his race, Isaiah marvelled at God's excessive mercy in granting such a favour to a race that is so sinful.

9. As for us, since the greatness of this gift, which the prophet had foreseen,[18] has been revealed to us, since the sacrifice[19] has now been performed for us and we are bidden to celebrate its memorial in this liturgy we are witnessing, we stand *with eyes cast*

---

[13]*Oikonomia.*

[14]1 Thess. 4.17. I.e., it is not until the next life that we shall be fully united with the angels in worship.

[15]Lk. 20.36.

[16]Is. 6.5.

[17]Gen. 8.21.

[18]T regards Isaiah's words quoted in the last section as an obscure prophecy of the whole *oikonomia.*

[19]I.e., Christ's definitive sacrifice on the Cross. For a discussion of the element of 'awe', to which so much importance is attached in this paragraph, see Introduction, pp. 59-66.

down in such great reverence that we cannot even look upon the majesty of this liturgy. We make the words of the invisible powers our own to express the greatness of the mercy which has been unexpectedly lavished upon us. The feeling of awe does not leave us; throughout the liturgy, both before and after the exclamation 'Holy',[20] we keep our eyes on the ground ... The bishop also joins his voice to that of the invisible powers, praying and glorifying God. He too is in awe at what is taking place. For it is only right that he should experience fear and trembling no less than the rest, or rather even more, since he is performing this dread liturgy on behalf of all.

10. When all present have exclaimed: *'Holy, holy, holy'* and *fallen silent again,* the bishop continues the liturgy. First he says: 'Holy is the Father, holy is the Son, holy is the Holy Spirit'. These words are a profession of faith in his holy and eternal nature and a proof that he has interpreted the hymn of the Seraphim accurately.[21]* Then he proclaims the transcendent mercy that God bestowed on us when he revealed his plan[22] for us in Christ. For Christ, 'though he was in the form of God,' determined to 'take the form of a servant';[23] he assumed[24] a perfect and complete man for the salvation of the human race, thus cancelling the ancient and cruel burdens of the law[25] and death's long-established hold over us, and conferring upon us favours beyond our description or comprehension. For Christ our Lord accepted the passion in order to exterminate death utterly by his resurrection; and he has promised that we too can share with him in the enjoyment of this future.

---

[20]I.e., the Sanctus.

[21]I.e., the trinitarian implications of the Sanctus explained in sect. 6.

[22]*Oikonomia* again. The narrative section of the Canon, which in the first Eucharistic Prayer of the Roman rite commemorates only the Last Supper, is extended here (as in the fourth Eucharistic Prayer, and the Byzantine Liturgy of St Basil (Jasper and Cuming, *Prayers of the Eucharist,* pp. 118-119)) to include the whole 'oikonomia', leading up perhaps to the words of institution at the end of this section. T attaches no special significance to them; it is the Epiclesis that transforms the bread and wine. See introduction, pp. 48-49.

[23]Phil. 2.6-7.

[24]See note 4.

[25]Cf. Col. 2.14.

So it was necessary for Christ to give us this mystery with its power to lead on to our future. Through it we are born again in the sign of baptism, commemorate our Lord's death by this dread liturgy, and receive his body and blood as our immortal and spiritual food. When he was about to go to meet his passion, he bequeathed this food to his disciples, so that we might receive his body and blood by means of this bread and wine — we who all believe in Christ and continue to commemorate his death ...

Epiclesis over the Offering

11.... . But *by virtue of the sacramental actions, this is the moment appointed for Christ our Lord to rise from the dead and pour out his grace upon us all.*[26] This can take place only by the coming of the grace of the Holy Spirit, by which the Holy Spirit once raised Christ from the dead. Two quotations from St Paul prove this. First: 'designated Son of God in power according to the Spirit of holiness, by his resurrection from the dead, Jesus Christ our Lord'. Secondly: 'If the Spirit of him who raised Jesus Christ from the dead dwells in you, he who raised Christ from the dead will give life to your mortal bodies also through his Spirit which dwells in you.' Our Lord himself said: 'It is the spirit that gives life, the flesh is of no avail.'[27]

12. Accordingly, the bishop is obliged by the liturgical rules to entreat God that the Holy Spirit may come and that grace may descend from on high on to the bread and wine that have been offered, so showing us that the memorial of immortality is truly the body and blood of our Lord. For our Lord's body is of the same nature as ours: it was originally by nature mortal but by means of the resurrection passed to an immortal and unchanging nature ... Just as our Lord's body was clearly revealed as immortal when it had received the Spirit and his

---

[26]The Epiclesis, through which the bread and wine become the body and blood of Christ, occurs *after* the words of institution, if one assumes that they are referred to in sect. 10 (cf. Introduction, p. 46). At this moment, in T's view, the bread and wine, which have *symbolised* the *dead* body of Jesus, *become* his *risen* body.

[27]Rom. 1.4; 8.11; Jn. 6.63.

anointing,[28] so too in the liturgy the bread and wine that have been offered receive at the coming of the Holy Spirit a kind of anointing by the grace that comes upon them. From this moment we believe that they are the body and blood of Christ, free from death, corruption, suffering and change, like our Lord's body after the resurrection.[29]

Epiclesis over the People

13. *The bishop also prays that the grace of the Holy Spirit may come upon all the assembly.* The new birth has made them grow into a single body; now they are to be firmly established in the one body by sharing the body of our Lord, and form a single unity in harmony, peace and good works.[30] Thus we shall look upon God with a pure heart; we shall not incur punishment by communicating in the Holy Spirit[31] when we are divided in our views, inclined to arguments, quarrels, envy and jealousy, and contemptuous of virtue. By our harmony, peace and good works, and by the purity of heart with which our soul looks upon God, we shall show that we are awaiting to receive the Holy Spirit. In this way, by communion in the blessed mysteries, we shall be united among ourselves and joined to Christ our Lord, whose body we believe ourselves to be, and through whom we 'become partakers of the divine nature'.[32]

---

[28]At his baptism Jesus received an anticipation or sign of the immortality which the Holy Spirit was to confer on him at his resurrection (cf. BH 3.22). It is in his Spirit-given risen life that he is present in the Eucharist.

[29]Cf. BH 5.26.

[30]The effect of both baptism and Holy Communion is to unite the people with one another in Christ. Baptism begins the process: the Eucharist deepens it.

[31]Cf. 1 Cor. 11.29: 'For any one who eats and drinks without discerning the body eats and drinks judgment upon himself.' There is such a close connection between the presence of Christ and of the Holy Spirit that communion can be described as 'communicating in the Holy Spirit'. So too in the modern Byzantine Liturgy of St Chrysostom, when the deacon shows the congregation the sacred species they are about to receive, he describes them, not as the body and blood of Christ, but as 'the fulness of the chalice of faith, of the Holy Spirit', and 'the boiling water of faith, full of the Holy Spirit'.

[32]2 Pet. 1.4.

Commemoration of the Living and the Dead

14. The bishop performs the divine liturgy in this way, and *offers a prayer for all whom it is always customary to name in church; and then passes on to the commemoration of the dead.* For this sacrifice obtains protection for us in this world, and on those who have died in the faith it confers after death the fulfilment of that transcendent hope which is the desire of the goal of all the children of Christ's mystery.

The Breaking of Bread and the Mingling

15. *After these prayers the bishop pauses, then takes the sacred bread in his hands and looks up to heaven,* directing his gaze upwards as an expression of thanks for such marvellous gifts. Then *he breaks the bread,*[33] at the same time *praying for the people that the grace of Jesus Christ may come upon them ... The people reply in the usual way* expressing agreement. *He traces the sign of the cross over the blood with the bread and over the bread with the blood.* He brings them together as a sign that, though they are two distinct things, they are one in power and are the memorial of the passion and death that affected our Lord's body when he shed his blood on the cross for us all ... A human body is one with its blood, which is diffused throughout every part of it. This is why, wherever you make a cut, be it big or small, blood must flow from the place of the incision. This was true of our Lord's body before the passion: a great quantity of blood inevitably flowed from wounds inflicted by the crucifixion.

---

[33]T suggests three reasons for the breaking of the bread: (1) so that the Body and the Blood can be brought together, thus showing that both belong to the same Lord and derive their power from him (sect. 15); (2) so that the bread can be shared out to the congregation (sect. 19); (3) in imitation of Jesus, who 'shared himself out' to small groups of the disciples in his risen appearances (sect. 17-18). He does not, however, regard it as a symbol of the breaking of Christ's body in the passion (as, e.g., Peter Chrysologus did: '... that Christ may be your bread and as bread be broken for the forgiveness of your sins; that Christ may be your cup which is poured out for the remission of your offences.' Serm. 30; PL 52.286); nor as imitation of Christ's breaking of the bread, which seems an obvious reason for the ceremony. T can be too subtle. For the Mingling, see Introduction, pp. 52-53.

16. When our Lord gave his body and blood, he said: 'This is my body which is broken for you for the forgiveness of sins,' and 'This is my blood which is shed for you for the remission of sins.'[34] The first saying referred to his passion, the second to the cruelty and length of it, which caused so much blood to be shed. So it is appropriate that we too should follow this tradition and set both bread and wine on the altar as a sign of what took place and as a reminder that the two are one in power, because both belong to the one who underwent the passion — i.e., both the body of our Lord and the blood that was shed from it ...[35]

17. *For this reason it is laid down that he should drop the life-giving bread piece by piece into the chalice.* This action shows that the two elements are inseparable, that they are one in power and that they confer one and the same grace on the receiver.

When the bishop breaks the bread, this is no meaningless ceremony. He does it because Christ our Lord showed himself to all his followers after his resurrection from the dead. First he appeared to the women, then gradually, in small groups, to the eleven disciples and to all the faithful, for example to Cleophas and his companions; he wished in this way to show himself to them in his risen form and to tell them that they would share with him in the great gifts which he spoke of in his greeting.* He urged them to rejoice in the expectation of the promised blessings. Thus when he appeared to the women immediately after the resurrection, he said: 'Peace be with you.'[36]

18. This is why the bishop, now that he has duly completed the liturgy, follows our Lord's example — for this is the memorial of his death and resurrection[37] — and breaks the

---

[34]Cf. 1 Cor. 11.24-25; Mt. 26.26-28 and par. See Introduction, pp. 51-52.

[35]T only hints at a point stressed with little justification by some theologians, that the separate presentation of the body and blood in the Eucharist denotes the separation of them in the passion. Still less does he regard the priest's action in bringing them together as a sign of the resurrection; he takes it rather as a sign that, though the sacrament is received under two kinds, it remains a unity.

[36]In fact these words were addressed to the disciples in the upper room (Jn. 20.19). 'Peace' is presumably the gift Christ 'spoke of in his greeting'.

[37]T refuses to regard the Eucharist one-sidedly as the memorial of the death alone. This wider view accords with his central teaching that the effect of the sacraments is not to be confined to the forgiveness of sin, but involves the beginning of risen life in the Spirit.

bread just as our Lord shared himself out in his appearances, appearing to different people at different times, and finally to a great gathering. In this way everyone was able to come to him. So too now people have a high regard for the gift that has been revealed to them; they adore our Lord and acknowledge the great reward that came to him; and they receive him in their hearts by eating the consecrated bread so that they too may enjoy sublime communion with him. With great delight and joy and in strong hopes we are led in this way to the greatness which through the resurrection we hope to experience with him in the world to come.

19. Eventually, then, all the bread is broken, so that all of us who are present can receive a share. When we receive one little mouthful, we believe that in this mouthful we each receive Christ whole. For it would be scandalous if the woman with the flow of blood received a divine favour simply by touching the fringe of his garment,[38] not even part of his body, while we believed that we did not receive him whole in a fragment of his body. Again, when we kiss, we ordinarily do so with the mouth; it is a small part of the body, but by means of it we intend to embrace the whole body. We often walk in pairs hand in hand, taking this part of the body as a sign of our fellowship.

20. With a view to what is to happen afterwards, the bishop who offers this sacred, sublime sacrifice must begin by performing the same action;[39] he begins to break the bread. This is an appropriate action, for from this point we must picture Christ our Lord in our minds by means of this bread, for in each one of the fragments he comes to the receiver. He greets us and reveals his resurrection and gives us a guarantee of the promised blessings ...

Preparation for Communion

21. When all this has been done, the Church herald speaks out again and reminds us briefly of those for whom we should all pray. First he announces: *'We must pray for the one who has*

---

[38]Cf. Lk. 8.43ff.
[39]I.e., the bread must be broken before communion can be given.

brought this holy offering. [40] That is to say, we have been granted the privilege of making this offering; let us continue to pray that we may become worthy of looking at it and staying close to it and sharing in it. The bishop concludes the prayer by asking that God may approve of the sacrifice and that the grace of the Holy Spirit may come upon the world, so that we may not be punished for sharing in the sacrament, although it is infinitely above us.*

22. When the bishop has concluded the Eucharistic Prayer in this way, *he blesses the people and wishes them peace; all present make the usual response with heads bowed in due reverence.* When the prayer is completed and all are intent on receiving Holy Communion, *the Church herald proclaims: 'Let us attend' ... The bishop announces: 'What is holy for the holy.* [41] For our Lord's body and blood, which are our food, are indeed holy and immortal and full of holiness, since the Holy Spirit has come down upon them. Not everyone may receive this food, but only those who have been sanctified, and therefore only the baptized who have undergone a new birth, and 'have the first fruits of the Holy Spirit',[42] which enables them to receive the favour of sanctification. This is why the bishop says: *'What is holy for the holy'*, and urges everyone to recall the dignity of what is laid on the altar ...

23.... . You must lead good lives so as to strengthen in your own persons the gift which has been given you and to be worthy of the food you require.* For every animal which is born of another animal God has made a food which suits its nature; every animal is born of its like and feeds on its like. A sheep is born of a sheep and feeds by the nature[43] of a sheep. So too a

[40]I.e., presumably, the donor(s) of the bread and wine. T enlarges the scope of the prayer to include all the participants.

[41]This liturgical phrase is probably inspired by Mt. 7.6: 'Do not give dogs what is holy'. Cyril of Jerusalem (MC 5.19) also connects these words with the descent of the Holy Spirit on the offerings. The dialogue — 'What is holy ...', 'Let us attend', 'One holy Father ...' — is present in the Byzantine Liturgy of St Chrysostom.

[42]Rom. 8.23.

[43]Just as the young animal sucking its mother's milk can be said to feed on its mother's 'nature', so we in the Eucharist receive the one divine 'nature' that all three Persons share.

horse or any other animal is born of a mother of the same species as itself and feeds from its mother's nature. You too have been born in baptism by the grace of the Holy Spirit and his coming and received this sanctification; accordingly you need to receive food of the same kind by the grace and the coming of the Holy Spirit, so that this sanctification you have been given may be strengthened and grow, and the promised blessings may be fulfilled in the world to come where we shall all enjoy complete holiness. This is the meaning of *'What is holy for the holy'*. With these dispositions, with this profession of faith, with this eagerness, we approach this sublime communion; we must receive this holy, immortal food in fear combined with love.

This is what the bishop's words mean. *All reply: 'One holy Father, one holy Son, one Holy Spirit'*,[44] acknowledging that there is only one holy nature, the nature of the Father, the Son and the Holy Spirit; alone it exists from all eternity, alone it is unchanging, alone it can confer sanctification on whoever it wills. *They add: 'Glory be to the Father and to the Son and to the Holy Spirit for ever and ever. Amen'*. For all who acknowledge the holy nature owe it a debt of praise.

Communion

24. Once the liturgy has been concluded in this way, *then we all eagerly receive the offering*. We receive from the dread, ineffable altar an immortal and holy food. Those who have charge of the divine liturgy and stand near the altar approach it to receive the divine food; the others receive away from the altar. But this makes no difference to the food itself; for there is only one bread, and only one body of Christ our Lord into which the bread that has been offered is transformed by the one coming of the Holy Spirit, and we all receive it equally because we are the one body of Christ our Lord and are all nourished with the same body and blood ... 'For by one Spirit we were all baptized into one body — Jews or gentiles, slaves or free'. And again,

[44]Cf. Cyril of Jerusalem, MC 5.19.

'Because there is one loaf, we who are many are one body, for we all partake of the same loaf.'[45] Since we all eat the same body of Christ our Lord and since this food gives us all communion with him, we all become the one body of Christ and receive communion and contact with him, our head. 'The bread which we break, is it not a participation in the body of Christ? And the cup which we bless, is it not a participation in the blood of Christ?'[46] St Paul teaches us that when we receive them, we are united with our Lord's body and blood, and so remain in communion with him and are ourselves Christ's body, while this communion strengthens the communion we received by the new birth of baptism. We have become his body. St Paul said: '*You* are the body of Christ', and again: Christ is 'the Head, from whom the whole body, nourished and knit together, grows with a growth that is from God.'[47]

25. The privilege of 'communion' in the mysteries is granted to us all without exception; for we all need it equally, as we believe that it confers the possession of eternal life. *Accordingly the bishop, who is performing the ceremony, is the first to come forward and receive.* This regulation shows that the sacrifice is offered by the bishop on behalf of all, and that he needs to communicate just as much as the others.*[48] Our Lord showed by his words that the efficacy of the sacrament lay in the eating and drinking: 'He who eats my flesh and drinks my blood will live for ever.'[49] He does not say 'He who celebrates', but 'He who eats'; and this all do equally ...

All alike have the right to communicate; but a person receives more, if by living in love, faith and virtue he shows himself to be worthy of receiving — insofar as one can do so, for clearly no one can be truly worthy. For how could a mortal man, subject to corruption and sin, show himself to be worthy of receiving this body which has become immortal and

---

[45] 1 Cor. 12.13 (adapted); 10.17.
[46] 1 Cor. 10.16 (adapted).
[47] 1 Cor. 12.27; Col. 2.19.
[48] Once again T is emphasizing the equality of bishop and laity. Cf. BH 4.41 with note 73.
[49] Jn. 6.54, 58.

incorruptible, and now in heaven at God's right hand is universally honoured as Lord and King? But we place our confidence in our Lord's mercy, who gave us these gifts. We come forward with all the fervour and attention we can muster, in order to do so as worthily as human nature permits. With these hopes we all approach Christ our Lord. He gave us a new birth in holy baptism and made us his own body, his own flesh, his offspring — 'Here am I, and the children God has given me' —;[50] and with a love like that of a natural mother he devised a way to feed us with his own body. To use other symbols, he set the bread and the chalice before us, and they are his body and blood, by which we eat the food of immortality while the grace of the Holy Spirit flows down on us, feeding us and so making us immortal and imperishable in hope; by means of them, in a way that is beyond description, he leads us to share in the blessings that are to come, when we are fed by the grace of the Holy Spirit in simple fact, without sacraments and signs, and so become by nature completely free from death, corruption and change.

26. Now by means of these commemorations and signs that have been performed, we all approach the risen Christ with great delight. We embrace him as joyfully as we can, for we see him risen from the dead and hope ourselves to attain to a share in the resurrection. In the symbols that have been enacted, he rose out of the dead from the altar, as if from a tomb;[51] he appears and comes close to us; and when we receive him in communion, he announces to us his resurrection. Although he shares himself when he comes to us, he is entire in each part and close to each of us, giving himself to each of us for us to seize and embrace him with all our might and show him whatever love we choose to give ...

27. *Then we each come forward, with eyes cast down and both hands extended.* By our lowered eyes we pay the debt of fitting adoration, making a public act of faith that we are receiving the body of the King who became Lord of all by union with the divine nature and is worshipped as Lord by all creatures alike. Our

---

[50]Heb. 2.13, quoting Is. 8.18 (LXX).
[51]On the importance of the Epiclesis in this process see BH 5.11-12.

two hands stretched out together acknowledge the value of the gift we are about to receive. *The right hand is stretched out to receive the offering, and the left hand held underneath.* This is a sign of great reverence: the right hand is stretched out uppermost because it is to receive the royal body; the other hand supports and guides its sister and partner, for it is not ashamed to play the part of a servant to its equal in deference to the royal body that the right hand is carrying.[52]

28. *As he gives communion, the bishop says: 'The body of Christ'.* These words teach you not to pay attention to the appearance, but to put yourself in mind of what has happened to the offering, which by the coming of the Holy Spirit has become the body of Christ. You should come up in great fear and with much love because of the greatness of the gift — fear because of its great dignity, love because of its grace. *So you say 'Amen' to his words,* confirming and subscribing to the bishop's declaration. *You receive the chalice in the same way.*

When you have received the body in your hands, you adore it, acknowledging the authority of him who is placed in your hands and recalling our Lord's words to his disciples after his resurrection: 'Authority in heaven and on earth has been given to me.'[53] With a great and sincere love you place it on your eyes,[54] kiss it and address to it your prayers as to Christ our Lord who is now with you, for you possess the great source of confidence[55] you hoped for, now that you have come to him and taken hold of him. As you pray you confess your weakness and your many sins, and acknowledge that you are utterly undeserving of such a gift; you pay him the glory that is his due for giving you these gifts and for favouring you with such help that, by becoming free from all evil and always performing his will, you have become worthy of receiving the offering.

---

[52]Cf. Cyril of Jerusalem, MC 5.21: 'Make your left hand a throne for your right, since your right hand is about to welcome a king.'

[53]Mt. 28.18.

[54]Cyril also describes this detail (MC 5.21).

[55]Cf. Heb. 10.19ff.: 'Therefore, brethren, since we have *confidence* to enter the sanctuary by the blood of Jesus, ... let us draw near.'

29. In such dispositions as these *you receive and swallow* your share in the sacrament. The grace of the Holy Spirit does not only feed the body; by this dread communion it also feeds the soul as well as the body, and even more than the body; when it makes the body immortal in the world to come, it also makes the soul immune to change and to all sin.[56] *After you have received, you offer up on your own account the thanksgiving and blessing that are due to God,* so as not to be ungrateful for this divine gift, *remaining with all the congregation to pay this debt of thanksgiving and blessing in accordance with the Church's custom.* For it is only right that all who have received this spiritual food should give thanks to God in common for this great gift ...[57]

Correct Dispositions and Forgiveness of Sin

33. The whole of this world exists only in appearance; in the apostle's words[58] it is not 'lasting' and is doomed to certain decay. But we look to the world 'which is to come', which will last for ever. Therefore we must all order our lives with a view to the world to come. This is the destiny which is in store for us and for which we hope; for we have fed on the sacramental food and communicated in the sacred mysteries.*

We should not allow faults due to human weakness to keep us from communion in these mysteries.[59] For while habitual

---

[56]Although it has usually been held in the Church that the soul is of its nature immortal, there is another tradition, not altogether consistent with the first, that immortality is the fruit of the Eucharist. This tradition, which T supports here, derives from such texts as: 'If any one eats this bread, he will live for ever' (Jn. 6.51). T believes that the effect on the soul is mediated by the effect on the body. Cf. Cyril of Jerusalem, MC 4.3: 'We become bearers of Christ, since his body and blood enters all our limbs'; Tertullian, *de Resurrectione Mortuorum*, viii.23 (PL 2.806): 'The flesh (*caro*) is the hinge (*cardo*) of salvation ... The flesh feeds on Christ's body and blood, so that the soul also may feed on God.'

[57]Three sections have been omitted; they repeat what has gone before, and then consider the moral dispositions appropriate to one who receives Holy Communion.

[58]Cf. Heb. 13.14.

[59]T has at last to admit that sin is possible even after the new birth of baptism (cf. BH 3.13 with note 29). T does not see 'faults due to human weakness' as a bar to receiving communion; on the contrary, communion obtains forgiveness for such sins (section 35. The Council of Trent was to repeat this teaching). However,

sinners should not come forward to receive them without fear, those who have their salvation at heart should come to Holy Communion, remembering that, just as we need food to support this life, so too the dispensation[60] of Christ will provide us with spiritual food for the life to come.

34. So we should neither abstain from communion altogether nor receive it carelessly, but be as attentive as we can when we receive this favour. We should come to communion attentively and eagerly, realising that if we allow aimlessness a complete hold over our lives, so that we sin without scruple and do what we please, how we please, with no thought of the good, we are condemning[61] ourselves when we receive this ineffable food and drink. But if we are careful how we live and are eager for the good and always keep it in mind, our faults will be indeliberate or due to weakness and will do us no harm. On the contrary, we shall gain considerable strength from receiving communion. Our Lord's body and blood and the grace of the Holy Spirit which the sacrament confers will help us to perform good works and strengthen our dispositions by driving away unprofitable thoughts and completely extinguish our faults — provided of course that we have fallen against our wills or inadvertently or through human weakness, and address God with great sadness and keen sorrow for our sins.*[62]

35. Receiving Holy Communion will certainly obtain for us forgiveness of such sins. For Christ our Lord said explicitly: 'This is my body which is broken for you for the forgiveness of sins'; and 'This is my blood which is shed for you for the

---

like Cyril of Jerusalem (MC 5.23) he discourages certain sinners from receiving the sacrament. Cyril does not explain what kind or degree of sin constitutes an obstacle; T here makes the criterion habit, in section 39 definitive rejection of the Law. (Later moralists observed that habit can in fact lessen the gravity of a sin.) Neither T nor Cyril had arrived at a clear distinction between mortal and venial sins, though T approaches it in sect. 39.

[60] *Oikonomia.*

[61] Cf. 1 Cor. 11.29, 32.

[62] T's attitude to sins 'due to human weakness' is perceptive and subtle: such sins cause us sorrow, but at the same time we should understand that they 'do us no harm'. In other words, we must learn to live with ourselves without lowering our ideals.

forgiveness of sins'; and again: 'I came not to call the righteous, but sinners'.[63] If then we sin through carelessness, it will go hard with us if we approach the holy mysteries; but if we earnestly do what is right, avoid evil and sincerely repent of any faults we may commit, we shall find in Holy Communion the gift of forgiveness of our sins; for though we are sinners, we have been chosen for repentance which will lead to the life and salvation of us all, simply out of the mercy of God who called us. This is the meaning of our Lord's words, and the words of Isaiah can teach us the same lesson.[64]

36. Isaiah saw an awe-inspiring vision, which signified that through the dispensation[65] of Christ our Lord, the whole universe was to be filled with God's praise, to learn the mystery of the Trinity and to receive instruction, and to be taught the creed and to be baptized in the name of the Father and of the Son and of the Holy Spirit. To teach Isaiah this lesson the Seraphim spoke this hymn in a loud voice: 'Holy, holy, holy is the Lord; heaven and earth are full of his glory'.[66] When the prophet saw this in his vision, he fell on his face at the thought of the weakness of sinful and tainted human nature. One of the Seraphim was sent to him and took a burning coal from the altar with tongs and laid it on the prophet's lips saying: 'Behold, this has touched your lips; your guilt will be taken away and your sins forgiven.'[67] The burning coal on the altar stands for the sacrament which was to be given to us. The coal was originally black and cold; but when it came in contact with the fire, it became bright and warm. The food of the holy mystery was to resemble the coal in this: what is offered is ordinary bread and wine,[68] but by the coming of the Holy Spirit

[63]Cf. Mt. 26.26, 28; 1 Cor. 11.24-26; Mt. 9.13.

[64]Isaiah received on his lips the burning coal (= the Eucharist filled with the Holy Spirit) after he had acknowledged his sins, and as a result he received forgiveness.

[65]*Oikonomia.*

[66]Is. 6.3 (adapted). Cf. BH 5.6-8.

[67]Is. 6.7 (LXX).

[68]Cf. Cyril of Jerusalem, MC 3.3: '... the bread of the Eucharist after the invocation of the Holy Spirit is *no longer just bread*, but the body of Christ.' Cf. also MC 1.7.

it is changed into the body and blood and so assumes the power of spiritual and immortal food ... The Holy Spirit also came down from heaven on to the apostles in the form of fire, and through them the gift of the Spirit entered into the whole human race. And just as the Seraph went up to the prophet and cleansed him and took away all his sins, we ought to believe that our debts are all cancelled by our sharing in the holy mysteries, provided that we repent of our sins with grief and compunction in our hearts.

37. When the prophet had received this favour, he fell on his face and said: 'Woe is me! For I am lost; for I am a man of unclean lips; for my eyes have seen the King, the Lord of hosts!'[69] These are the words of a man pierced with sorrow and tormented by his conscience because of his sins. It was while he was in this state that it was given to him to hear these words and the Seraph came to him with the burning coal. If we try to imitate the prophet, the grace of the Holy Spirit will certainly help us to do what is right, and will abolish all our sins just as fire consumes thorns.

38. Now the Seraph did not take the burning coal in his hand, but in tongs. This vision shows that even the Seraphim fear to touch the sacrament without some intermediary. The bishop acts in this capacity for you, when he gives you the sacrament with his hand saying: 'The body of Christ'. Not that he counts himself worthy to pick up such gifts and present them; instead of tongs he possesses the grace which made him a priest and gives him the confidence to present such gifts. He picks them up with his hand to give us confidence to receive them in our hands. Not only are we free from fear at their greatness; grace even gives us confidence. The burning coal touched the prophet's lips without burning them; so when the bishop gives you this gift with his hands in the confidence engendered by the grace of the Spirit he possesses for this ministry, you too should receive it with confidence and great hope.* The greatness of the gift makes you afraid; but you receive it, trusting in the mercy of him who had presented

[69]Is. 6.5.

mankind with these gifts and has given the bishop also such confidence, not only for his own sake but for the sake of all who need God's mercy. For, as St Paul says, he was ordained 'to offer sacrifices for his own sins and for those of the people'.[70]

39. This is the disposition and the love that are demanded of us if we are to receive Holy Communion. If we have committed a serious sin of any kind which implies the rejection of the Law once for all, we must abstain from communion, but we should not allow ourselves to stay away from it indefinitely.[71] For what good would this do us if we persevered in our sins? No, we must stir up our consciences with all our might so as speedily to attain due contrition. We must not leave the healing of these sins to ourselves;[72] for we know that, just as for the diseases of the body God has arranged remedies with which experts can treat us, so too, since our souls are subject to change, he has given us the remedy of contrition according to rules which have been laid down on this matter from the beginning. The priests[73] and experts must follow the discipline and wisdom of the Church in adjusting the treatment which they give to penitents according to the severity of their sins.*

40. That is why our Lord said: 'If your brother sins against you, go and tell him his fault between you and him alone. If he listens to you, you have gained your brother. But if he does not listen, take one or two others along with you, that every word may be confirmed by the evidence of two or three witnesses. If he refuses to listen to them, tell it to the church; and if he refuses to listen even to the church, let him be to you as a Gentile and a tax collector'.[74] This is the treatment of sins that

---

[70]Cf. Heb. 7.27.

[71]The word 'indefinitely' is not contained explicitly in the Syriac.

[72]Just as in sickness we consult a doctor, we have recourse to a priest or 'expert' when we seek to be cured of our sins (cf. section 44). The function T assigns to the priest is that of imposing a proportionate penance; although he thus implies that forgiveness comes through the Church, he does not regard the *priest* as the agent of forgiveness. In fact, the Church's discipline in this regard took several more centuries to become fixed.

[73]This is the word which has generally been translated 'bishop'. T is probably not implying a distinction between priests and experts.

[74]Mt. 18.15-17.

God has devised and entrusted to the priests of the Church, so that they can use it with all diligence in treating human faults.

41. St Paul also says: 'Be urgent in season and out of season, convince, correct and console.'[75] 'Convince' the guilty, he says, 'in patience and in teaching', so that they may come to realize their faults for themselves. 'Correct' them in such a way that they receive correction as a precept, and so learn to help themselves. He also tells Timothy to 'console' when the conviction and corrections have brought sinners to the stage where they show themselves anxious to amend and to turn away from evil and eager to embrace the good. All this, St Paul says, must be done with 'patience' and 'teaching'. He recommends patience, because at each one of these stages, conviction, correction and consolation, the penitent learns by word of mouth what suits his condition and helps him to recover.

42. St Paul seems to have acted in this way when he learnt at Corinth that a misguided man was 'living with his father's wife'.[76] He ordered that the man should be 'delivered to Satan', that is, expelled from the Church. He gives this reason: 'for the destruction of the flesh, that his spirit may be saved in the day of the Lord Jesus Christ'. It is as if he said: I command that this should be done in order that the man may be tormented in this life, and so recognize his faults and accept conviction; by way of correction he is to be punished, so that, learning wisdom, he may turn from sin and return to righteousness; thus, when he has abandoned sin, he will receive fullness of life in the world to come. For he received the grace of the Spirit when he was baptized, but abandoned it when he sinned and persisted in his sin. When St Paul says: 'His spirit may be saved', he means that the man will turn from his sins and receive in full the Holy Spirit, who will restore his former state. According to his Second Epistle, written immediately after the man had repented, St Paul gave orders that the man should be received

---

[75] 2 Tim. 4.2 (adapted). T wishes the sinner to accept correction, first out of respect for the corrector, but eventually because he sees for himself the wisdom of the correction.

[76] 1 Cor. 5.1ff.

as follows: 'For such a one this punishment is enough; so you should rather turn to forgive and comfort him, or he may be overwhelmed by excessive sorrow. So I beg you to reaffirm your love for him. Any one whom you forgive, I also forgive.'[77] In other words, St Paul ordered that the sinner should be allowed to recover the confidence he had before; for he had accepted correction and amended his life and by severe penance obtained forgiveness of his sins.

43. St Paul went on to lay down rules for such situations: 'If anyone bears the name of brother and is guilty of adultery or greed, or is an idolator, drunkard, reviler or robber — one should not even eat bread with such a one. For what have I to do with judging outsiders? Is it not those inside the church whom you are to judge?'[78] He declares that we ought not to offer correction to strangers but to members of our own family, to those who have done what they are told and accept correction from us in the proper spirit. He goes on to indicate the advantage that this judgment will bring to those within the Church: 'God judges those outside'.[79] He means that if 'those outside' remain without correction, they will certainly be punished as strangers to religion; but as for 'those of the household of the faith',[80] if they are willing to accept correction, it will bring them remission of their sins and free them from the threat of punishment in the world to come. So, as there are some who reject the correction that is offered to them, St Paul says: 'Drive out the wicked person from among you',[81] as if to say: Let him be completely excluded from your company. This remark recalls our Lord's words: 'If he refuses to listen even to the church, let him be to you as a Gentile and a tax collector.'[82]

---

[77]2 Cor. 2.6-10. It is not in fact certain that St Paul is referring in the two epistles to the same man.

[78]1 Cor. 5.11-12 (adapted).

[79]1 Cor. 5.13.

[80]Gal. 6.10.

[81]1 Cor. 5.13.

[82]Mt. 18.17.

44... . Therefore we should approach priests with great confidence and reveal to them our sins.[83] With the greatest care, compassion and charity they treat sinners according to the rules I have already explained to you. They will not make public anything that should not be revealed, but keep to themselves the sins that have been committed; for like true, watchful fathers, they must respect their sons' sense of shame when they impose upon their sons' bodies the treatment that will cure them.

In this way, by putting our lives in order, by recognising the greatness of the mysteries, that invaluable gift to which we have been invited and which will put us in debt all our lives long, and by taking due care to correct our faults, we shall show ourselves worthy of our future hope. With this end in view we have obtained by God's grace the favour of celebrating this mystery now, and of enjoying the kingdom of heaven and all the indescribable blessings which will last for ever and which we shall all receive by the grace of our Lord Jesus Christ. To him with the Father and the Holy Spirit be glory now and for ever. Amen.

[83]Although 'private confession in any form even approaching our modern understanding of it did not exist in the ancient church' (J. Dallen, *The Reconciling Community, the Rite of Penance,* New York, 1986, p. 66), T's words here, as in sect. 39, seem to imply the existence of a penitential discipline which involves an element of private confession.

Bibliography

The Scriptural quotations in this publication are, where possible, from the Revised Standard Version of the Bible, copyrighted 1946 and 1952 by the Division of Christian Education of the National Council of the Churches of Christ in the U.S.A and used by kind permission. Sometimes, however, I have had to depart from this version, when the Fathers follow a different text; they may, for example, have been using the Septuagint or a translation based on it. Such cases I have generally indicated in the notes, for example by adding to the reference the letters LXX.

T. C. Akeley, *Christian Initiation in Spain c. 300-1100*. London, 1967.

K. Aland, *Did the Early Church Baptize Infants?* London, 1963.

B. Botte, 'Apertio Aurium', in RAC vol. 1, pp. 487ff.

B. Botte, *Le Canon de la Messe Romaine* (Textes et Etudes Liturgiques, 2). Louvain, 1935.

B. Botte, *Ambroise de Milan: Des Sacrements, des Mystères, Explication du Symbole* (Sources Chrétiennes, 25 bis). Paris, 1961.

L. Bouyer, *Eucharist*. Notre Dame and London, 1968.

F. E. Brightman, *Liturgies Eastern and Western*. London, 1896.

S. P. Brock, 'The Transition to a Post-Baptismal Anointing in the Antiochene Rite', in *The Sacrifice of Praise*, ed. B. D. Spinks (Rome, n.d.), pp. 215-225.

S. P. Brock, *The Holy Spirit in the Syrian Baptismal Tradition* (Syrian Churches Series, 9). Kottayam and Paderborn, 1979.

P. Brown, *Augustine of Hippo: a Biography*. London, 1967.

J. B. Bury, *History of the Later Roman Empire*. London, 1923.

R. Cabié, *The Eucharist* (*The Church at Prayer*, ed. A. G. Martimort, vol. 2). Collegeville and London, 1986.

R. H. Connolly, *The Liturgical Homilies of Narsai*. Cambridge, 1909.

J. D. Crichton, *A Short History of the Mass*. London, 1983.

J. G. Cuming, 'Egyptian Elements in the Jerusalem Liturgy', in JTS 25 (1974), pp. 117-124.

J. G. Cuming, 'The Shape of the Anaphora', in *Studia Patristica*, 20.ii (1989), pp. 333-345.

E. J. Cutrone, 'Cyril's Mystagogic Catecheses and the Evolution of the Jerusalem Anaphora', in *Orientalia Christiana Periodica*, 44 (1978), pp. 52-64.

J. Daniélou, *The Theology of Jewish Christianity*. London, 1964.

J. G. Davies, *The Architectural Setting of Baptism*. London, 1962.

J. G. Davies, 'Orientation', in *A New Dictionary of Liturgy and Worship* (2nd edn., London, 1986), p. 421.

G. Dix, *The Shape of the Liturgy*. 2nd edn., London, 1945.

A. J. Doval, *The Authorship of the Mystagogic Catecheses attributed to Cyril of Jerusalem* (unpublished D.Phil. thesis). Oxford 1992.

J. R. K. Fenwick, *Fourth Century Anaphoral Construction* (Grove Liturgical Study 45). Bramcote Notts, 1986.

J. D. C. Fisher and E. J. Yarnold, 'Initiation; the West from about A.D. 500 to the Reformation', in SL, pp. 144-152.

R. A. Greer, *Theodore of Mopsuestia, Exegete and Theologian*. London, 1961.

R. P. C. Hanson, *Allegory and Event*. London, 1959.

J. M. Hanssens, *La Liturgie d'Hippolyte* (Orientalia Christiana Analecta, 15). Rome, 1959.

P. W. Harkins, *St John Chrysostom: Baptismal Instructions* (Ancient Christian Writers, 31). Westminster, Maryland and London, 1959.

F. Homes Dudden, *The Life and Times of St Ambrose*. Oxford, 1935.

R. C. D. Jasper and G. J. Cuming, *Prayers of the Eucharist: Early and Reformed*. 3rd edn., New York, 1987.

G. Jeanes, 'Early Latin Parallels to the Roman Canon?' in JTS 37 (1986), pp. 427-431.

J. Jeremias, *The Eucharistic Words of Jesus*. London, 1966.

J. Jeremias, *Infant Baptism in the First Four Centuries*. London, 1960.

C. Jones, G. Wainwright, E. Yarnold and P. Bradshaw (ed.), *The Study of Liturgy*. 2nd edn., London and New York, 1992.

J. A. Jungmann, *The Mass of the Roman Rite*. New York, 1951-1955.

H. A. Kelly, *The Devil at Baptism*. Ithaca U.S.A. and London, 1985.

J. N. D. Kelly, *Early Christian Doctrines*. 4th edn., London, 1968.

G. Khouri-Sarkis, 'Prières et Cérémonies du Baptême', in *L'Orient Syrien*, 1 (1956).

A. Archdale King, *Liturgies of the Primatial Sees*. London, 1957.

A. F. J. Klijn, *The Acts of Thomas*. Leiden, 1962.

P. Kruger, 'Le sommeil des âmes dans l'oeuvre de Narsai', in *L'Orient Syrien*, 4 (1959), pp. 196-210.

G. W. H. Lampe, *The Seal of the Spirit*. 2nd edn., London, 1967.

H. Leclercq, 'Bapistère', 'Flabellum', 'ICHTHYS', 'Sputation', in DACL, vols. 2, 5, 7, 15 respectively.

H. Lietzmann, *Mass and the Lord's Supper*. Leiden, 1953-1976.

H. Lietzmann, *A History of the Early Church*. London and Cleveland, 1961.

L. P. McCauley and A. A. Stephenson, *The Works of Cyril of Jerusalem* (The Fathers of the Church, vols. 61 and 64). Washington, 1969-1970.

R. H. Malden, 'St Ambrose as an Interpreter of Holy Scripture', in JTS 16 (1915), pp. 509-522.

L. L. Mitchell, *Baptismal Anointing*. London, 1966.

R. Murray, *Symbols of Church and Kingdom: a Study in Early Syriac Tradition*. Cambridge, 1975.

M. P. Nilsson, *Geschichte der griechischen Religion*. 3rd edn., Munich, 1967.

O. Perler, 'Arkandisziplin', in RAC, i. 667ff.

A. Piédagnel and P. Paris, *Cyrille de Jérusalem: Catéchèses Mystagogiques* (Sources Chrétiennes, 126). Paris, 1966.

A. Piédagnel, *Jean Chrysostome: Trois Catéchèses Baptismales* (Sources Chrétiennes, 126*bis*). Paris, 1988.

J. Quasten, 'Theodore of Mopsuestia on the Exorcism of the Cilicium', in *Harvard Theological Review*, 35 (1942), pp. 209ff.

A. Raes, 'Attouchement des sens avec l'eucharistie', in *L'Orient Syrien*, 3 (1958), pp. 488-489.

H. Rahner, *Greek Myths and Christian Mystery*. London, 1963.

M. Righetti, *Storia Liturgica*. 3rd edn., Milan, 1964-.

H. Rondet, 'La Croix sur le Front', in *Recherches de Science Religieuse*, 42 (1954), pp. 388ff.

B. D. Spinks, *Addai and Mari – the Anaphora of the Apostles* (Grove Liturgical Study 24). Bramcote Notts, 1980.

D. Stone, *A History of the Doctrine of the Eucharist*. London, 1909.

H. L. Strack and P. Billerbeck, *Kommentar zum Neuen Testament aus Talmud und Midrasch*. Munich, 1922-1961.

T. J. Talley, 'From Berakah to Eucharistia', in *Worship*, 50 (1976), pp. 115-137.

T. Thompson and J. H. Srawley, *St Ambrose on the Sacraments and on the Mysteries*. London, 1950.

R. Tonneau and R. Devreese, *Les Homélies Catéchétiques de Théodore de Mopsueste* (Studi e Testi, 145). Vatican City, 1949.

A. Wenger, *Jean Chrysostome: Huit Catéchèses Baptismales* (Sources Chrétennes, 50). Paris, 1957.

E. C. Whitaker, *Documents of the Baptismal Liturgy*. 2nd edn., London, 1970.

M. Wiles and M. Santer, *Documents in Early Christian Thought*. Cambridge, 1975.

J. Wilkinson, *Egeria's Travels*. London, 1971; rev. edn., Jerusalem, 1981.

G. Winkler, 'The Original Meaning of the Prebaptismal Anointing and its Implications', in *Worship*, 52 (1978), pp. 24-45.

E. J. Yarnold, 'Baptism and the Pagan Mysteries', in *Heythrop Journal*, 13 (1972), pp. 247-267.

E. J. Yarnold, 'Ideo et Romae Fideles dicuntur qui baptizati sunt: a Note on De Sacramentis 1.1', in JTS 24 (1973), pp. 202-207.

E. J. Yarnold, 'The Authorship of the Mystagogic Catecheses attributed to Cyril of Jerusalem', in *Heythrop Journal*, 19 (1978), pp. 143-161.

E. J. Yarnold, 'Initiation: Sacrament and Experience', in *Liturgy Reshaped*, ed. K. Stevenson (London, 1982), pp. 17-31.

E. J. Yarnold, 'Who Planned the Churches at the Christian Holy Places in the Holy Land?', in *Studia Patristica*, 18.i (1985), pp. 105-109.

E. J. Yarnold, 'Anointing in Baptism', in *Living Stones*, 1 (1987), pp. 27-31.

E. J. Yarnold, 'The Early Syrian Rites', in *The Study of Liturgy*, ed. C. Jones *et al.*, pp. 127-129.

Index